D1391724

Making
Miniature Furniture

John Davenport

Making Miniature Furniture

B.T. Batsford Ltd, London

ISBN O 7134 4898 9

Typeset by Servis Filmsetting Ltd, Manchester
and printed in Great Britain by
The Bath Press, Bath
for the publishers
B.T. Batsford Ltd
4 Fitzhardinge Street
London W1H 0AH

Dedicated
to
my Grandson
Kieran

Acknowledgements

I would like to thank my wife Julie for putting up with my impossible demands while I compiled this book. Without her help I would probably not have succeeded. Also my son and daughter, David and Mitzi, who helped with objective criticism.

Two others who deserve thanks for their kind help and information are Sara Salisbury from *Nutshell News* and June Stowe of *International Dolls' House News*.

Contents

Acknowledgements

I Introduction 9

II Approaching the work 13
Golden rules 13
Apprentice pieces and other scales 16

III Timber 20
Obtaining timber 20
Which wood to choose 21
Walnut 22
Cutting wood 23
Storing your wood 26
Making the most of the wood grain 26

IV Tools 30
Basic tool kit for miniature cabinet work 30
Block plane 30
Files 31
Chisels 33
Knives and rulers 35
Saws 36
Working to the $\frac{1}{12}$th scale 41
Adjustable sliding bevel 42
Marking gauge 45
Cramps 45
Vices 47
Sharpening stone 48
Small machinery 53

V Wood tools and joints 66
Boards and supports 66
Wood joints 73

VI Cleaning up process 81
Sandpaper 81
Using sanding blocks 82

VII **Finishing** 84
    Wood staining 84
    Wood filler 84
    Applying polish 85
    Varnishing 85
    Dulling 86

VIII **Projects** 87
    1: Making a carcass for a simple drawer and door 87
    2: The better made drawer and door 95
    3: Collector's cabinet 106
    4: Victorian davenport desk 113

    Appendices 124
  I Supplementary tools 124
  II Museums to visit in Britain 129
 III Museums to visit in America 134
 IV Shops selling miniature furniture 138
  V Tool suppliers 140
 VI Magazines 141

    Bibliography 142

    Index 143

I *Introduction*

For me, the gradual slide into this fascinating world of miniatures happened almost by accident. My hobby started in the 1960s, when I was in my mid-twenties. At that time I never dreamt that I would make miniatures professionally, most to a scale of $\frac{1}{12}$th.

After completing my apprenticeship as a cabinet maker, I sampled three or four jobs in the next five years, eventually going into partnership with my father, restoring antiques. He was a french polisher by trade and had run a small business for many years in Sussex and badly needed the extra help of a cabinet maker.

The work in this field is fascinating – so many different pieces of furniture turn up to be repaired, never the same thing twice and always a new challenge, unlike most cabinet work today, which involves a lot of mass production and repetition.

I worked as a furniture restorer for about 18 months until one morning a large dollshouse arrived on my bench, brought in to be restored by one of our

1 Saleroom apprentice
piece made in
yew wood

customers. It had been bought from some 60 miles away, and all the furniture had been taken out for the journey; the roof looked as though a 15-stone man had sat on it, but I could see at a glance the skilled work that had gone into its making. Looking back, I remember how absorbed I became in the process of restoring this $\frac{1}{12}$th model. Of course, I was still ignorant of the vastness of this hobby and unaware that so many people were dedicated collectors of miniature furniture.

The dollshouse was collected in due course, paid for and taken home; the owner was delighted and suggested that I should be making them, not just repairing them. I only began to take this comment seriously several years later when working on three apprentice pieces: two chests of drawers in mahogany, and a bureau in walnut. They were beautifully inlaid and banded and I was struck by their superb quality. I decided that I would like to buy such items, but was not able to afford saleroom prices. Therefore, my only option was to make them myself.

2 Reproduction apprentice piece inlayed with marquetry ($\frac{1}{4}$ scale, $7\frac{3}{4}$in.) (197mm high)

3 Walterhausen miniatures ('Duncan Phyle' $\frac{1}{12}$th scale) inspired me when I was looking for apprentice pieces.

The first piece I did manage to buy in those early days was a small chest (fig. 1). It was reasonably priced but not accurately proportioned.

4 Early attempt at $\frac{1}{12}$th scale bureau bookcase made in satin walnut – note that the handles are out of scale

11

As well as realizing that the miniatures were not always good, frequenting antique sales showed me how eager people were to bid for the models.

My first attempt at a $\frac{1}{12}$th model was disappointing (fig. 4); I had neither the knowledge nor the requisite expertise, nor had I examined museum pieces or been to miniature shows. However, my skills improved as I acknowledged and made up for my deficiencies. I visited museums and shows and was amazed at the varieties of exhibits and the differing degrees of skill involved in each item.

I did notice with closer research into $\frac{1}{12}$th scale pieces in the museums that many were out of scale; of course, many were delicately made masterpieces, but I could see others had odd proportions and were not correctly jointed. This is very important in a good quality miniature, and the type of joints must be of the period in question. I was ready now to undertake the challenge of making high quality, true-to-the-life reproduction miniatures.

I have undertaken many challenges in the making of miniature models since those early days and still enjoy making them; I hope it will be a challenge you will enjoy too.

5 Miniature walnut chest-of-drawers ($\frac{1}{50}$th scale)

12

II *Approaching the work*

Because of the small proportions involved in $\frac{1}{12}$th scale and closeness of the work, it is easy to become frustrated with your work and make mistakes as a consequence. Rule number one, therefore, is to take frequent breaks and leave your work until you are well rested. Do not get too disappointed too quickly if things go wrong; remember, if it were that easy, everyone would be making magnificent miniatures.

Often, magazines or books include very professional drawings – splendid to look at but possibly too complex for a beginner with little experience and limited tools. For sophisticated pieces you would need a bandsaw for shaped pieces, a milling and drilling machine for rebates and mouldings, a lathe for the turns, and Flexi drill and burrs for shaping moulding and very fine carving and so on. Such equipment is very expensive and not worth investing in until you are committed to your craft. It is more important to lower your sights and begin with a basic tool kit.

Golden rules

1   Keep the pink things at the end of your hands *behind* the cutting edge. Of course this applies to all work with tools and machinery, but when handling tiny pieces of wood the ends of your fingers are used so much more than in most other hobbies.

2   Always keep your workshop tidy. The tendency is to work right up to the last minute, especially if you have little spare time to devote to the hobby. Again, the smallness of the parts you work with makes it paramount that you work in a tidy environment. So, although it might seem a waste of time, make yourself *tidy up*. Put tools away every time you leave the bench.

3   Because of the small scale you will be working in, lighting is also very important. Natural daylight is the best environment to work in – a skylight over the bench is ideal, but not always possible to achieve. Try to place your bench near a window, at least, but not face on as this will cast a shadow on the front of your work however strong the light is. Place the bench side on to the window – this will give you a good light on one side and the front of your work. If the light in your work room is inadequate you must use artificial light. A portable lamp is preferable to a fixed light – it is better to be able to alter the light source without you yourself having to move. When purchasing a lamp choose one with a swivel arm (fig. 6). Of course, these are

13

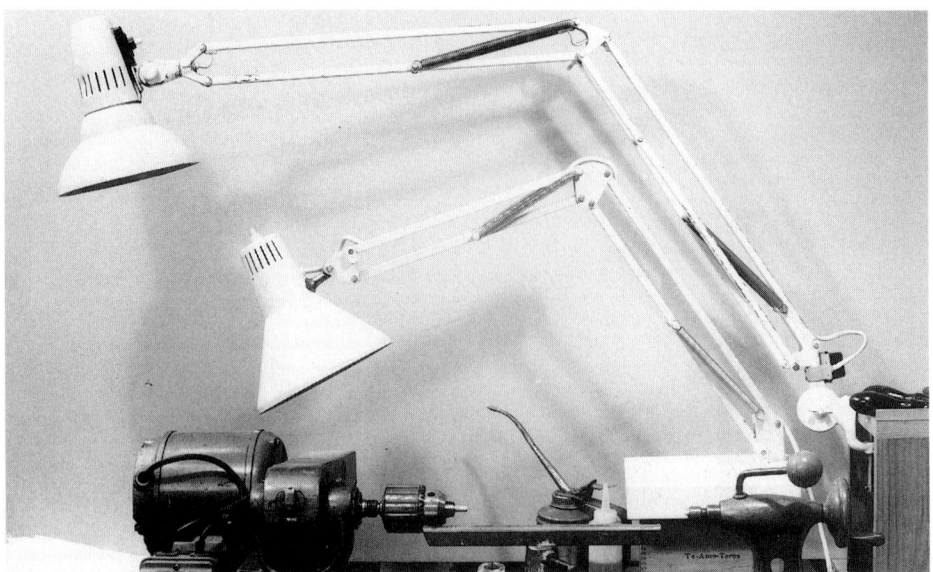

6 Working lamps

more expensive, but I believe well worth the extra cost for the area they cover. It can be a frustration trying to stretch a short arm further than it can go. I have also found that a small light for each machine is the ideal set up (fig. 7).

 If you are sitting for a long period using the lights, do not have them too close to your face as in time they become too hot and make you uncomfortable. Use a brighter bulb and move the lamp further away from you.

4 When setting up your workshop make your bench as heavy as possible, it will not do to have it move every time you push against it. This also applies to your lights – they should all have a sound base to prevent them moving when the machine vibrates.

5 When you have finished for the day, always drop a cover over your machines, especially if you are going away for a few days. Dust tends to settle on the metal surfaces, moisture is absorbed into the dust and your machines can slowly go rusty. This applies to your tools, also; if you lay them on shelves or hang them up, at least clean them regularly.

6 Always keep a pair of goggles close to your machines to use when the need arises.

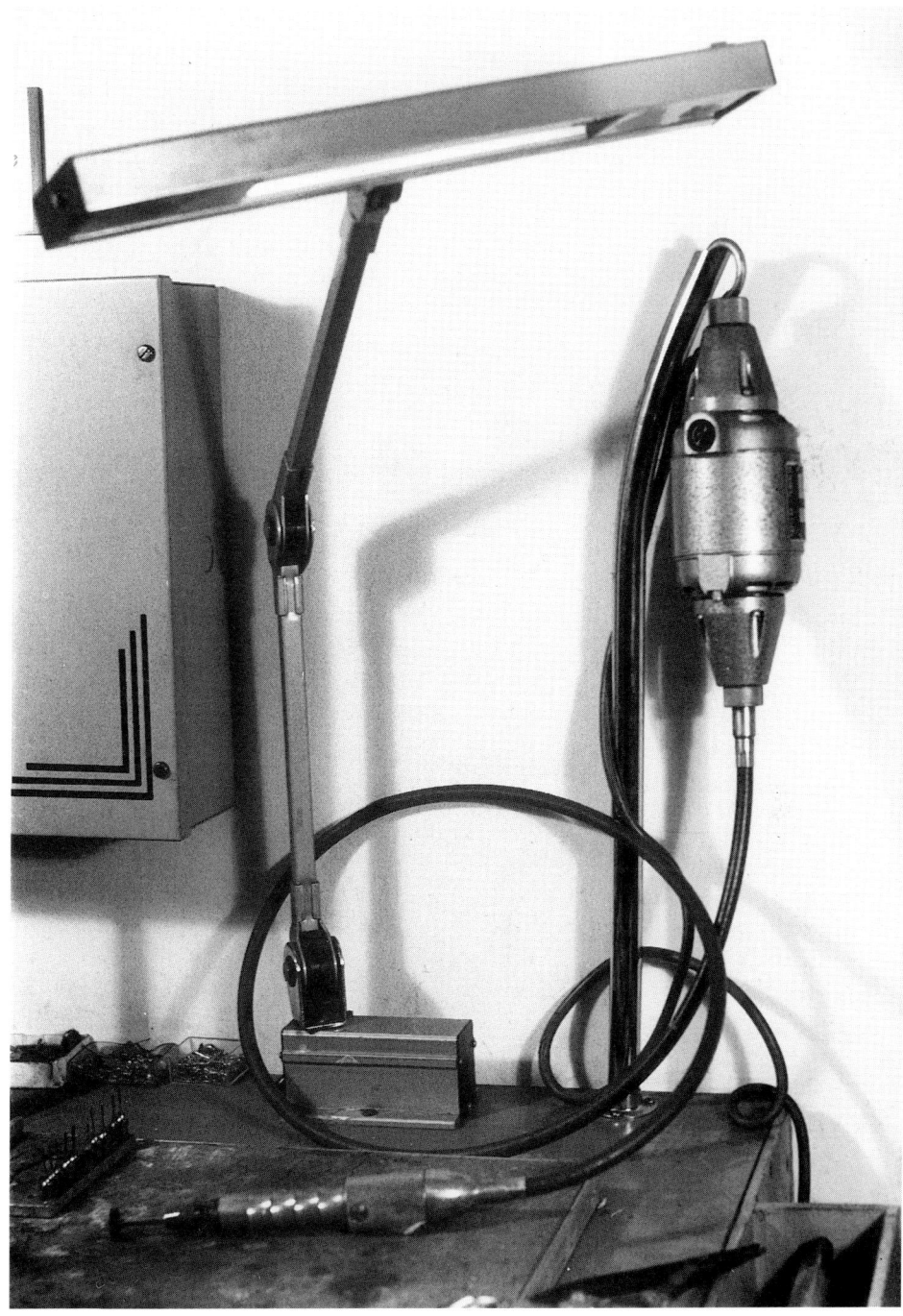

7 Use a separate light for each machine

Apprentice pieces and other scales

I am often asked by would-be miniature makers which model is the most difficult to make – the $\frac{1}{12}$th scale or the larger apprentice scale? I have to say that the $\frac{1}{12}$th scale is more difficult, especially the more complicated pieces with intricate shapes and many drawers. The larger scales are also easier to make from the point of view of obtaining tools – you will need only the usual cabinet maker's tools, but those for $\frac{1}{12}$th work are generally smaller in scale and therefore more difficult to obtain.

What is an apprentice piece? There is no strict definition and there are other terms that are applied to the same sort of pieces. These include: exhibition pieces, second size miniatures, salesman's samples and travellers' pieces.

Apprentice pieces are thought to have been made by woodworking craftsmen at the end of their apprenticeship to show their skills. Many of these

8 Military chest, 8in. (20cm) high, in teak with brass corners and handles ($\frac{1}{4}$ scale)

16

are now in museums along with sample pieces or travellers' samples; there are no standard sizes enabling you to distinguish which is which. Travellers' pieces or salesman's samples were probably originally smaller than the genuine apprentice piece but not as small as the $\frac{1}{12}$th scale. Ideally, they would have been small enough to carry four or five in a case or a bag, and a chest of drawers would have measured about 5in. (127mm) high. The equivalent apprentice piece was more likely to have been 8 or 10in. (203 or 254mm) in height and too bulky to have been carried around. Travellers' pieces were then of a very high standard and most likely made by one of the top craftsmen in a company.

By the end of the eighteenth century, sample pieces were made redundant by the introduction of illustrated catalogues, which were cheaper to produce and much easier to carry. When I repaired many of these samples or apprentice pieces I noticed that some were of poor quality and badly jointed. I concluded that these had been made by amateurs, before coming into the hands of dealers and acquiring the misnomer of apprentice pieces, although I am sure that most apprentices would have been embarrassed to have laid claim to them.

The miniature four drawer chest shown in fig. 9 is a copy of a genuine piece I

9 Mahogany chest with four drawers, banded in rosewood. It is smaller than the apprentice piece being $\frac{1}{6}$th scale. The pieces on the left are $\frac{1}{12}$th scale.

10 Red
lacquered
bureau
bookcase
with 36
interior
drawers. It
is made
from
walnut like
the original

bid for at a saleroom years ago; the price went way over my head, but I did have the presence of mind to take the measurements. Although sold as an apprentice piece, its small size led me to think it was a traveller's sample. It could have easily fitted into a case with others and not taken up too much room, whereas the apprentice pieces are usually too large for carrying around.

Figure 10 is 27in. (686mm) high. It is a reproduction of a red lacquered bureau bookcase, which I made some years ago. The piece I copied was too large to be called an apprentice piece. Instead, it was probably made for exhibition purposes and probably comes under the category of masterpieces. Masterpieces are models of especially high quality cabinet work; they were made as test pieces by craftsmen wishing to join a guild and are usually larger than apprentice pieces.

III *Timber*

11 The workshop

Obtaining timber

Whenever possible use old wood for making miniatures. If you find it impossible to gain access to old hardwood, by all means try the new hardwood, but do try for the old seasoned wood first.

The first timber I used for a miniature in the $\frac{1}{12}$th scale came from an old mahogany table bought in second-hand furniture shop. The base of all the legs had been sawn off many years before for some reason, and it was offered very cheaply. When cleaned down, it had a lovely, close-grained top; I cut the top down into strips of a useful size and stacked it away for later use, as in fig. 12.

12 Timber preparation

Fine grain timber

I am often asked where I get particular types of wood from with such fine close grain; there is no particular secret source. Anyone can do it, with a bit of patience. Most of the best hardwood comes from second-hand furniture shops or auction salerooms. Look around for something old, not antique, as this would cost too much. If something is broken or incomplete, even better, as the item will probably be much cheaper. Look out for mahogany or walnut. It is sometimes hard to identify when you are not experienced, so look inside and underneath where the surface has not been polished or waxed – the surface finish may be nothing like the real colour of the wood. Pull a drawer out and inspect the sides.

Which wood to choose

One advantage in making miniatures is that you do not need a mass of timber. I once bought a Regency teatray that had been burnt but the undamaged wood

13 Tip-top dining table banded in yew with various types of veneer inlays ($\frac{1}{12}$th scale)

was a beautiful walnut. I made three fine miniatures from that one tray, one of which is shown in fig. 13.

Later, when you have obtained an old piece of furniture and cut a sample strip off, you may find it is not to your liking and you have to try again. But when you do find the right piece, you will probably have enough to make many miniatures. Finding the right timber with that close grain and good colour to suit the small scale is all part of the work.

Figure 15 shows a rosewood desk that I made from a set of rosewood door-push plates (fig. 14), which came from an old converted public house in Brighton. I often wonder how many hands pushed against those plates in the years they were in use.

Walnut

Seasoned walnut is one of the best all round hardwoods to work with and, more to the point, easier to find than most. So much furniture was made from this timber in the last hundred years in England, and it is ideal for miniature work. The expansion and contraction in varying temperatures is limited, and walnut is also much less likely to warp, especially if seasoned.

14 Rosewood for $\frac{1}{12}$th miniatures

One important tip with walnut is to keep pieces that come from different sources separately. Timber can come from many parts of the world, and the variations in figure, colour and density can vary considerably. Sometimes you will be lucky, and the different sources of walnut will match. However, it is better to be safe and keep the pieces separate until you have experimented with a few samples by coating them with polish to see the finished colour your surface will give you.

Cutting wood

If you haven't your own bandsaw, find a timber yard or cabinet or joiner's shop. They will cut your wood to a workable size for a fee. You might also need

23

15 Davenport desk in rosewood with ivory inlay ($\frac{1}{12}$th scale)

16 Mahogany wardrobe door, approximately eighty years old; a piece of this was cut out to make a table (fig. 18)

to take it back to be recut when you have worked out sizes closer to your drawings. Be sure there are no nails or screws left in the wood when you break it down; the machinist will be obliged to charge you extra if it damages the teeth of the saw. I once cut an old drawer front on a circular saw, but somehow forgot to take the back of the lock plate off. As a result the saw hit the plate and broke four of its teeth.

You will be able to manage for a while in this way without a small circular saw or bandsaw, but if you continue to make progress, a machine saw will have to be your first buy. I have had both a circular saw and a bandsaw for many years now, but the bandsaw is the best buy. Choose a saw that will cut at least 1in. thick hardwood as shown in fig. 56.

Figure 16 shows a piece cut from a Victorian wardrobe door which is 80 years old.

17 A miniature cabinet before completion. This is a reproduction of a $\frac{1}{12}$th miniature of a very fine George I bureau cabinet. The carcass drawers and doors are carefully chosen, well-seasoned oak; the cabinet doors and flap were veneered in selected burr-amboyna. There are working locks and the usual parchment drawers, candles slides and secret drawers appropriate to these finer-made full-size bureau cabinets; the bandings are in kingwood.

Storing your wood

Once you have cut your wood into various sizes and thicknesses, stack it for three weeks with tiny spacing slats between each piece to allow air of an even temperature to flow on each side of the wood (see fig. 12). Also make sure that your stored wood is in a warm place with a temperature of 21°C (70°F) and no higher. Do not forget to cut extra pieces in case you spoil the ones you are working on or need some more.

18 Telescopic dining table in mahogany ($\frac{1}{12}$th scale)

It is important to stack and store wood this way even though it may be many years old. This is because the wood can warp once it has been cut. A period of three weeks gives the wood time to settle down to a new thickness – any warping can be trimmed off or the wood can be rejected if too badly twisted.

As your work improves you will have to pay more attention to your selection of woods. Your choice of figure, colour, texture and feel are all important for the end product to be satisfactory. The amount of work you put in always warrants you choosing the best wood available.

Making the most of the wood grain

Figure 19 is an example of how you can make the most of the grain of the wood by cutting it in different ways. All the pieces are cut from a 1in. square strip of stock: the walnut and satin walnut on the right are cut across the annual rings and the pieces on the left with them.

If you should acquire, for example, a strip of 2in. × 2in. (51mm × 51mm) walnut, just cut a small 3in. long piece *with* the grain, then another piece *across* the grain also 3in. (76mm) long (fig. 21). Clean them both up on one side only, then just brush with a quick coat of polish. This will immediately bring the grain to life and show you which way to cut the rest of your wood for the finest surface figure. Then you will be able to cut the rest (or have it cut) into convenient-sized strips. For most walnut you will find for miniature cabinet work, including satin, cuts across the annual rings will give the best results.

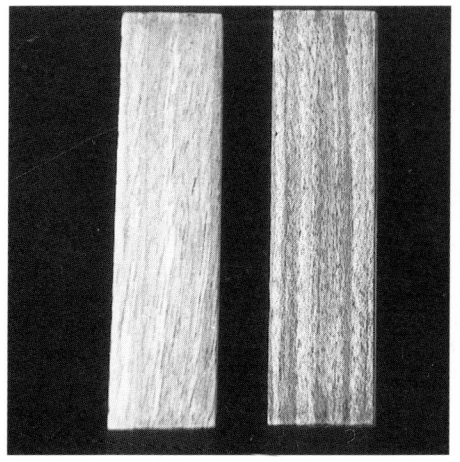
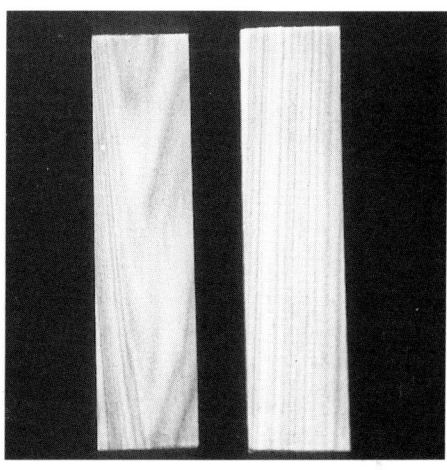

19 (*Left*) Walnut cut with the grain;
(*Right*) Walnut cut across the grain

20 (*Left*) Satin walnut cut with the grain;
(*Right*) Satin walnut cut across the grain

21 Cut your wood both *across* and *with* the grain. After coating both pieces, decide which looks best.

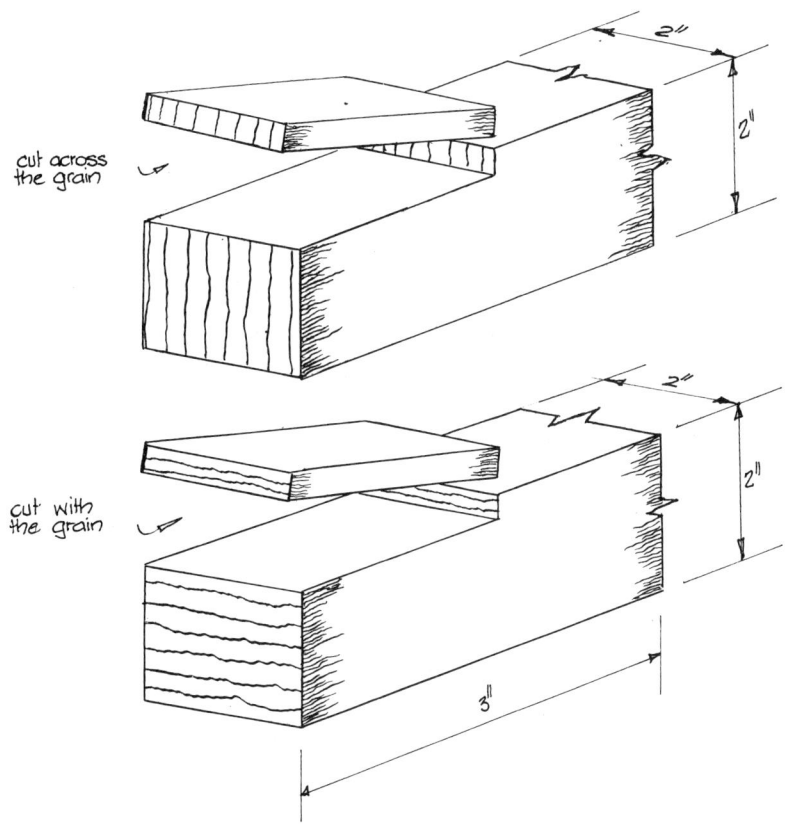

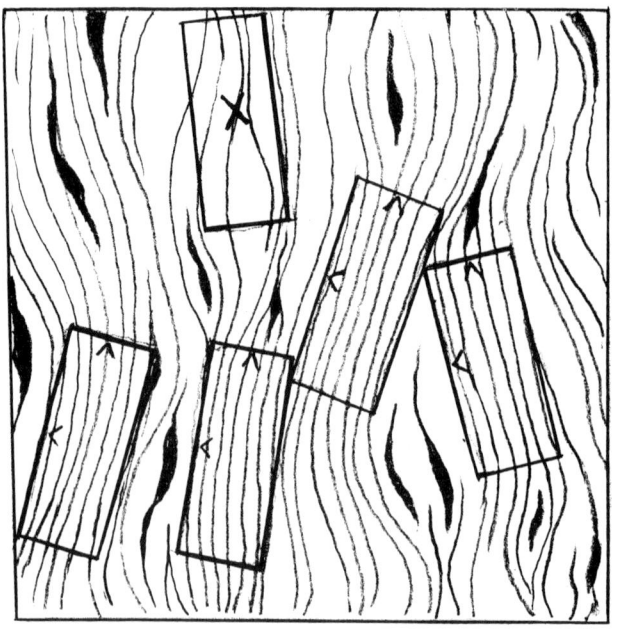

22 Selecting close grain on four small panels

Mahogany is not so simple as there are so many different kinds of wood. Figure 22 shows a method of selecting a close grain to make four small panels for a $\frac{1}{12}$th scale miniature; the wild grain in the sketch has been exaggerated to show the obvious mistake in the fifth panel on the top left corner, where the wide gap in the grain makes it totally unsuitable for a small door front.

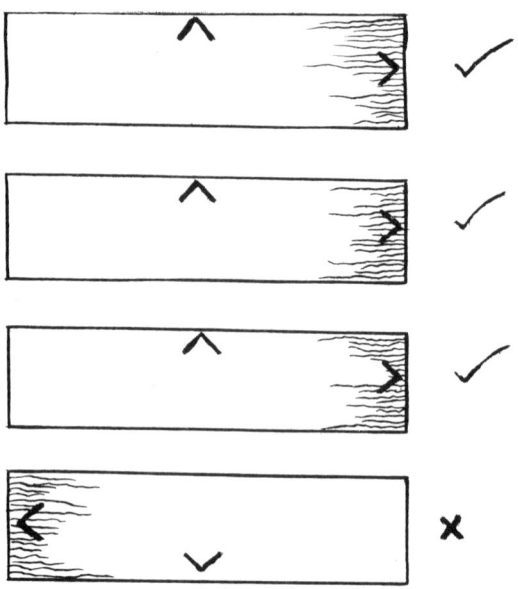

23 The importance of marking the door panels. The grain on one drawer front is facing in the opposite direction to the other three and may look different

When cutting out a set of drawer fronts or doors, make sure you mark the top and one side before cutting, **as in fig. 22**. This will ensure that the grain and colour variations will all face the same way; if one is inadvertently turned, as in fig. 23, when polished, the colour can be altered quite considerably. Before starting to clean the face of these drawers, transfer the markings to the edges; this way you will always have the mark indicating the way they should all face.

IV *Tools*

Basic tool kit for miniature cabinet work

Ruler	Pin chuck for drills
Small hammer	Set of fine drills
Block plane	Set of very fine chisels
Set of needle files	$\frac{1}{4}$in. standard bevel-edged chisel
Needle files for metal	Small marking gauge
Gents saw	Adjustable bevel
Fret saw	Set of six small clamps
Piercing saw blades	Fine bradawl
Junior hacksaw	Half round 6in. file
Saws X-acto, fine cut, set of three	Calliper gauge
Small snips	Sharpening stone
Tweezers	Honing guide
Small square	Portable bench vice

Block plane

These small block planes in figs 24 and 25 are $6\frac{3}{8}$in. (162mm) long and especially useful in cabinet work for trimming end grain because of the very low angle

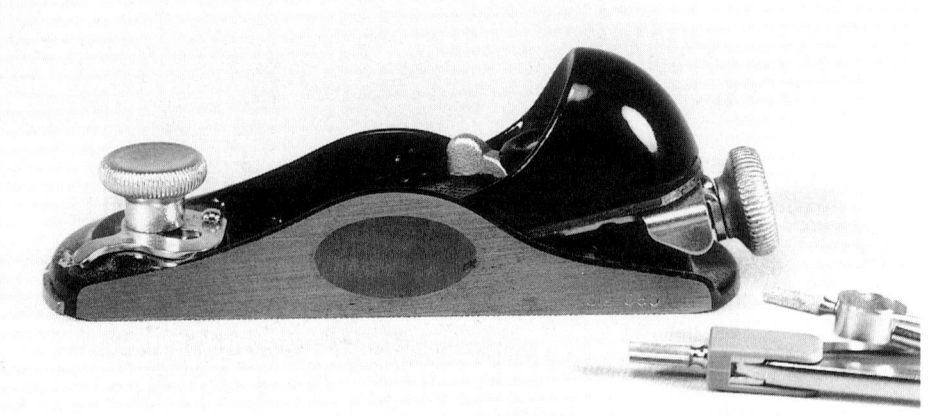

24 Block plane

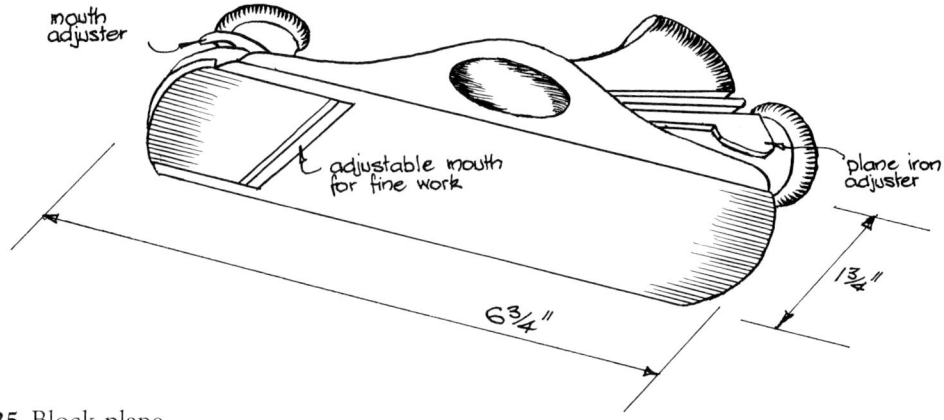

25 Block plane

blade ($13\frac{1}{2}°$) and easy adjustments (fig. 25). You can make very fine cuts with them without having to use too much pressure.

Files

You must have a good set of needle files, at least six to start with. They can be bought separately or in a set. There are so many makes on the market; buy the more expensive, better quality ones. Figure 26 shows six standard shapes to start you off with.

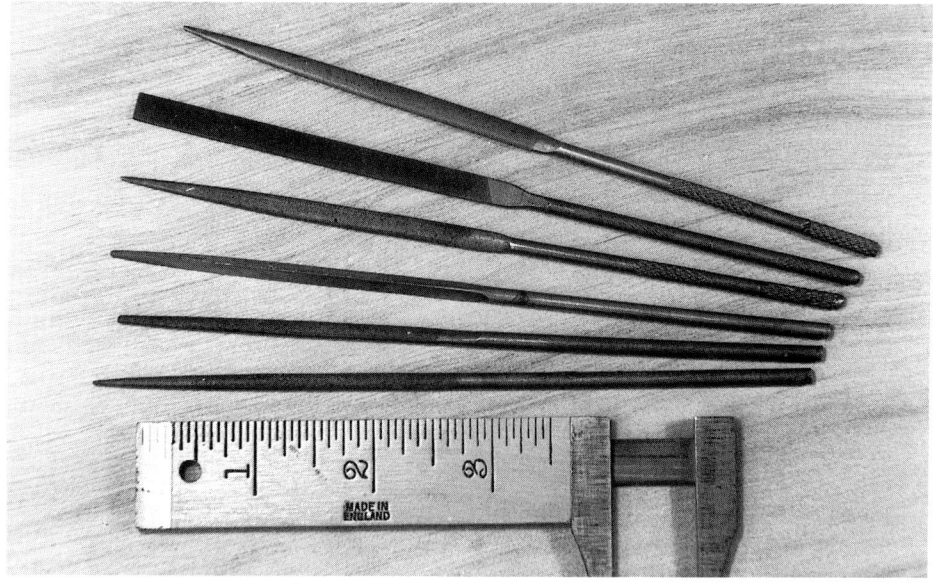

26 File shapes

three square	△
pillar	▭
half round	⌓
round	○
oval	○
square	▢

There are many more shapes available, but these six will be enough to start with. It is an advantage to have one smooth edge on at least two of your needle files – some makers do supply them like this. If you do have difficulties obtaining them, it is quite easy to hone one edge down smooth on the hand stone. Smooth edges are invaluable when trimming an inside corner where you must file one edge without damaging the other. Yet do remember that after making one smooth surface to a file, two edges are now quite sharp, especially if you hone down one edge on a three square file. I use a rubber finger stall if I am using this file for any length of time to safeguard my finger when pressure is applied.

You will find small knob handles on the needle files very useful. If you cannot obtain these knobs, any kind of small wooden knob will do. The knob prevents any soreness on the ball of your hand.

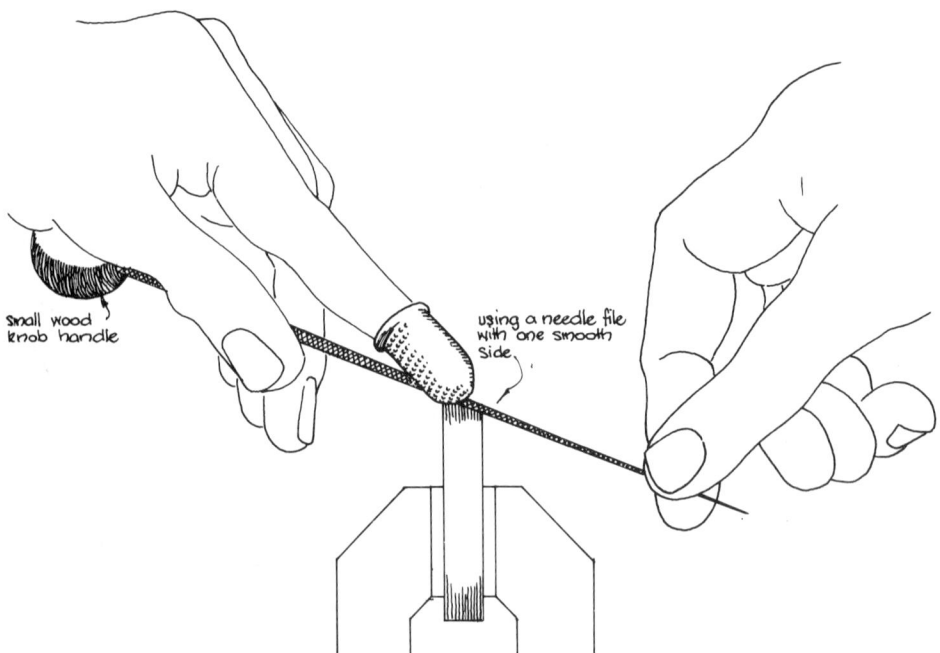

small wood knob handle

using a needle file with one smooth side

27 Small wood knobs attached to files make them more comfortable to grip

When purchasing these needle files remember they are graded according to the number of teeth per centimetre. The grade number should be marked on the handle. Finer grades are 4–5 and 6; coarse cuts are 0 and 00. These files are designed for metal work. For miniature woodwork I have found grades 2–4 are best.

Care of your files

Wood swarf tends to clog in these small files, especially hardwood, so invest in a file cleaner with the files you buy.

If you use needle files for any kind of metal work, especially brass work, do not use these same files on your woodwork, as small metal particles can easily become lodged in the grain. You will be unable to see them, but later when the polish goes on they can show up. Then, by this stage, it is hard to remove them without damaging the surface. I mark all files used for metal work with a little dab of red paint.

Chisels

Very fine chisels are a problem to obtain for miniature work, but if you have no small machinery to cut your rebate grooves and tenon joints you do need very fine chisels. An improvised set of thin miniature screwdrivers will serve to start

28 Improvising a set of miniature screwdrivers for temporary chisels

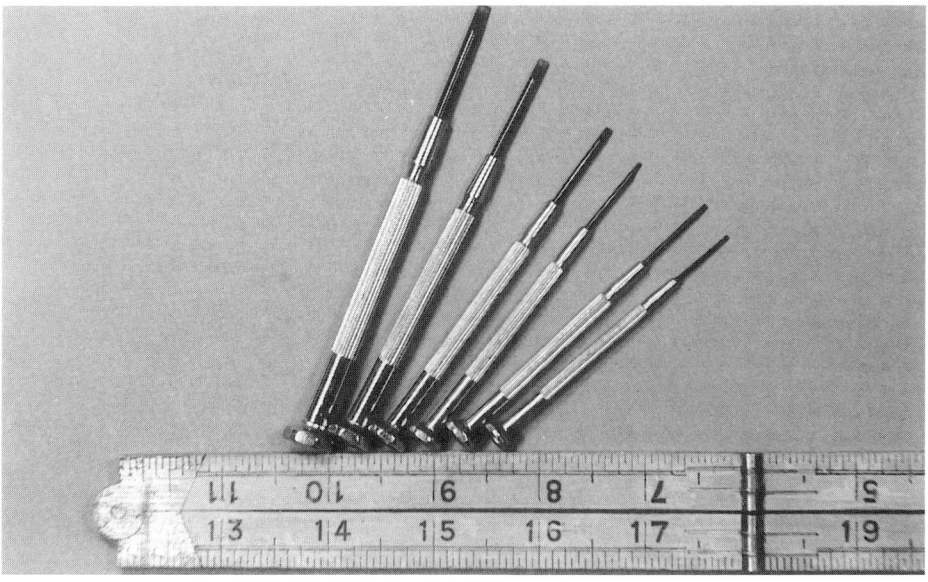

you off. They are quite flexible, being made from soft steel – not too much pressure is needed with this miniature cabinet work – and they will hold a sharp edge for a short time. These are available in most hardware tool shops or model shops, but it must be stressed they are only a provisional measure until you can buy and make up two or three really fine chisels.

Gravers

Real good chisels can be made from gravers. As well as being high quality steel, they are not expensive and are obtainable in square parallel. You can buy them in various sizes from 6mm down to 1.25mm; they are mostly sold in 6in. lengths, however.

Adapting your chisels

The best chisels for miniature work are those of the smallest gauges. The square parallel gravers, $\frac{1}{64}$in. (2mm) and $\frac{1}{8}$in. (3mm) wide and 6in. (152mm) long, are ideal and can be bought from jewellers' merchants and good quality tool suppliers.

Figure 29 shows four square parallel gravers that I made, sharpened and then fitted handles to them – one of $\frac{1}{8}$in. (3mm) and three of $\frac{5}{64}$in. (2mm). Do not buy gravers thinner than these.

Figure 30 shows a $\frac{3}{64}$in. (1mm) chisel which is made from a $\frac{5}{64}$in. (2mm) graver; to keep the shaft a little stronger, it is best to hone down on both sides about

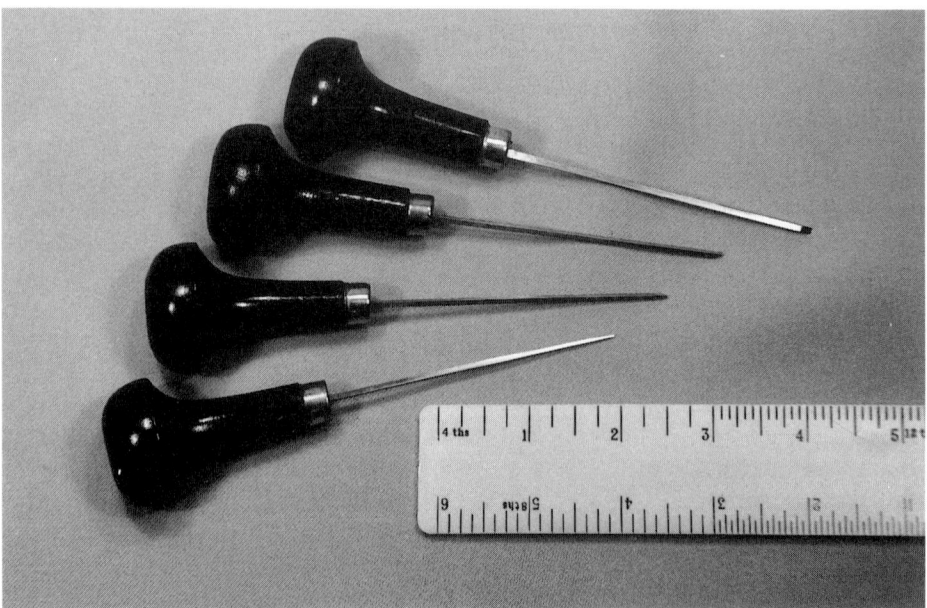

29 Fine chisels made from gravers

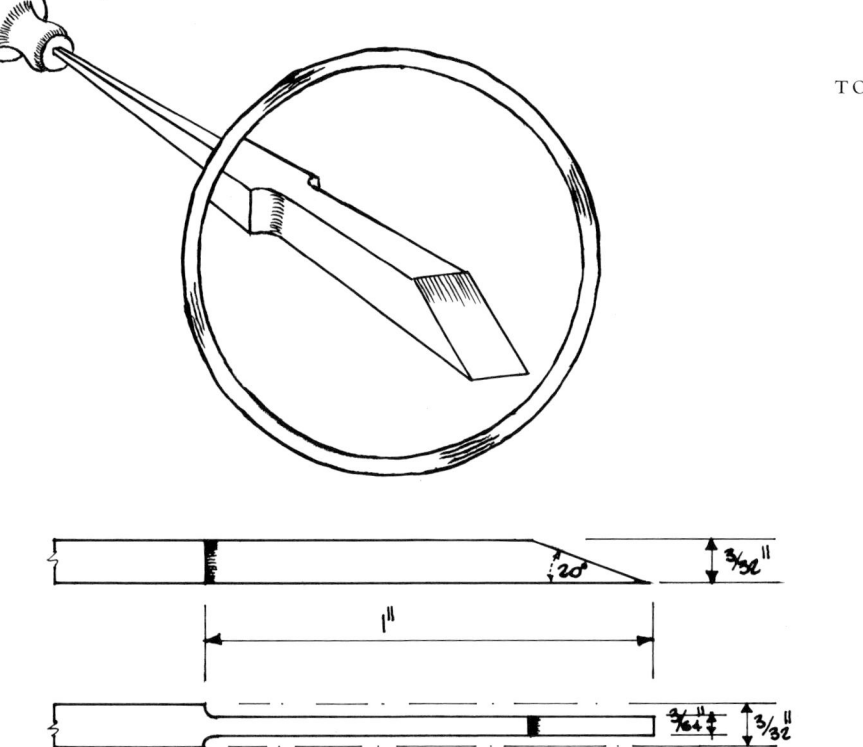

30 Chisel ($\frac{3}{64}$in.) – made from square parallel graver

$\frac{1}{100}$in. (0.25mm) from the tip to a length of 1in. (25mm) only, as shown. Then sharpen the tip to an angle of 20 degrees by honing down by hand – if you use a power grinder on these very thin gravers the shaft would quickly overheat and change the temper of the steel.

Lastly, to make the 6in. (152mm) shaft a little stronger and less flexible, make the graver shorter. I use 5in. (127mm) long gravers with 1in. (25mm) pushed into the handle.

Knives and rulers

You should really have more than one cutting knife. Figure 31 shows three examples. The very thin one is a surgical knife, stocked in many model shops, ideal for delicate carving and cutting veneers; however, it will snap easily when under too much pressure. The middle knife X-acto No. 2 has a multitude of assorted blades. It is ideal for deeper carving and *scribing* when you are marking to cut joints. The large Stanley knife (craft knife) is a general purpose workshop knife with a thicker blade; it is a heavy duty knife.

When scribing it is wise not to use your rule for this job; most are too thin, some only $\frac{3}{64}$in. (1mm) thick. If care is not taken as you scribe along the marked line the knife can easily ride up over the rule, blunting the edge of the knife and

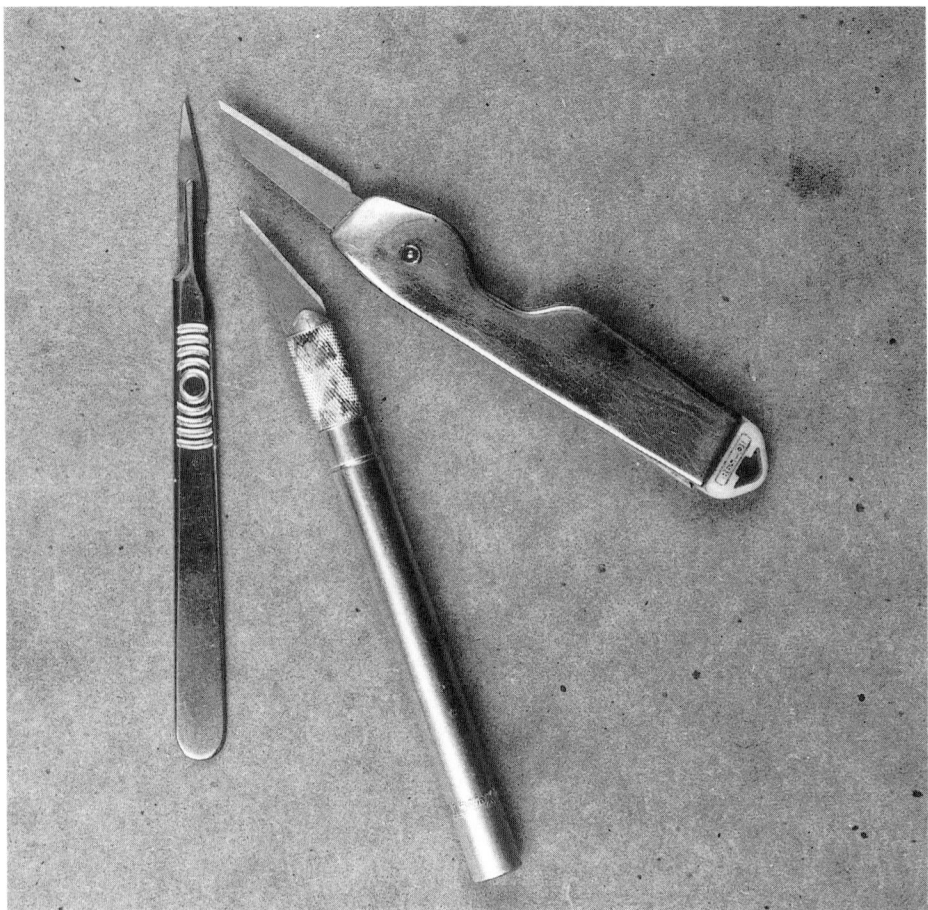

31 Useful workshop knives

possibly cutting your fingers before you have time to stop. I use a much thicker rule for this work, a steel rule taken from a carpenter's combination square is ideal, being $\frac{3}{32}$in. thick and much safer to use. To gain a better grip on the under side of this rule glue a strip of fine sandpaper to it. The only time you will have to use a thin flexible steel rod is over shaped surfaces (fig. 32).

Saws

In general cabinet making, many sizes of saws are necessary, from the rip saw for heavy work, right down to the dovetail saw and the small gent's saw; for miniature woodwork, however, you will need only the finer saws. A larger panel saw might be needed once in a while to cut longer pieces, if it is not

32 Flexible rule for
scribing over shapes

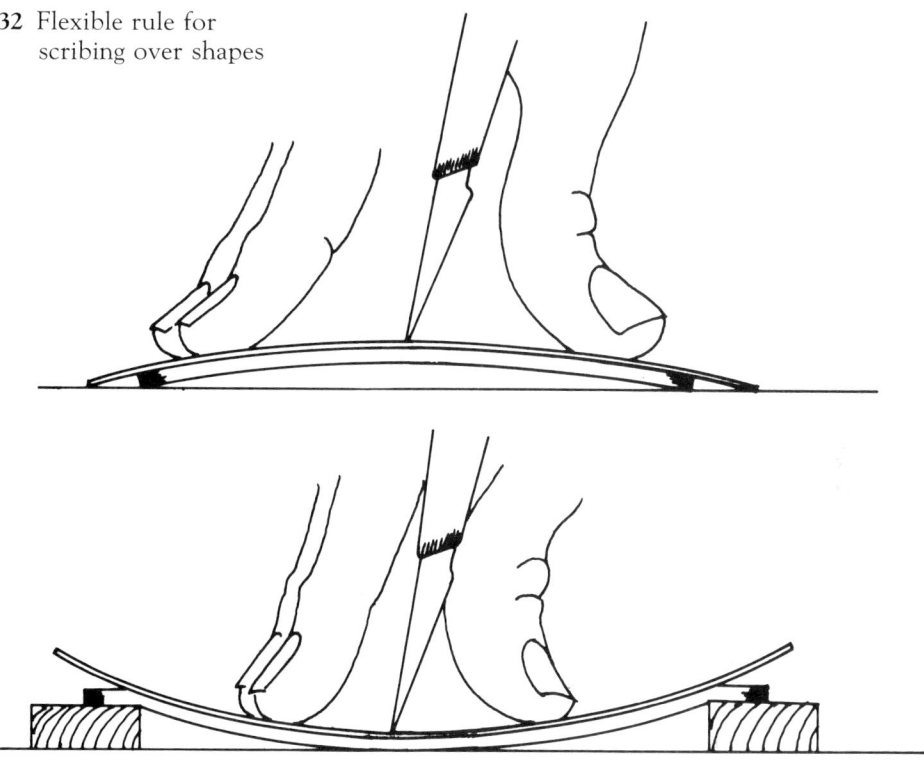

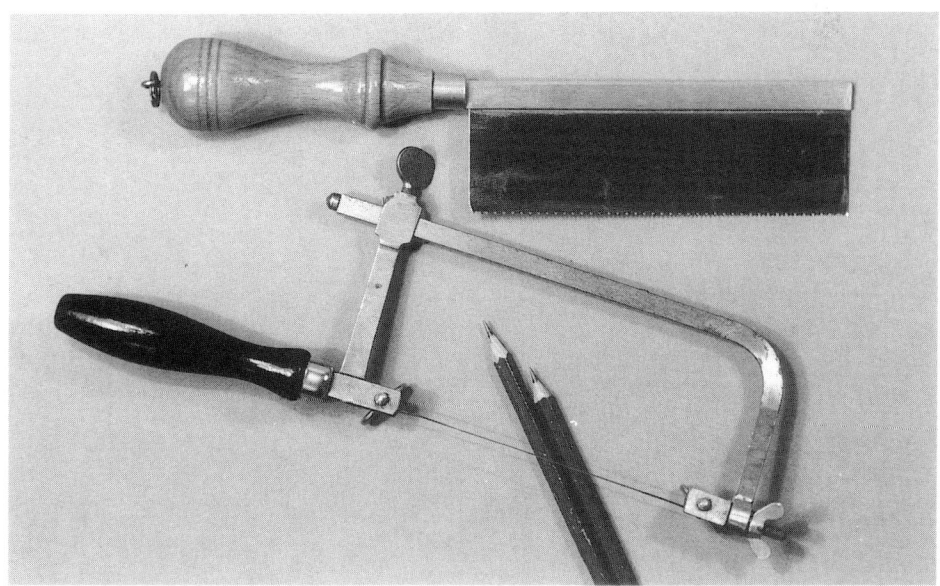

33 Gent's saw and adjustable fret saw frame

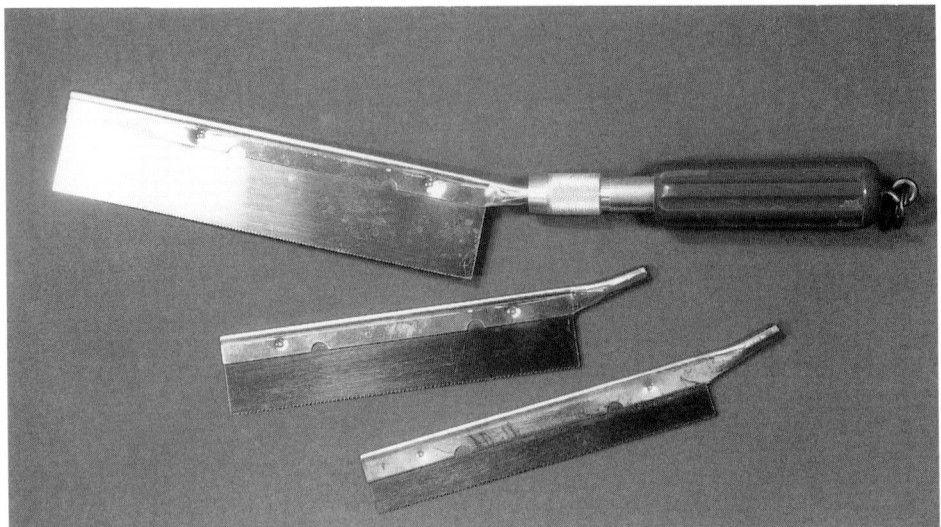

34 X-acto saws

possible for you to have them cut by someone who has a power saw. The gent's saw is, however, a must (fig. 33). Only purchase the larger tenon saw later if you think the gent's saw is not quite strong enough for some of the cuts you have to make. Again, do not buy the cheapest tools you can find. There are so many makes of saws on the market; seek advice before you buy.

The three saws with portable handles in fig. 34 are X-acto saws; they are reasonably priced and useful for very fine cutting, small joints, etc. Do not use them for cutting larger pieces of timber – if you should bend them by pushing too hard you will ruin their fine cutting edge. Revert to your gent's saw or tenon saw for larger work.

Fret saws

There are numerous types of fret saw on the market. The one in fig. 33 is perhaps one of the best buys. It has a tension wing nut at the front, which is much easier to adjust when the blade has to be tightened in the frame. Don't give it too much tension – just enough to keep the blade taut; too much and the blade will snap, especially the finer grades. Fret saws are available from jewellers' merchants (see page 141).

Grades of blade

When buying piercing saw blades, grade numbers are as follows: fine grades – 8/0, 7/0, 6/0, 5/0, 4/0, 3/0, 2/0, 1/0; coarse grades – 1,2,3,4,5, and 6. You won't need *all* of the finer grades, but you will need at least six grades, perhaps 1 dozen blades of each to cover various jobs and replace broken ones.

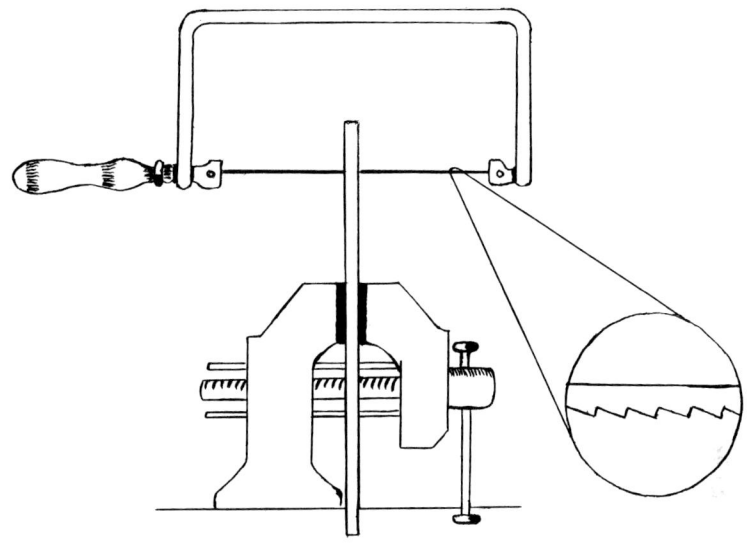

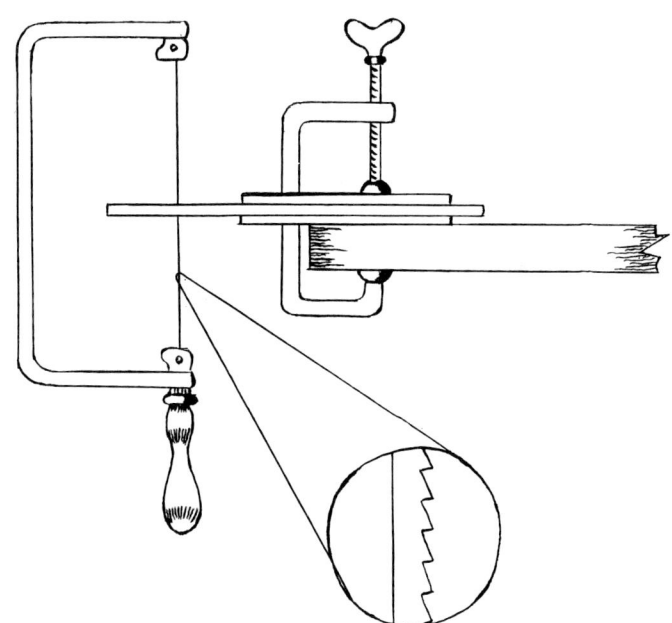

35 (*Top*) Method of cutting with blade teeth pointing away from the handle;
(*Bottom*) blade teeth pointing towards the handle

Tool shops do not carry very many different grades. The best place to find a large range is from a jewellers' merchant. I always ask for roundback blades – they are very good for tight turns, but they unfortunately are not always available.

Using the blades

One problem with blades is knowing how fine a grade to use to keep a thin cut without the blade breaking. If you keep breaking blades fit a slightly thicker grade, until you reach the finest you can work with without breaking it too often. Most people work with the blade teeth pointing towards the handle, as in fig. 35, but there are some instances where it is often much easier to work with the blade teeth pointing away from your handle (fig. 35). I would suggest you try both ways and use the method that is most accurate for you. Obviously, you must watch the cutting line carefully as you saw, but most of your

36 Fretwork ($\frac{1}{12}$th scale)

37 Rosewood davenport with ivory inlay

concentration should be given to keeping the piercing saw square to your work as you progress along the cutting line; do not worry too much if you break a few blades – they are not expensive. I break dozens in a year.

The fretwork in fig. 36 has been cut from a $\frac{1}{16}$in. (1.5mm) thick piece of walnut using a grade 3 piercing saw and is quite easy to achieve. The fretwork in fig. 37 has been cut from a $\frac{1}{32}$in. (0.8mm) piece of ivory, using grade 4/0 piercing saw blades much finer work and would require a little more practice. There are finer piercing saw blades than 8/0, but you should only use these for very delicate work.

Working to the $\frac{1}{12}$th scale

It is possible to find miniature furniture drawing ideas and sketches in craft books and miniature and model magazines. These are ideal to start you on the road to miniature making and will teach you many useful things, but as you progress you will feel the need to break away from the general simple type of miniature scale drawings and develop something of your own that pleases your eye and gives you more of a challenge.

Working on a drawing and making the measurements tally is all part of the fun and skill; even if you make many mistakes, eventually it will give you great satisfaction to know that you have really made it all by yourself. Do not be put off by scaling down, it really is quite easy.

The rulers shown in fig. 38 all have $\frac{1}{12}$th scale marked on one side and are still available. The one at the bottom, a steel ruler, is made by Picadore and has $\frac{1}{12}$th scale to the inch along the full length on one side and is subdivided into $\frac{1}{24}$th and $\frac{1}{96}$th. It can be obtained from Shestopal (see page 141).

The two white plastic rulers have the $\frac{1}{12}$th scale marked on one side only; the six inch ruler has three inches marked in $\frac{1}{12}$th scale, the twelve-inch ruler has six inches marked in $\frac{1}{12}$th scale. Made by Rolinox, they are very cheap and available in some stationers.

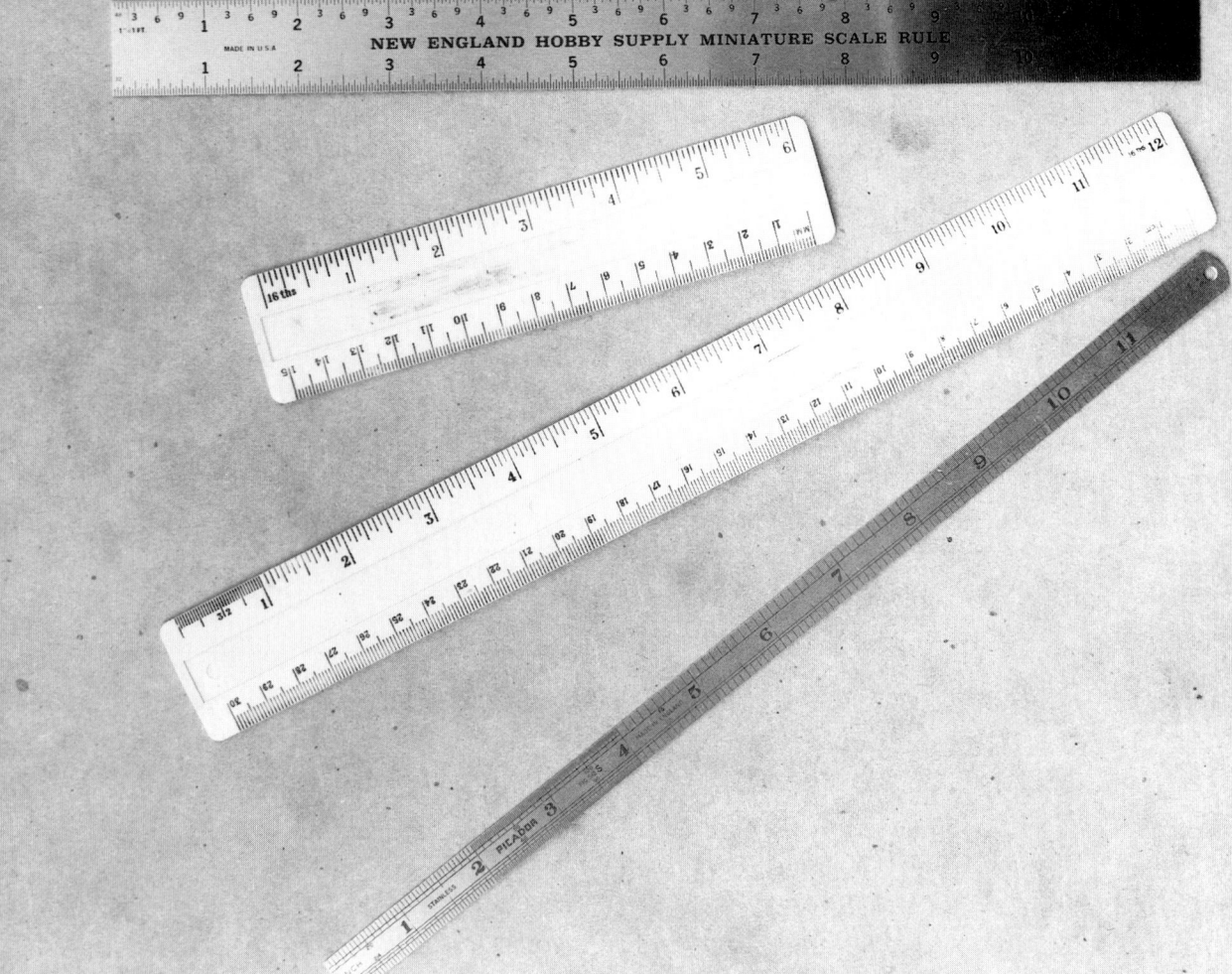

38 Rulers available with $\frac{1}{12}$th scale marked

The steel ruler at the top is easily the best of the four, made in America specially for miniature work; though not cheap, it is subdivided into forty-eighths along the full length of the rule. You can obtain these from a New England supplier (see page 141).

Adjustable sliding bevel

An adjustable sliding bevel is not easily available but most essential for complicated work. This steel one (fig. 39b) is ideal for miniature work.

The small adjustable sliding bevel with the black handle in fig. 39b is easier to make; it has been cut by hand and is well within the capabilities of anyone with the tool kit shown (see page 30).

I chose a small brass strip for the adjustable arm; this makes it easier to cut

39a Sliding bevels

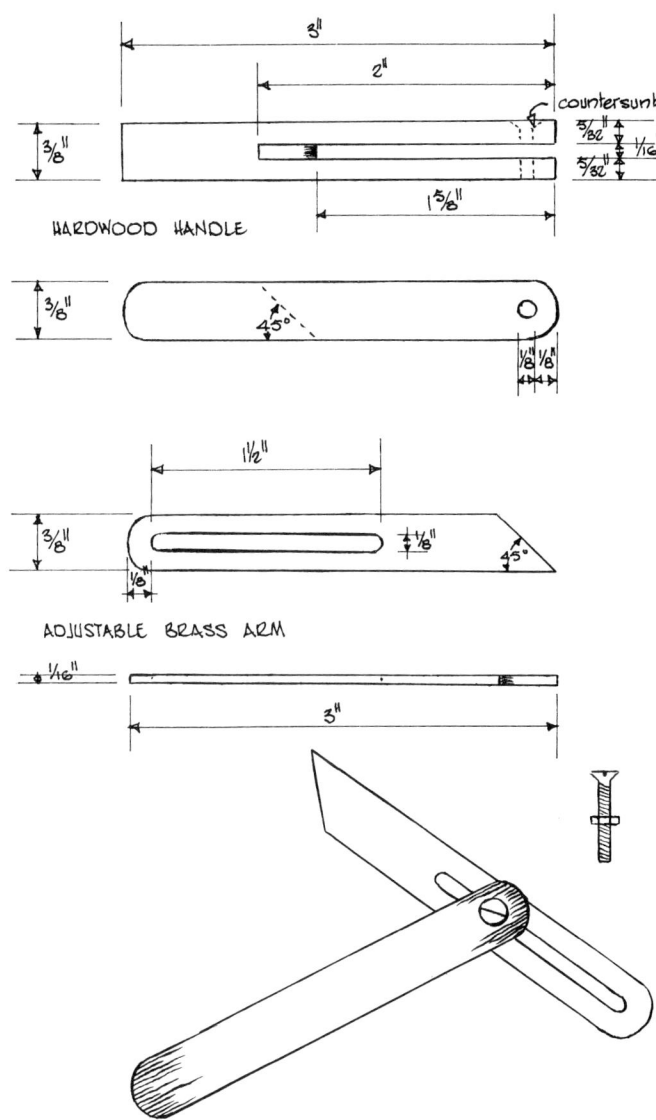

and shape. As this sliding bevel is used only for very fine work and has to take very little stress, brass is quite adequate for strength.

The handle is made of rosewood, but beechwood will do just as well. A small nut and bolt for the swivel arm will give you the adjusting point. The advantage of cutting a sliding arm is to enable you to manoeuvre the point into very small recesses

43

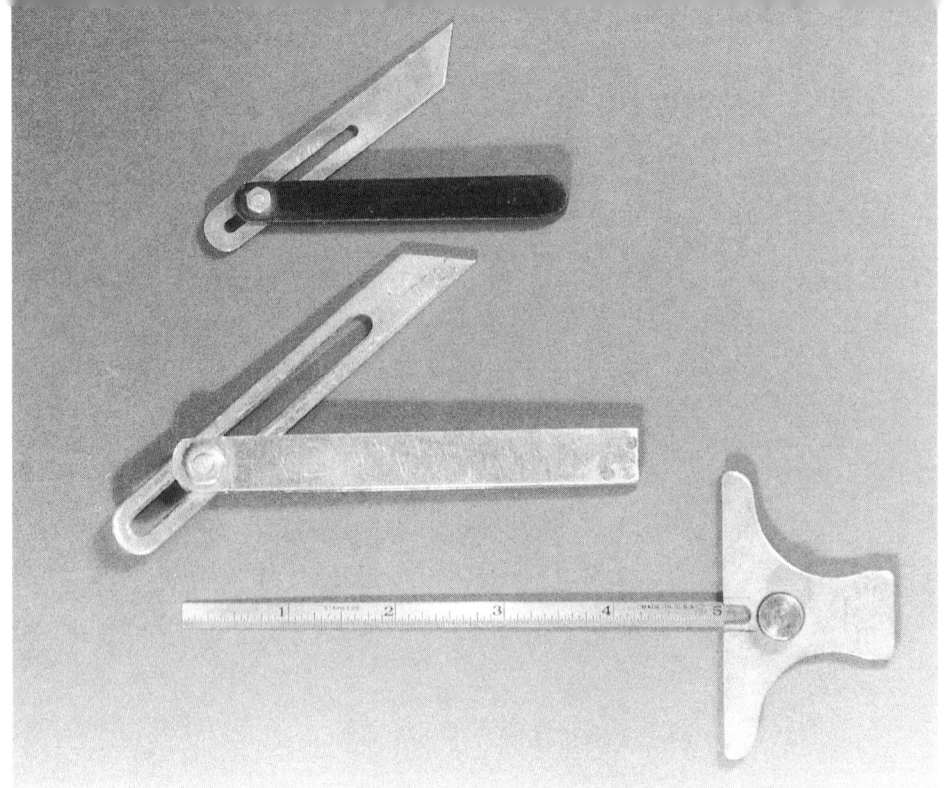

39b Bevels in use

40 Improvising to make a small marking gauge

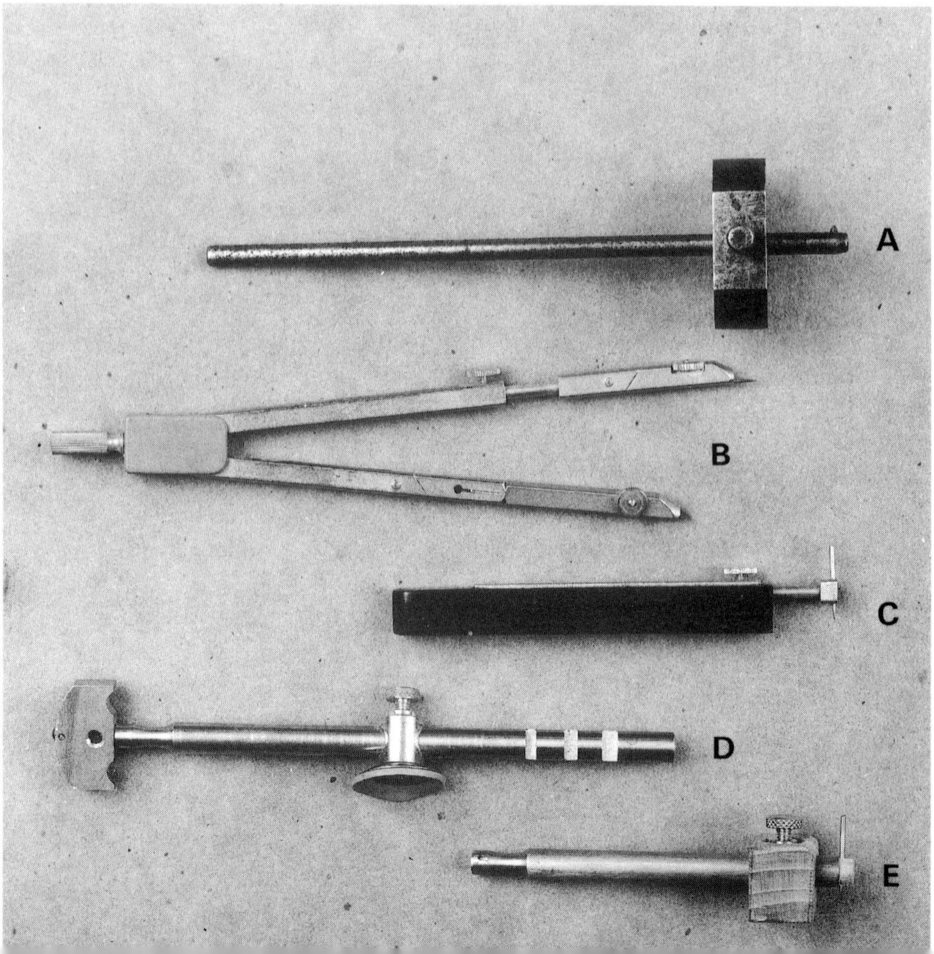

Marking gauge

A very small marking gauge is also hard to come by but essential for accurate work in this small scale. The three gauges in fig. 40 are all handmade; you can manage with just one gauge, but I have shown three to demonstrate how to improvise on them.

The top one (A) is all steel and again a little hard to make without metal work experience. The second gauge (C) has been cut out from a pair of callipers (B). A hardwood handle has been fitted to form a shoulder, and a small hole drilled through the head to take the marking pin. The bottom gauge, marked (E), is part of an old glass cutter marked at (D). A small beech block has been fitted to form a shoulder and a marking pin fitted in place.

These particular pins are old gramophone needles, wedged in tight. If you find it difficult to obtain hard steel pins of the right thickness, a needle cut down will do almost as well. Tips can also be ground to form a cutting edge for rebates. The steel gauge is the strongest of the three so I use this one for a cutting edge, as more pressure is sometimes needed for that particular job. But the other two gauges will do the job with a cutting edge formed on the marking pin. NB *It is easy to knock these pins out and replace them if they wear down with sharpening.*

Cramps

The assorted cramps in fig. 41 are all available from various tool merchants and hobby and model shops. You will need at least three pairs of different sizes, adding more later as you find a need for them. It really is essential to use small

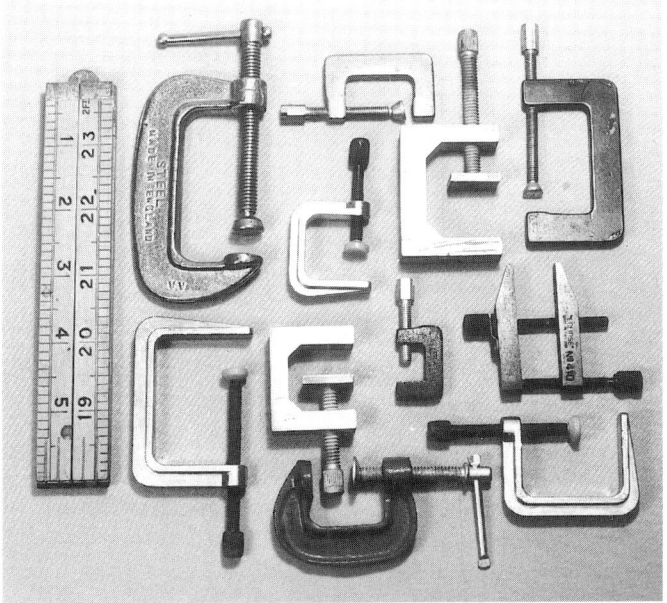

41 Assortment of small useful cramps

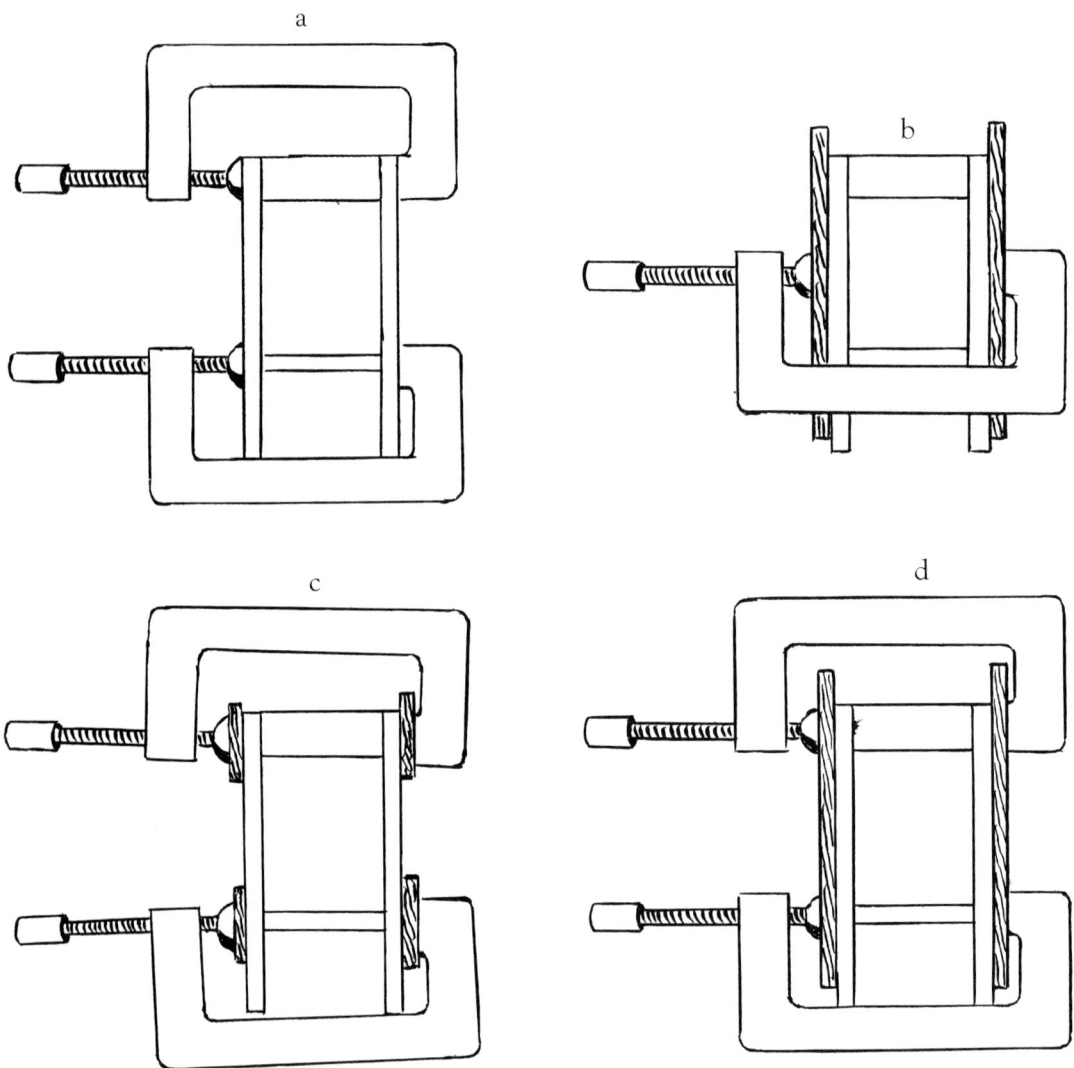

42 Using cramps to best advantage: (a) no protective blocks; (b) uneven pressure; (c) cramps out of line; (d) cramps placed correctly

blocks between the cramps and your work; without these blocks, small indents can easily form, even under slight pressure, and they are difficult to sand out later. Use a large cramp block to spread the pressure evenly over your work.

If at any time glue seeps through from your work and touches the cramp block, just place a small piece of plain paper between the two as a safeguard against sticking your block to the work.

Vices

There are so many types of small portable vices available on the market that it becomes difficult to know what to choose for your miniature cabinet work. The vice in fig. 43, or one similar, is not ideal for all jobs but good for most work that has to be held. It is not too expensive and has a swivel, enabling you to change the angles of the vice – a distinct advantage in miniature work.

If possible, it would be best to have two vices so you can fit softwood jaws on your first vice for general work. The second vice in fig. 44, with thin, hard, rubber strips as jaws, will enable you to work on the delicate and fragile pieces. Hard rubber will grip well without making any indents. The only disadvantage I have found with this rubber is that there will always be slight movement because the rubber gives a little. When it does become essential to hold your work rigid, revert to the softwood jaws. Never use a vice without any protection on the metal jaws for miniature woodwork. Cork strips can be useful to hold delicate work without damage (fig. 44). One last thing to mention: the vice is probably the tool you will use most of all. Look after it, oil the thread and guiding shafts very lightly from time to time and remember not to touch your work on the oiled parts.

43 Ideal vice for miniature work

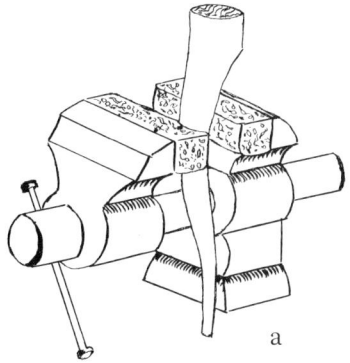

a

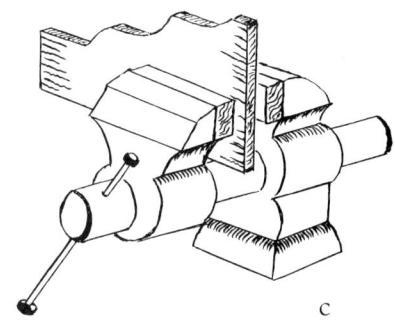

c

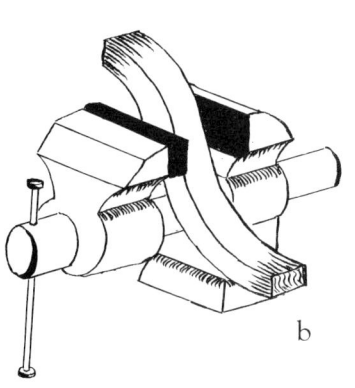

b

44 (a) Cork used for delicate shapes
(b) hard rubber for a grip without damage;
(c) soft wood for firm grip

47

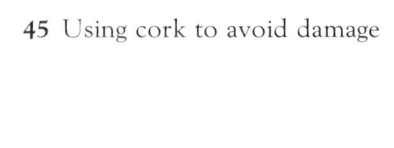

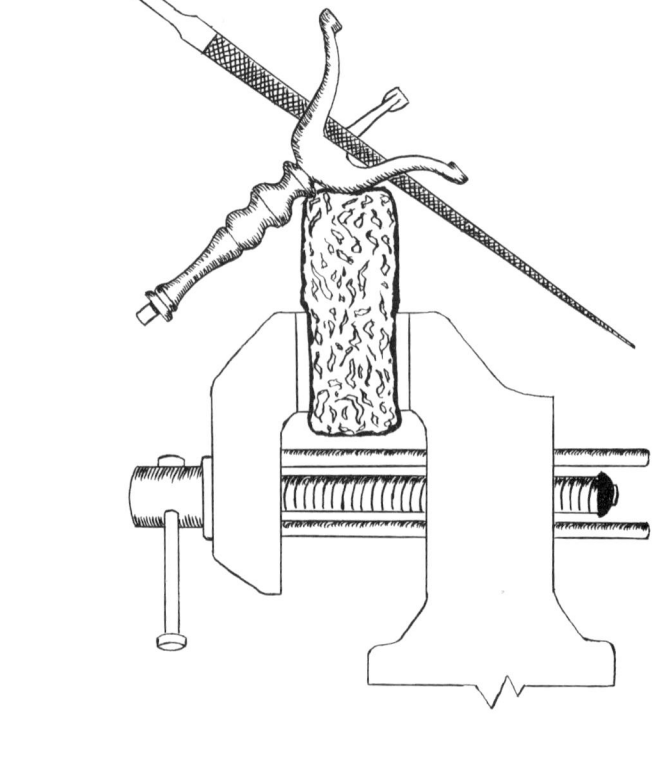

Sharpening stone

For a sharpening stone your best buy will probably be a combination oil-stone, with a fine grade one side and medium or coarse on the other. There is a large price range here, but do not buy the cheapest one you can find. It is difficult to give advice here without seeing the stone and reading the grade or quality on the box, but it is a very important part of your tool kit, so bear this in mind.

Later when you have practised a little sharpening and think your chisel or plane iron should be even sharper, you will probably have to buy a better quality oil-stone with a finer grade on one side for the sharper edge.

I have found it an advantage to make up a base for the combination stone with a small block either end, finishing level with the top (see fig. 46). The purpose of these blocks is to enable sharpening strokes of the honing guide to travel the full length of your stone; they help stop the wearing down that inevitably occurs in the middle of the stone, eventually making it hard to get that sharp finish you require to skim down the thin strips of stock you have cut.

48

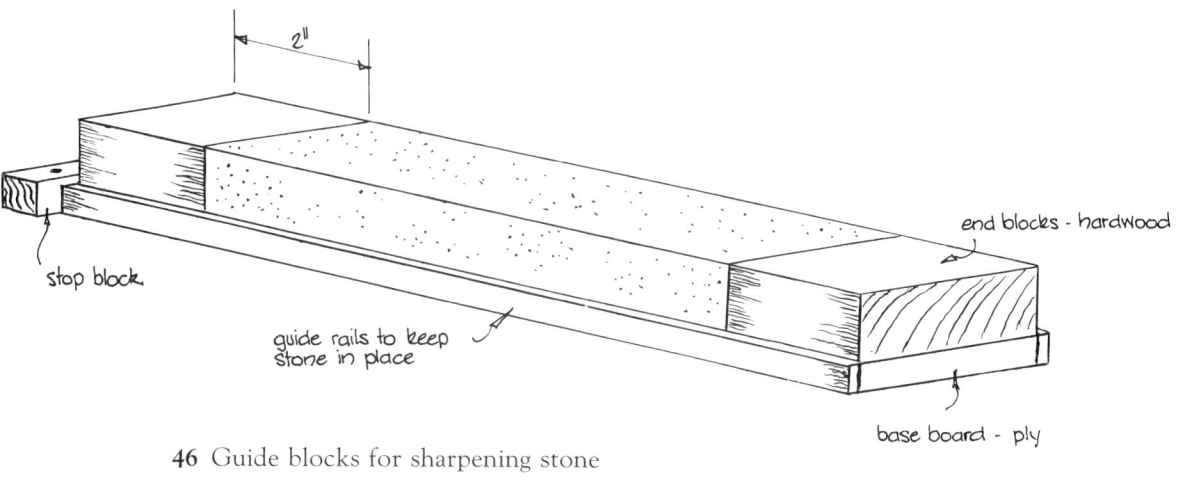

46 Guide blocks for sharpening stone

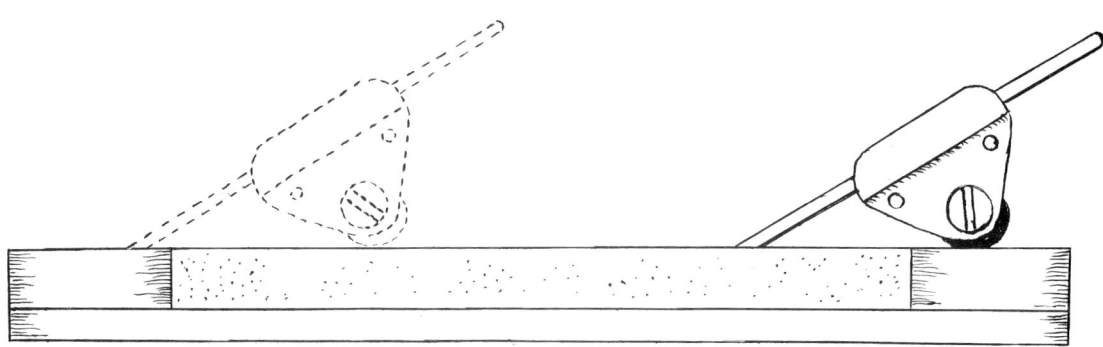

47 Obtaining full use of your sharpening stone

Of course, all stone wears down eventually, but this method will help keep the flat surface much longer (see fig. 47).

When the stone has become misshapen, spread carborundum powder on an old piece of glass; wet the stone down and rub until the surface is again flat. This does take some time but happily does not have to be done too often.

Most new chisels and plane iron tips are ground to an angle of 25 degrees but are not sharpened for use. The first thing you must do is to make sure the back of the iron is perfectly smooth and flat, using first the coarse and then the fine side of your stone – this part is just as important as sharpening the face side (fig. 48).

A typical angle for a chisel cutting softwood is shown in fig. 49. The same chisel used on hardwood should be at a slightly steeper angle to give best results for full size cabinet work. I would use these angles for making apprentice pieces, but the $\frac{1}{12}$th scale is so reduced that very little stress need be applied to chisel and plane irons alike. A much lower angle of 20 to 23 degrees can be used,

48 Preparing the back edge of your plane iron

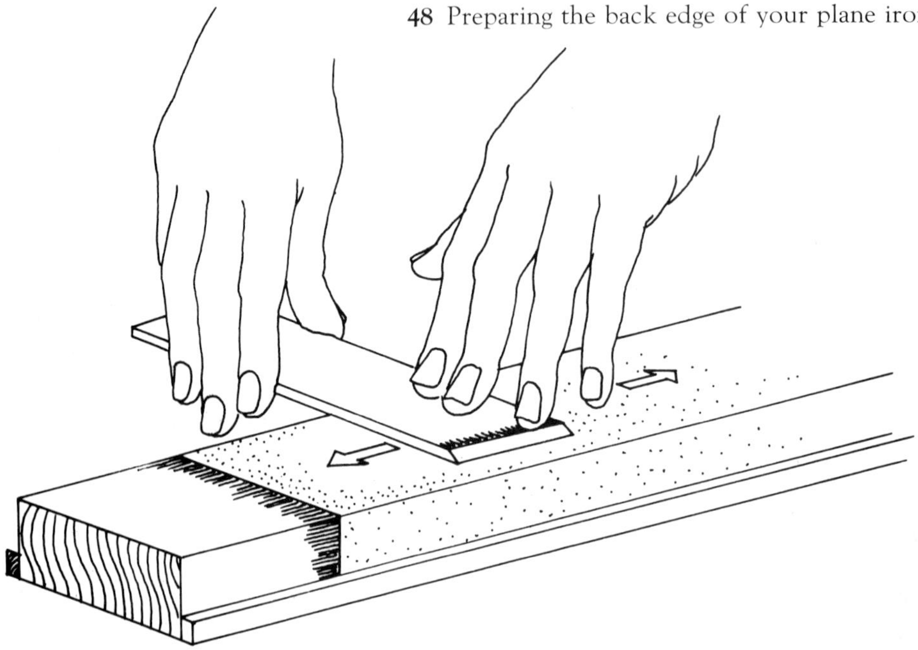

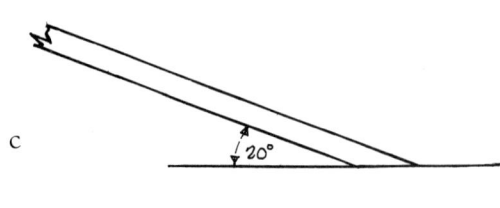

49 (a) Typical angle for chisel cutting softwood; (b) typical angle using the same type of chisel for hardwood; (c) suggested angle using chisels for $\frac{1}{12}$th scale miniature work

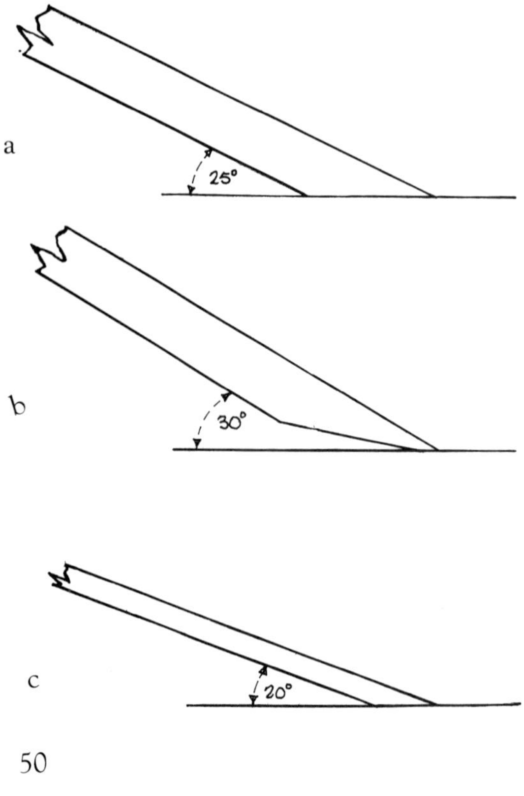

50 Keeping the plane iron true

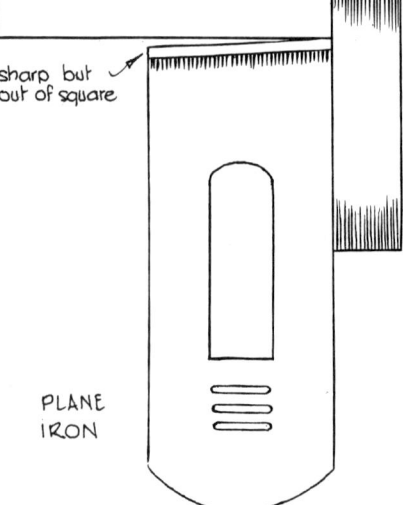

a

25°

b

30°

c

20°

sharp but out of square

PLANE IRON

51 Flush block placed at each end of your sharpening stone

giving you a very sharp edge. Use a 20 degree angle on plane irons even for hardwood in $\frac{1}{12}$th scale work, whether you sharpen by hand or with a honing guide (see fig. 49).

When sharpening the plane iron or chisel concentrate on applying even

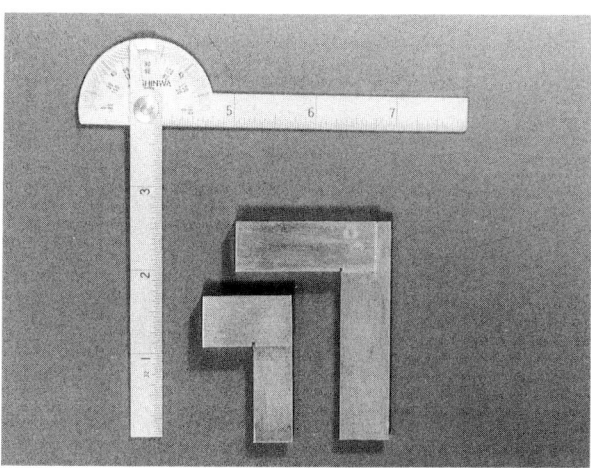

52 Tiny square cut down from a 2$\frac{3}{4}$in. (100mm) metal square

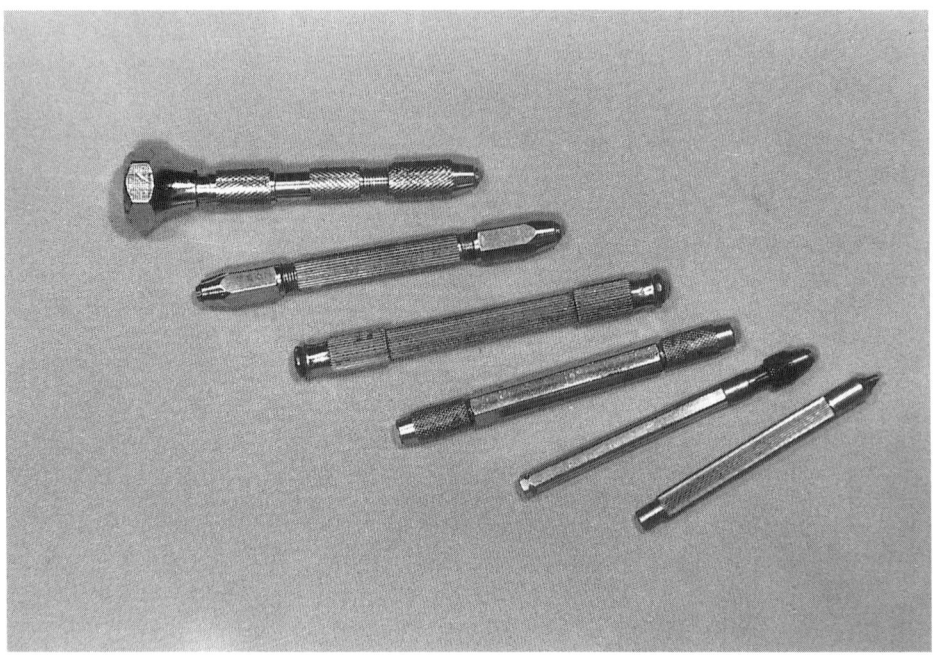

53 Various pin chucks that can be bought

54 Pin vice – large and small

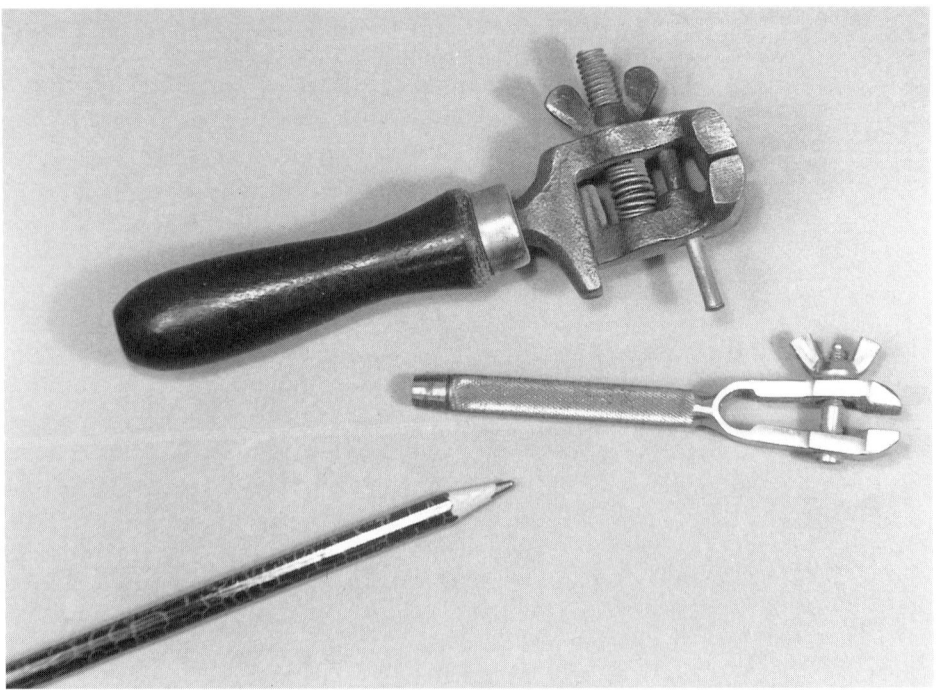

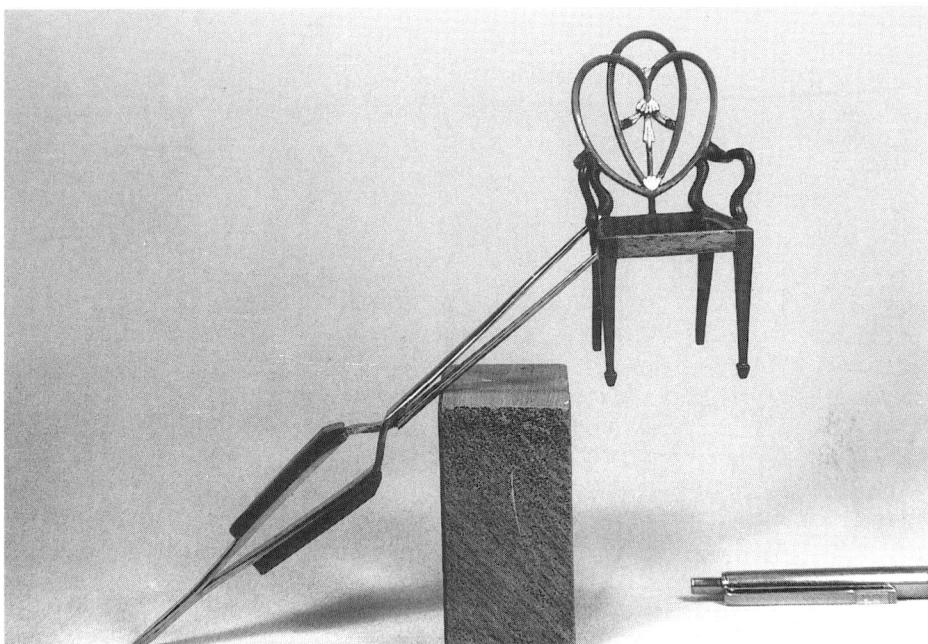

55 Gripping tweezers

pressure: there is a tendency to wear down one side, giving you a slant edge, as in fig. 50, so check with your square as you sharpen.

Do not swamp the stone with oil: only a little is necessary and always clean the stone when you have finished.

Use clean, thin oil for the next sharpening.

Buy a honing guide with which you can set to the required angle and obtain a good edge with very little practice.

Other small tools

Small machinery

There is an old quotation from a worker in a machine shop that goes: 'Treat them right and they won't bite.' Of course, this applied in a big machine shop, with large bandsaws, circular saws and planers, but it is still relevant to the small, light machinery. If it can cut wood, it can cut your fingers also, but I hasten to add that most of the small machines on the market now are very well designed and seem to improve each year with added guards and safety precautions. It is only if you do something silly while using them that they are dangerous. Just use common sense.

It will be advantageous to have at least some machinery, especially a lathe, but which should you buy first? This can be an awfully hard choice, for most of them are expensive and you want to make the right decision. It might be a long time before you can manage the next unit.

I have put the machines in order of preference for which to buy first, just as a guide line. Your preference could differ as you progress, but you have to start somewhere, so I hope this helps.

Bandsaw

The first I would suggest is a small bandsaw similar to the one in fig. 56. This particular one is made by Black and Decker. There are many other makes very similar, so making the choice can be confusing. The best advice I can give here is to make sure in your enquiries that the bandsaw will cut through at least 1½in. (38mm) hardwood, *across* or *with* the grain. Also, make sure the brand name is established; otherwise, when the blades do break (which is rare) you could have trouble obtaining spares. Purchase at least three grades, two of each type, and make sure the saw has an adjustable guide rail.

56 Bandsaw

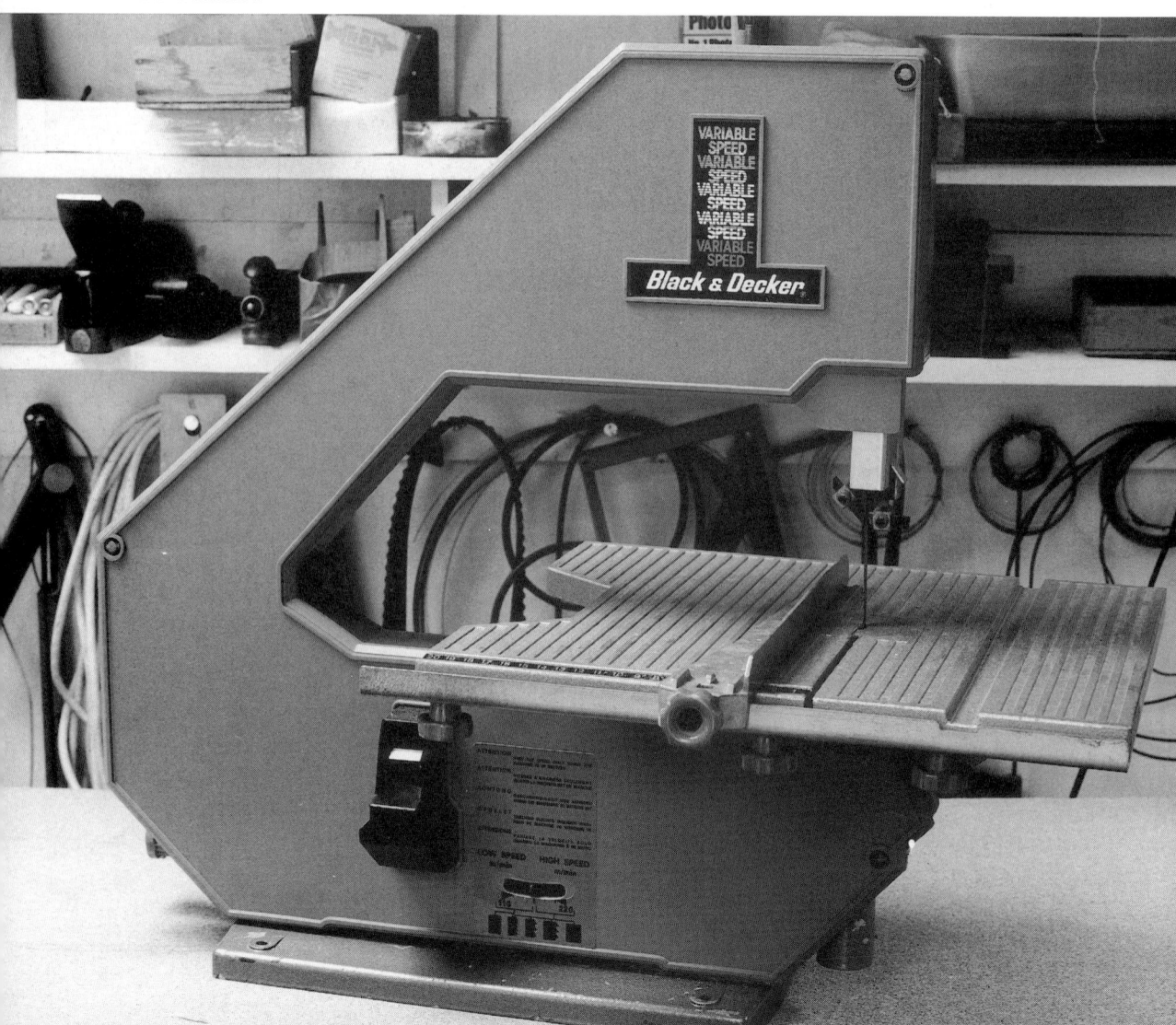

Lathe

It is true that many good tools, miniature drawings and small machines will give you endless help and information, but by far the most important asset is your own determination and ingenuity in overcoming small problems that arise. One example of this always comes to mind when I encounter a problem to do with a lathe. As a young man I spent a short time in the Sudan; a local craftsman working in the nearby village made his living turning out small handles from ivory (fig. 57). These small handles were later sold to a trader and used for making up ladies' vanity sets. His lathe was handmade, all wood except for four iron washers (fig. 58). It was held on the ground with a large stone at either end; he was very poor and had only seven or eight turning tools, all made by hand, except for a pair of shabby scissors. I had read somewhere of people turning, just using their own hand or foot power, but to see it done with such skill was

57 Ivory turns

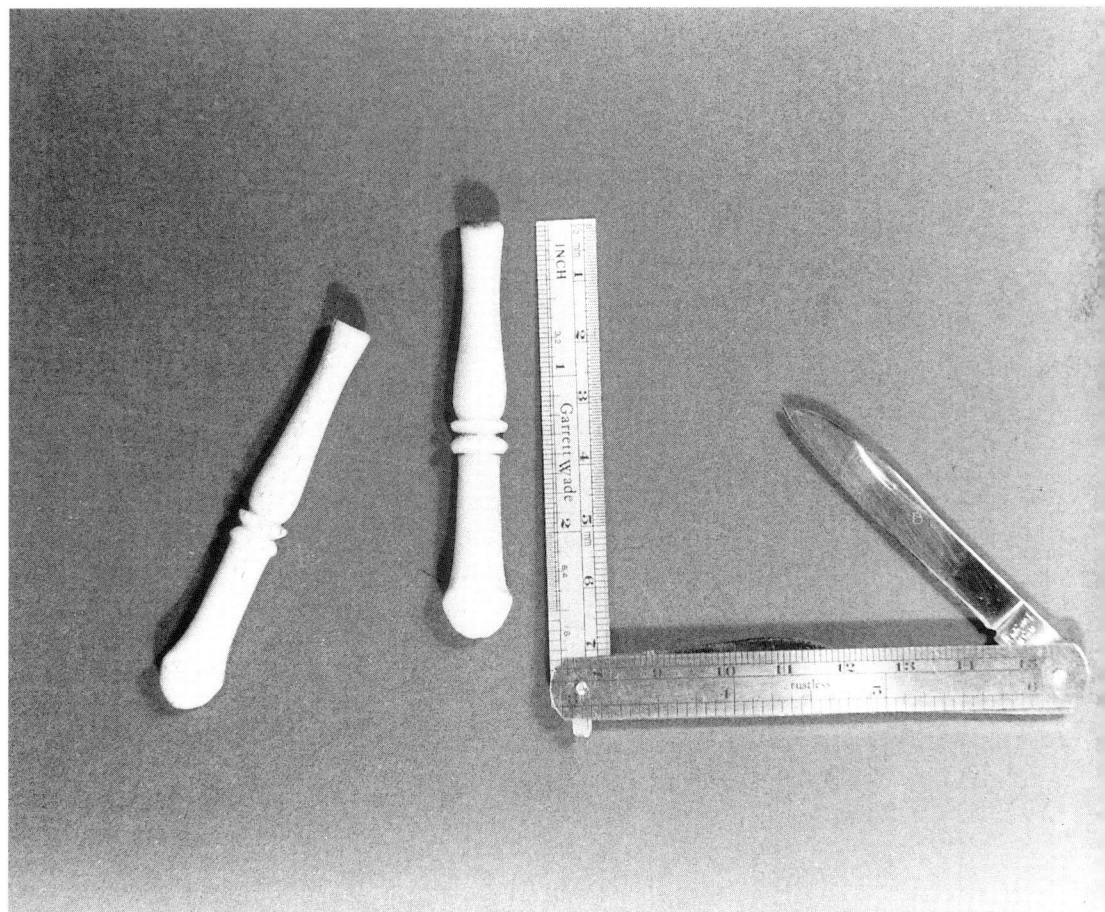

58 A foot-powered wood lathe

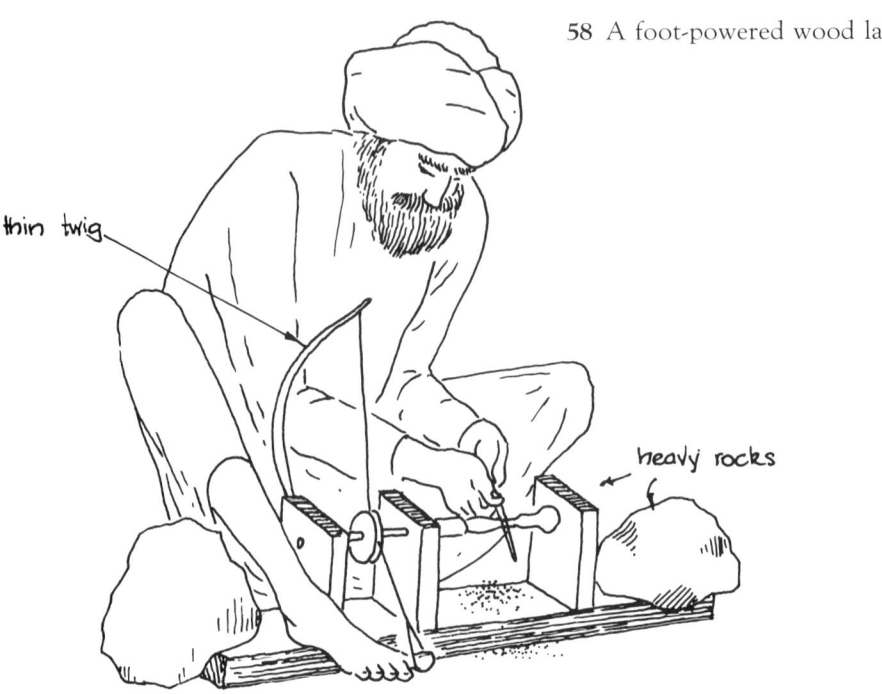

thin twig

heavy rocks

59 The Emco Unimat 3 lathe

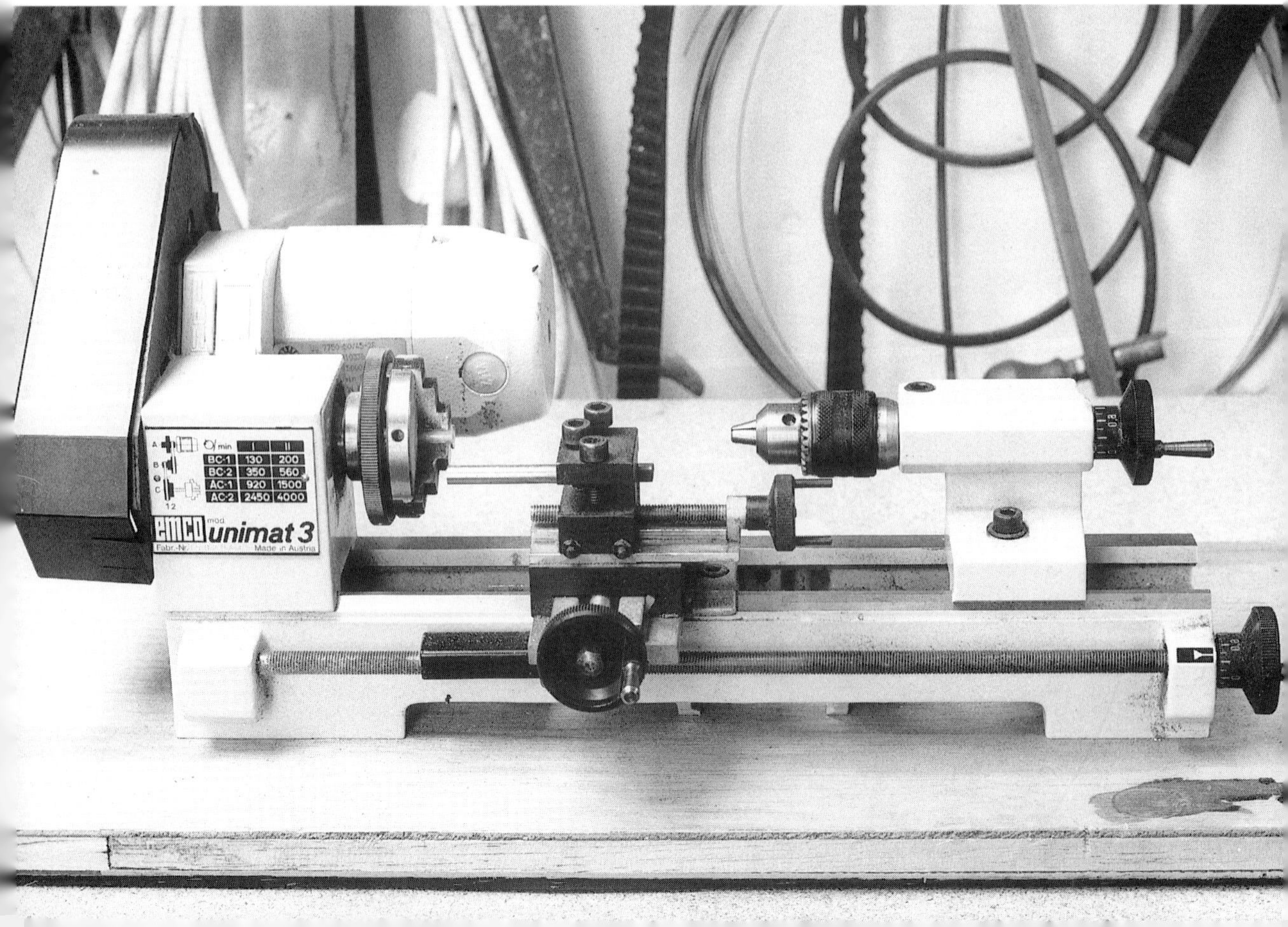

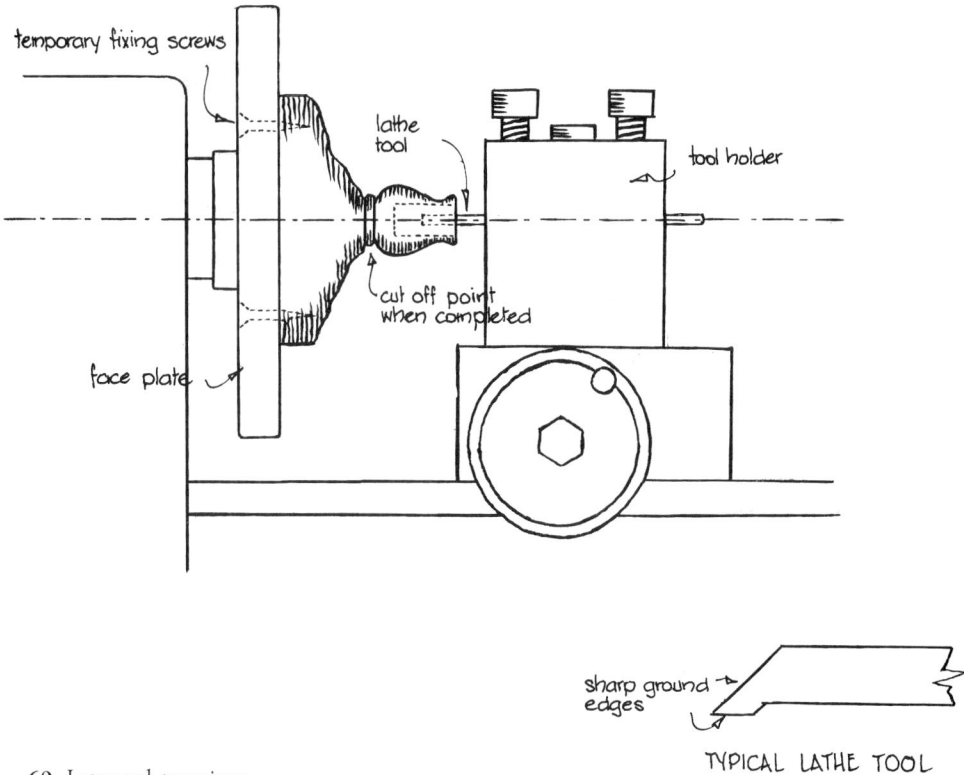

temporary fixing screws

lathe
tool

tool holder

cut off point
when completed

face plate

sharp ground
edges

TYPICAL LATHE TOOL

60 Internal turning

fascinating to watch; he co-ordinated all his movements to get the best result. The bowed piece attached to the string in fig. 58 is nothing but a piece of twig acting as a return spring. If he had the facilities most of us have access to he could easily have been a top craftsman. When I tried the lathe I found it virtually impossible to work.

There are so many lathes to choose from and such a vast range of prices; buy a good quality one and listen to advice. One of the best units I have now is the Emco Unimat 3; it is very versatile, good quality, and an ideal all-round lathe (fig. 59). You can add many accessories to this model: small circular saw, fret saw, flexible shaft for drilling and carving. A fixed drill and milling unit can also be added. Although I much prefer the separate machines, they are more expensive.

Figure 60 shows how the lathe can be used for internal turning operations. The usual way adopted in this process is to fit the face plate to the drive centre end of the lathe; centre and screw your work in hand to that plate. Then, with a small lathe tool fixed tight in the tool holder, fitted on the adjustable guide, work inwards, taking it slowly; remember, the collar will be thin and therefore delicate. Because this $\frac{1}{12}$th scale circumference at the base of these pieces is so small this face plate method is not always suitable.

61 Vases turned internally (dark – rosewood; light – yew)

62 Internal turning

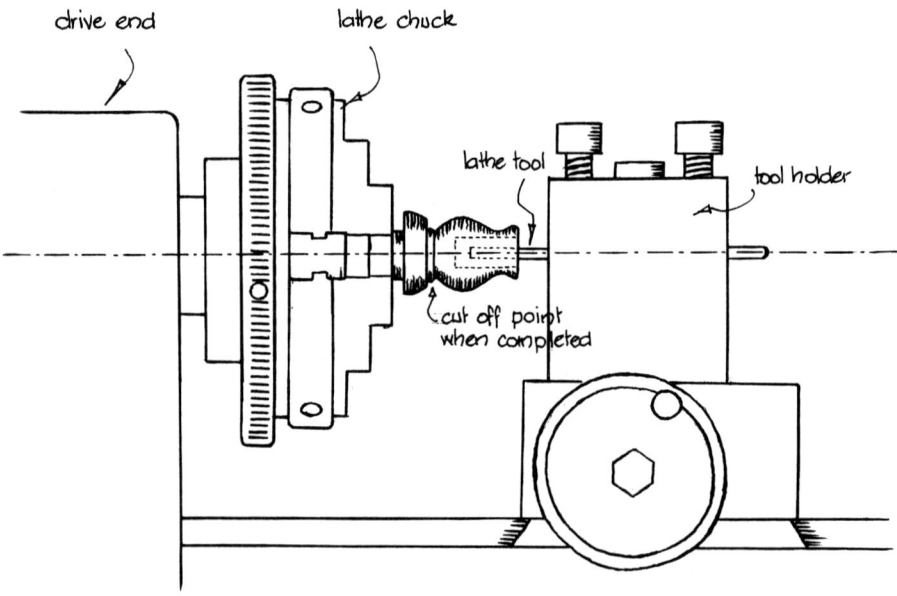

Another method is shown in fig. 61. Three small vases in fig. 62 are turned internally using the lathe chuck. Do try both methods.

63 Jewellers' lathe

The only other lathe I use now for fine work is a jewellers' lathe (see fig. 63). They are excellent but very expensive. The Unimat 3 or a very similar lathe will be ideal for most miniature turning.

Pendant drill

Choose a pendant motor with a flexible shaft and preferably a foot control with variable speeds (fig. 64). It is a little more expensive than the small hand drills, but well worth the extra as it is far easier to manoeuvre than a hand drill. The pendant drill also has a good range of accessory bits and will do countless small jobs.

64 Pendant drill with foot pedal

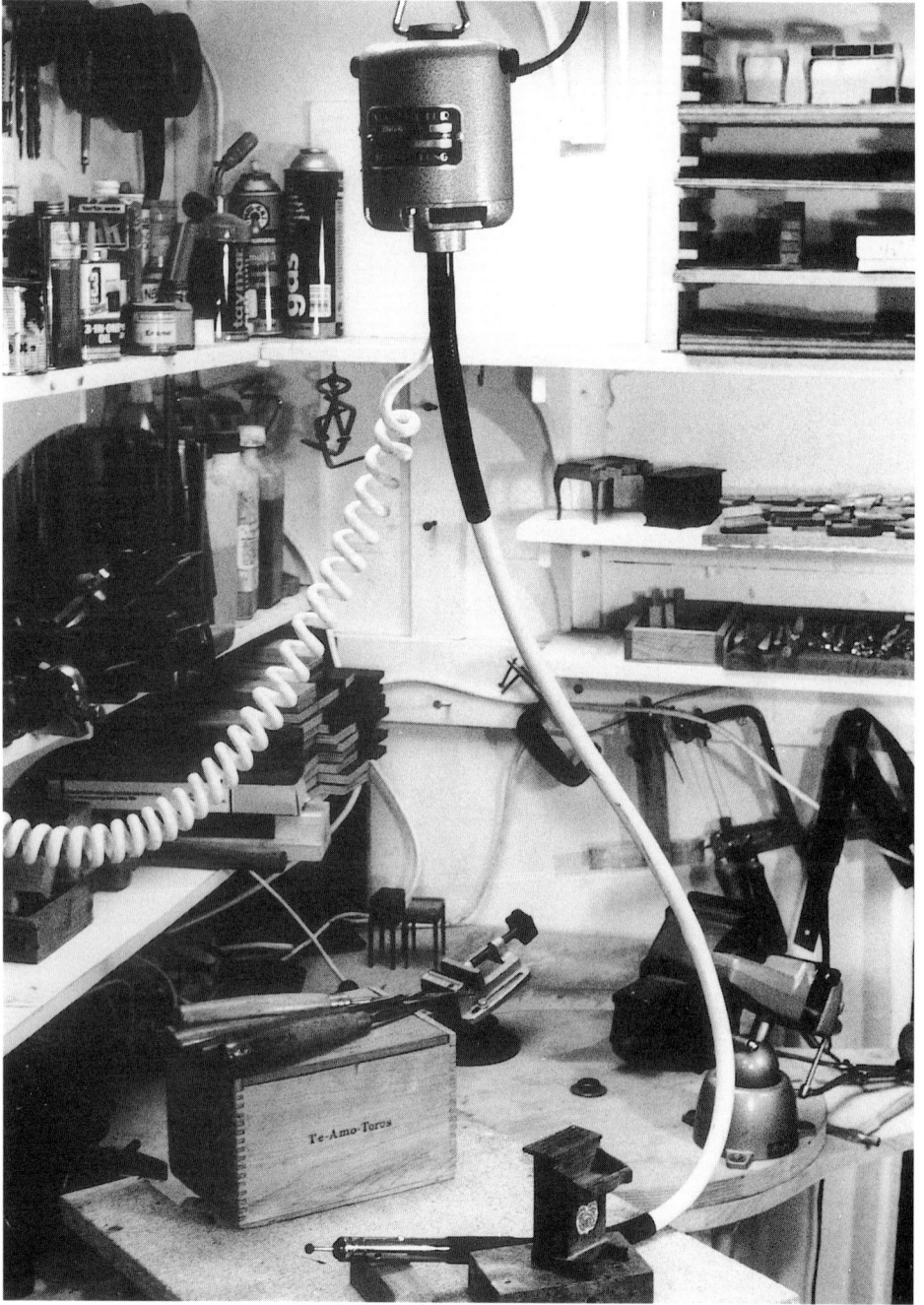

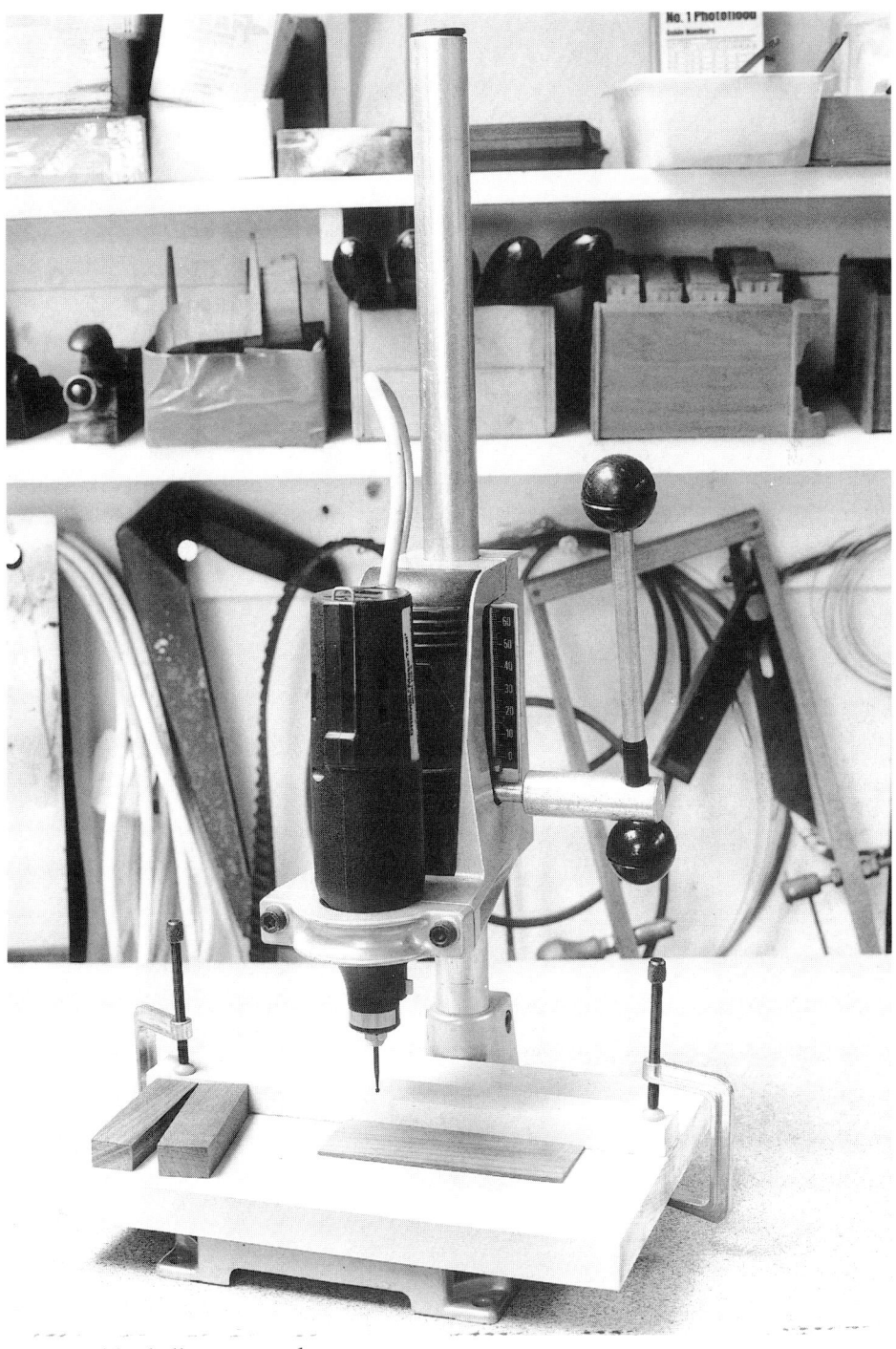

65 Portable drill on a stand

66 Cutting housings and rebates on a drill stand

If you should decide to buy a hand drill, first make sure there is a drill stand available on the market to fit it; you could use this then for fixed drilling and, with various small burrs and a guide rail, for rebating (as fig. 66 shows with this dremel drill). The burrs also come in a multitude of shapes and sizes (fig. 67)

67 Different burrs

Fretsaw

Perhaps the next choice is a small Vibrosaw or fretsaw (fig. 68). This type is made in Italy and very strong; the table is adjustable, making it easy to change when the blade begins to blunt in the one position. There are various other types and makes on the market that do the cutting just as well, but I mention this Vibro because in five years it has given me no trouble. Whichever one you do purchase try to obtain the roundback fretsaw blades – they give a much better clearance on tight turns.

68 Vibrosaw or fret saw

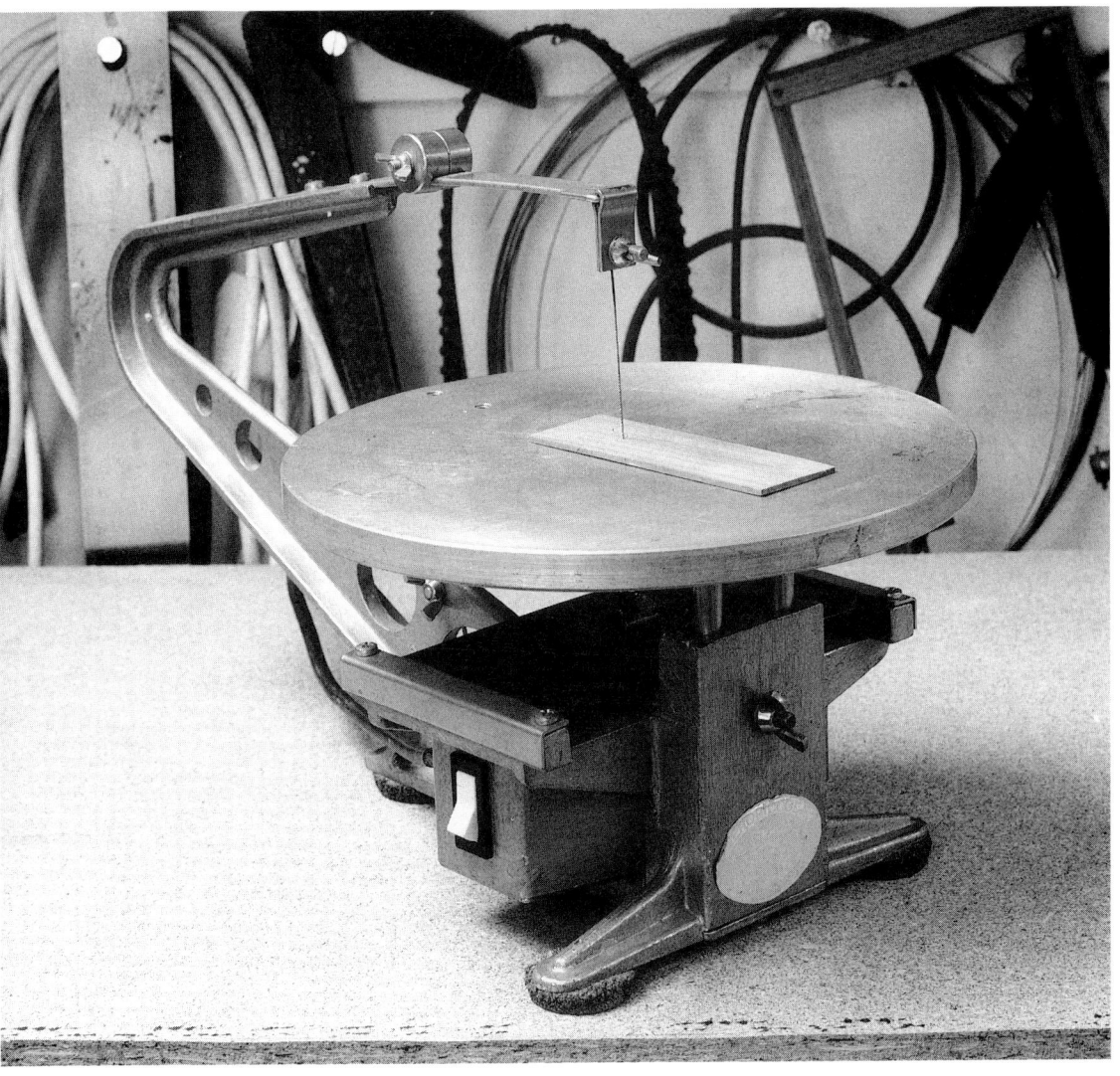

Grinder and polisher (fig. 69)

This is a small bench grinder suitable for light work, which has a $\frac{1}{5}$ h.p. motor, which is quite sufficient. I have another $\frac{1}{4}$ h.p. motor fitted to the bench with buffing mops. It would be advantageous to buy the combination unit available on the market with the grinding stone one side and a tapered screw spindle at the other for circular buffing mops.

69 Small bench grinding machine

1 A 1/12th scale walnut cabinet on a stand, banded in kingwood. (5¾ in. high)

2 A 1/12th scale collector's cabinet made in mahogany banded in zebrano veneer. (4 in. high)

*3 Miniature on miniature — a 1/12th scale military chest in mahogany;
on top is a 1/50th scale highboy in rosewood. (1⅝ in. high)*

Milling and drilling

Lastly, a milling and drilling machine is useful; this one is also made by Emco (fig. 71). The advantage with this unit is that you have much more control than with the adjustable milling table. A drill on a stand will do some of this work with a good measure of accuracy but will have a limited use for finer work.

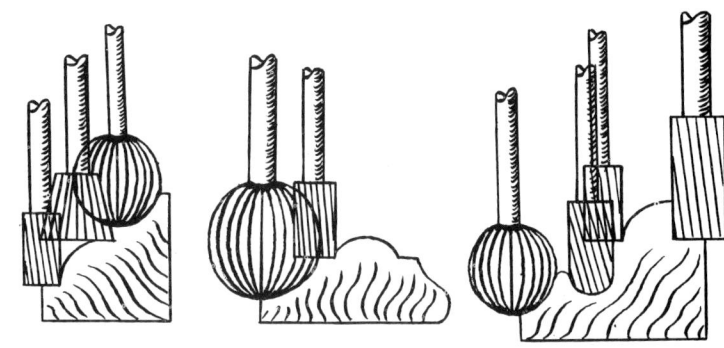

70 Fine shaped mouldings made with various burrs using the milling and drilling machine

71 Milling and drilling machine with adjustable table

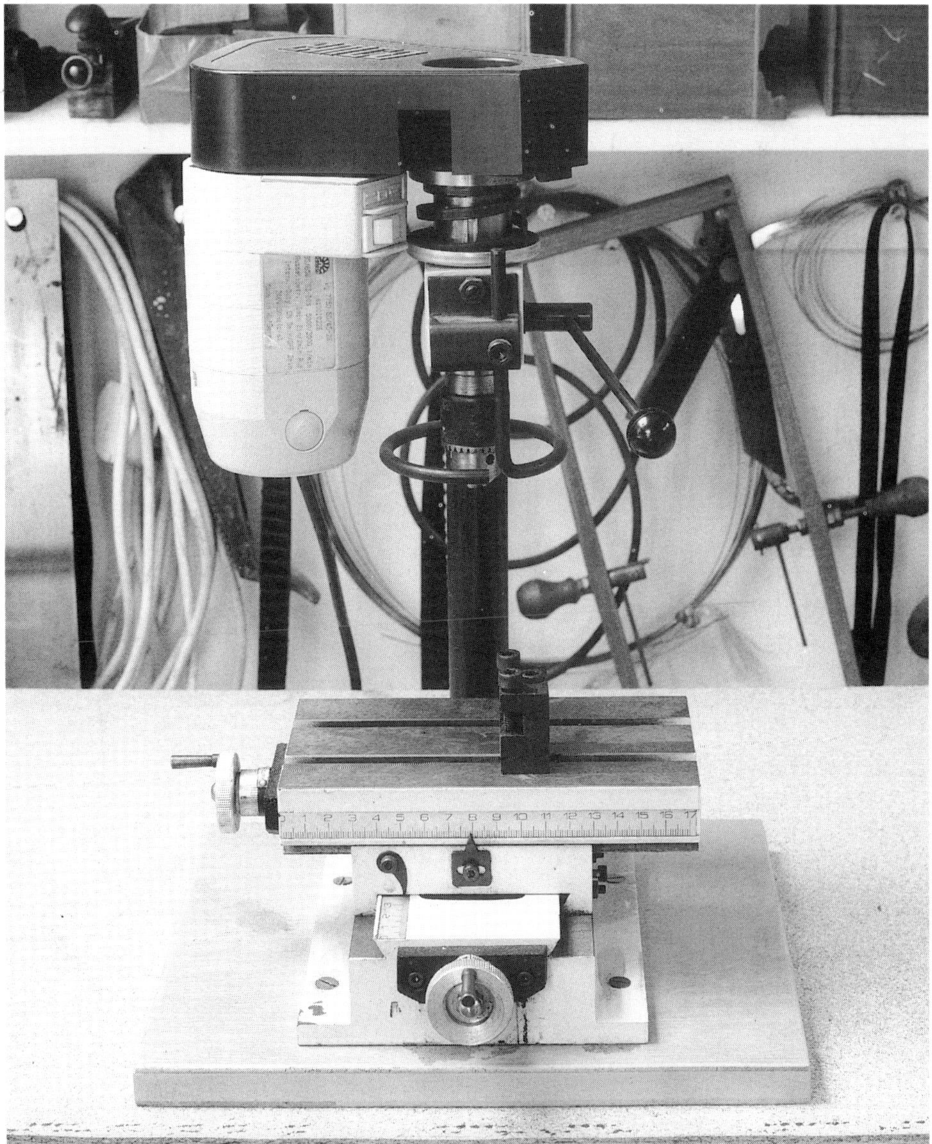

V *Wood tools and joints*

Boards and supports

When making up these wood tools I suggest $\frac{1}{2}$in. (13mm) good quality ply. Make sure the main surfaces are perfectly flat. The measurements given here are taken from the wood tools that I have made and used. It is not critical to stick to these exact thicknesses, though, if you find difficulty obtaining the correct sizes; just stay as close as you can to the drawing details.

Planing board (fig. 72)

With this board, the rough sawn pieces can now be trimmed down much closer to the finished thicknesses required to start cutting and jointing. Do not plane

72 Planing board

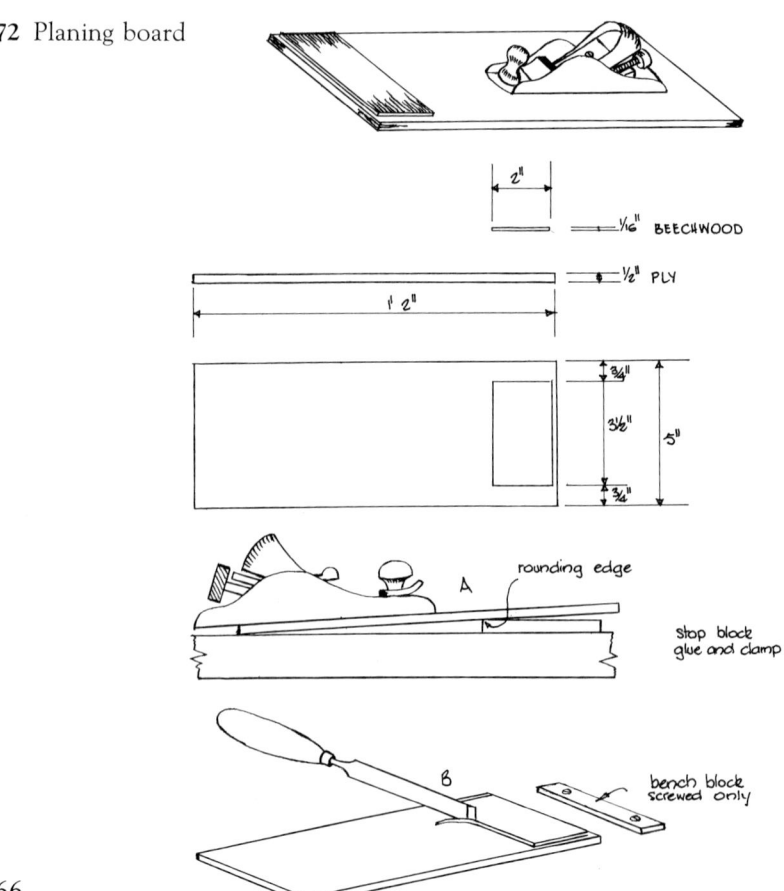

down to the exact thickness required; the piece has yet to be sandpapered, so allow a little thickness for this. Always plane with the grain and check all the time that you are not skimming down on one side too much. Because your stop block on the board has to be so thin, there is a tendency for the piece you are planing to ride up over this block (shown at A). To stop this happening as much as possible, a sharp edge must be kept on the hardwood stop block; later when the edge does wear down, trim sharp again (shown at B).

Small sawing block (fig. 73)

All parts should be glued and clamped except the waste board; this should be pinned only so that when worn with sawn cuts, it can easily be turned over or replaced. This sawing block has been made up for the small bench vice (c); a larger one can easily be made for the bench – just move the stop block to the front of your sawing block to hold against the bench.

73 (a) Small sawing block (b) cross section (c) side view

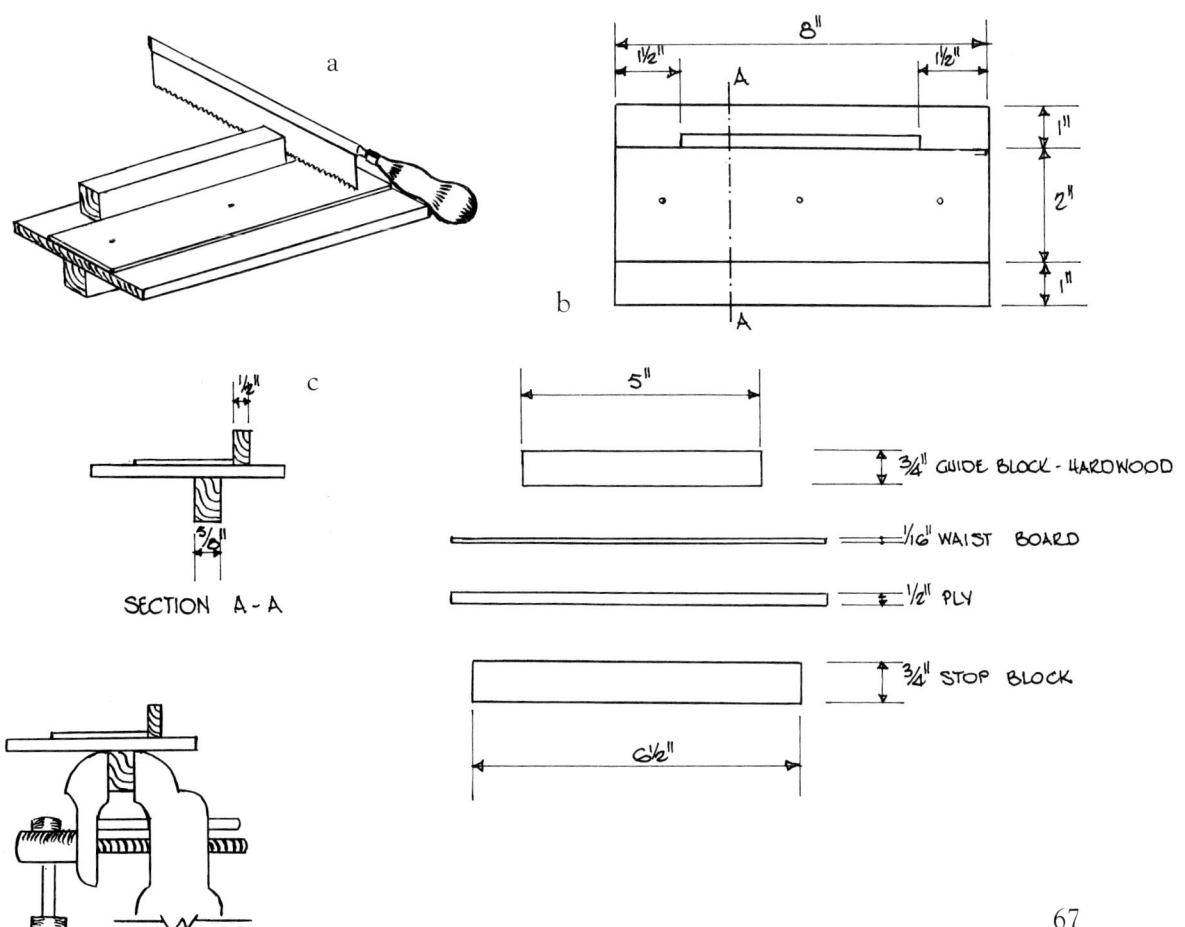

Squaring board

This is very useful if you find it hard to square the ends of your work. This squaring board can be used left- or right-handed. The stop rail should be glued and clamped to the guide block; this in turn must be glued to the base with the stop block also now glued in place. It is important to make sure the edge of the stop rail and the edge of the guide block are at right angles (fig. 74). When completed, place the board on the bench and the plane on one side, as shown in fig. 74 (a). Hold down your work on the guide block as shown (work in place to be squared), press quite hard, with your hand holding down your work and also keeping the squaring board tight to the bench.

Now push the plane along the guide line with the other hand. As the plane passes along the edge, use a slight pressure inwards – the plane will do the rest – keep repeating till the line is true.

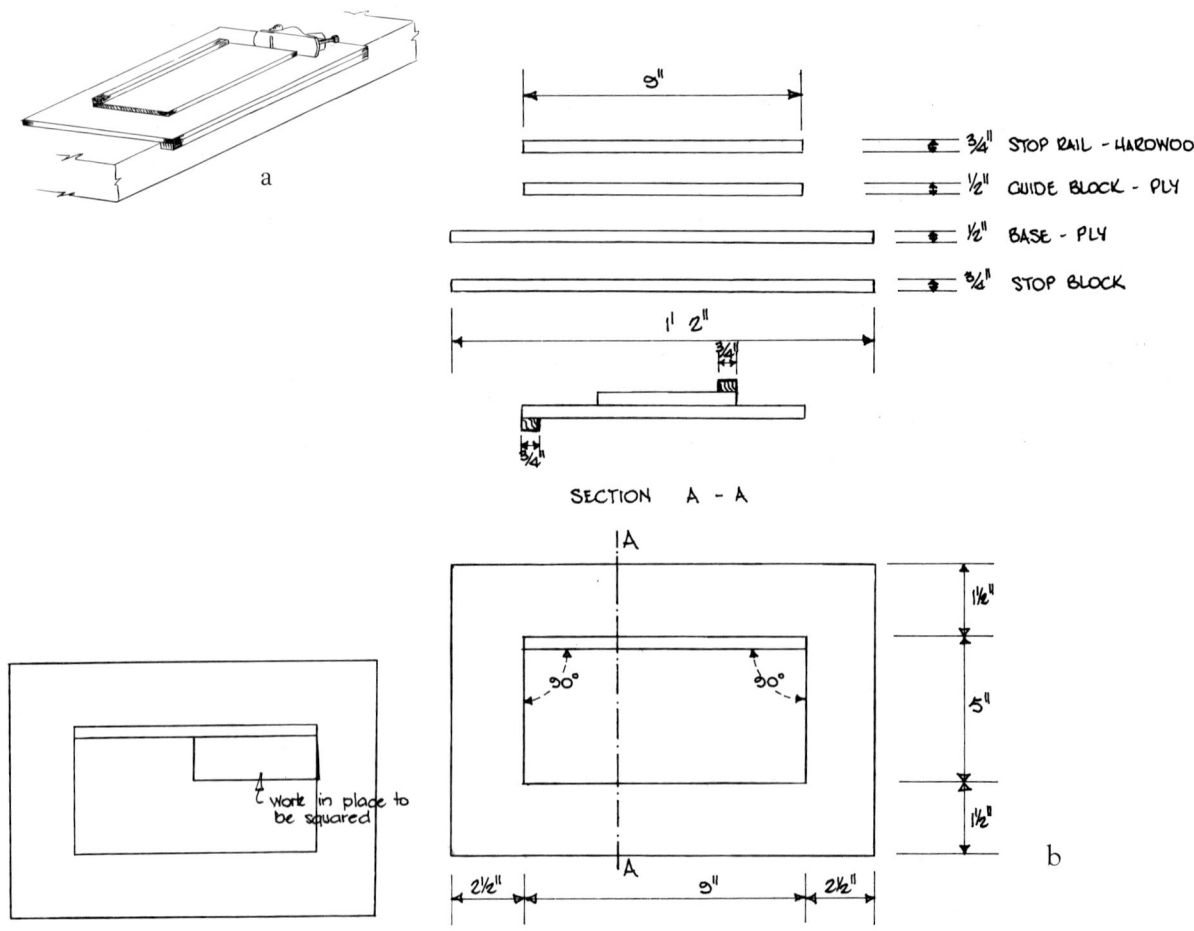

74 (a) Squaring board (b) cross section (c) squaring work

You will soon become more confident with a little practice. Pushing a small plane along on one side will seem very awkward at first, but it takes a little time to master.

Do not have the plane iron out too far or it will judder and make a bad cut.

Be careful not to trim down past your pencil line.

Felt boards

As the small separate pieces of your work take shape lay them down in sequence after cleaning and trimming for later glueing. If there are many pieces such as you would have for the making up of a chair, it is easy for a piece of your work to be pushed aside or mislaid in the general confusion and clutter on your bench. I have found it good practice to have two or three felt-covered boards handy; mine are 12×9in. and $\frac{3}{4}$in. (305×230mm and 20mm) deep with green felt glued on either side. If all the pieces are laid on the board when you have finished working on that particular miniature for the time being, it is then easy to lift it away to a safe place (fig. 75). This then does not disturb your layout and leaves the bench clear for another part of your work. The general idea of covering it with dark felt is to prevent tiny pieces from rolling or sliding about so much; they can be seen much easier, too, and this especially applies for small handles, pins and hinges you lay out for assembly.

A moulding placed round the edge will ensure no pieces fall.

75 Rough frame for stacking felt boards

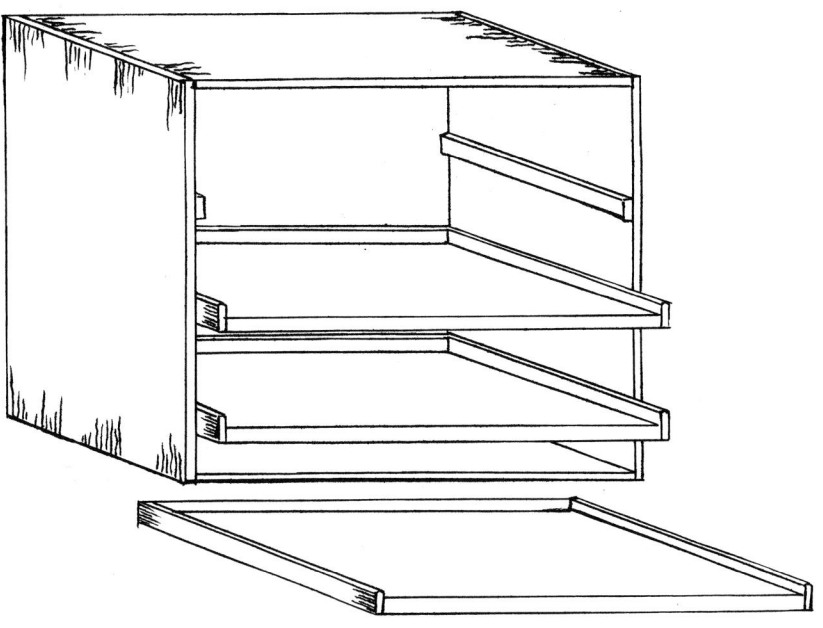

Small squaring block

These can be used to keep a frame square as shown in fig. 76. They are like a third hand when used properly and only one is needed with each frame or carcass. After you have satisfied yourself that all the pieces fit, in some instances you may have to glue them into a frame in one go. In this case it can become difficult to keep the whole square as you push and pull to manoeuvre parts into place. Just one block fitted will hold the frame square.

Therefore, use a cramp or elastic bands to keep the joints tight after glueing. You can now handle it to clean off any excess glue.

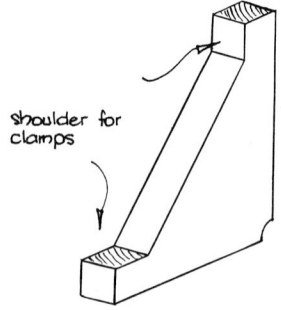

shoulder for clamps

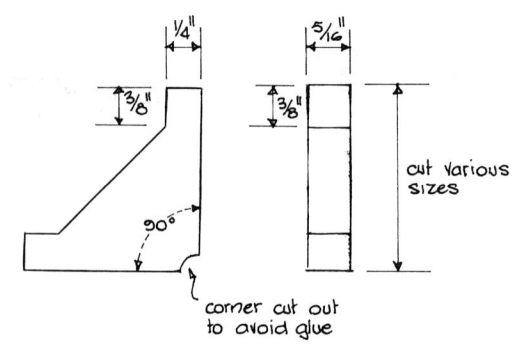

corner cut out to avoid glue

cut various sizes

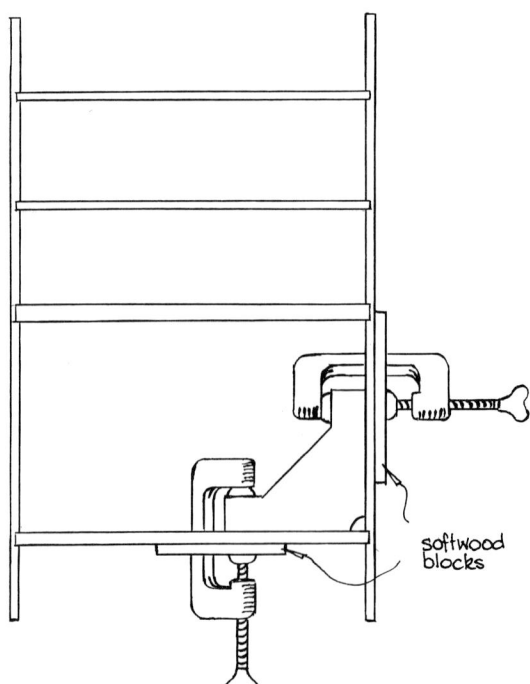

softwood blocks

76 Small squaring block

Of course, you will have to cut different sized blocks to fit different frames but they are easy to make.

Do not forget to use wood blocks on the outside of your frame when applying the clamps.

Mitre box (fig. 77)

This mitre box is very small and made to clamp into a portable swivel bench vice (fig. 77(c)), enabling you to turn your work to the best angle for cutting.

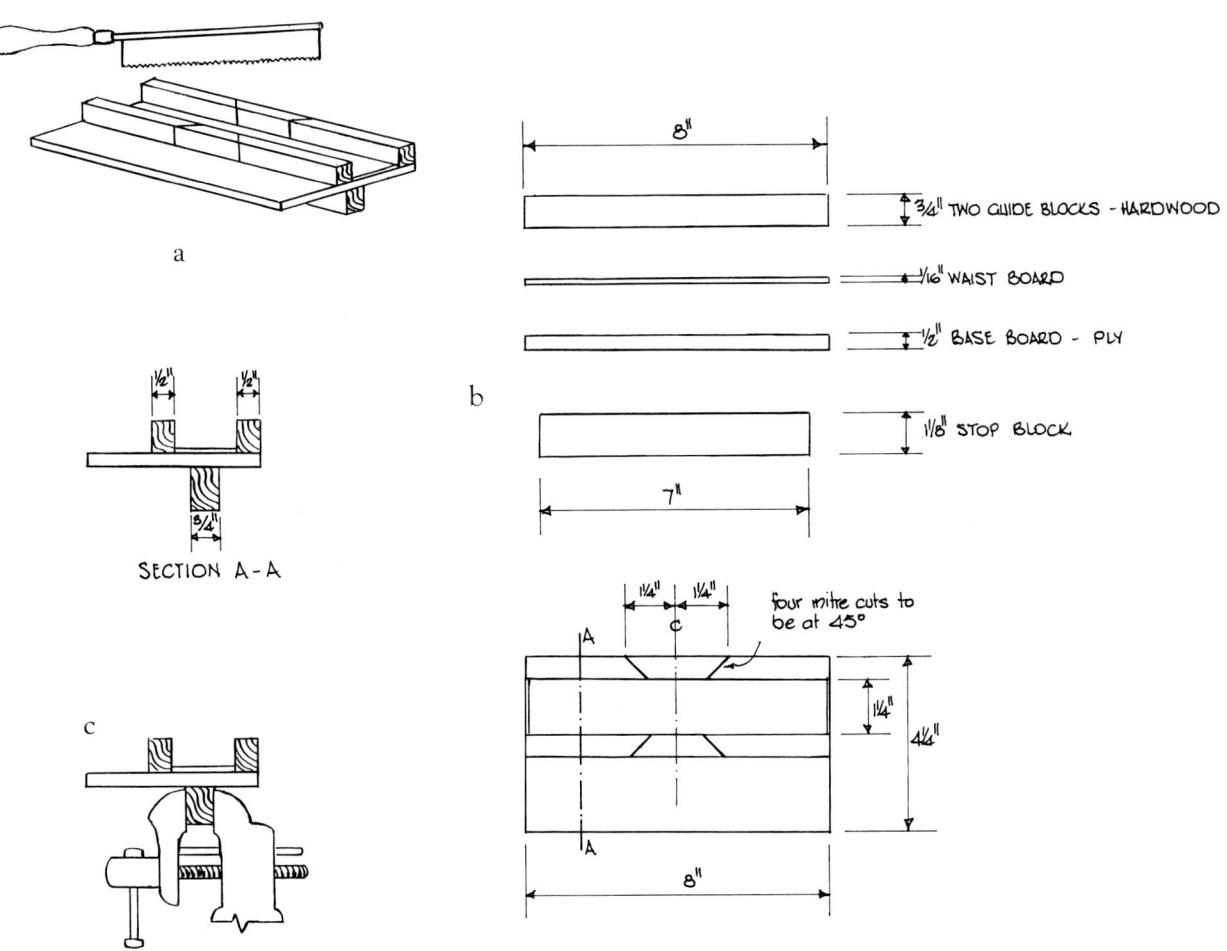

77 (a) mitre block (b) cross section (c) side view

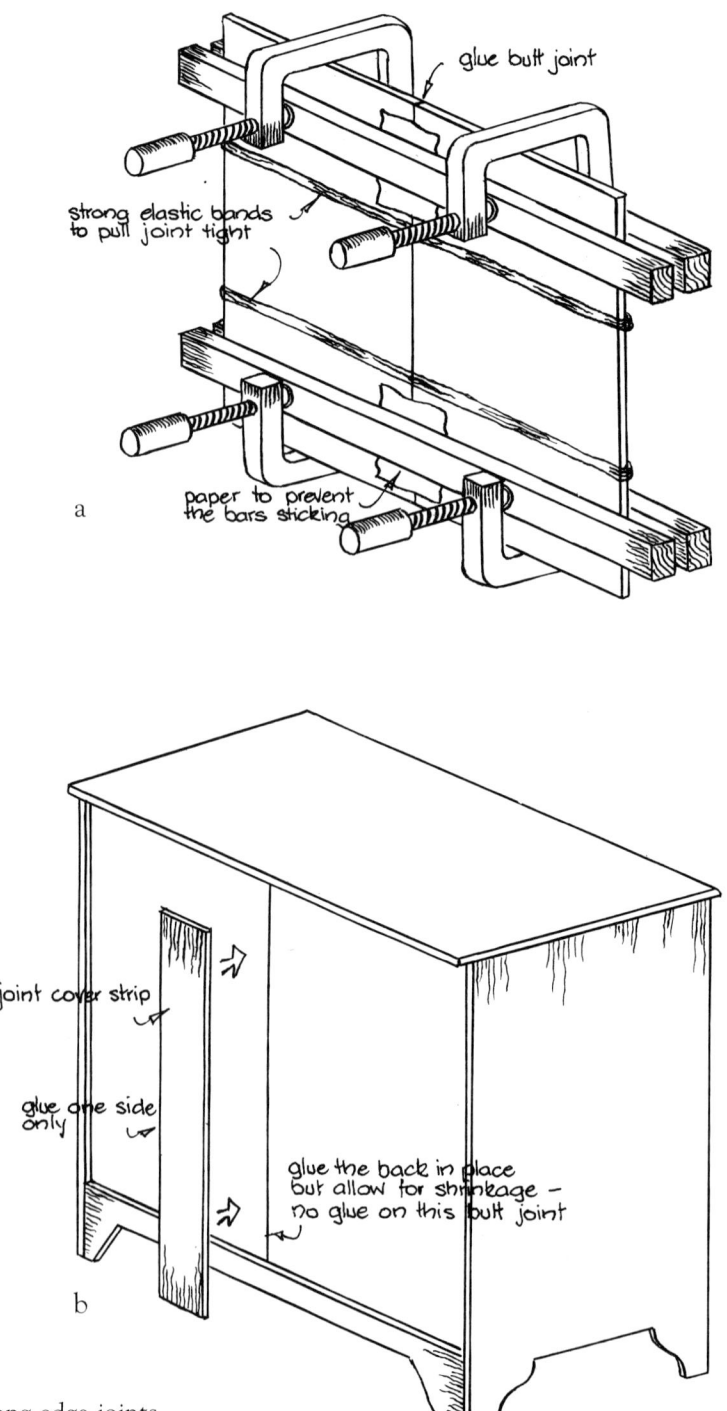

glue butt joint

strong elastic bands
to pull joint tight

paper to prevent
the bars sticking

a

joint cover strip

glue one side
only

glue the back in place
but allow for shrinkage —
no glue on this butt joint

b

78 Long edge joints

Glue and clamp the guide block and vice block, but do not glue the thin waist board; instead fix it with just two tacks.

As your saw cuts through the mitre it will leave slight cuts on the bottom board and in time become so cut about that the saw will slightly drop as it goes through, leaving a jagged edge on the underside of the mitre. Replace the waste board or turn it over when this starts to happen.

Wood joints

When making up surfaces more than 3in. (76mm) wide, for example a table top, do not be tempted to join two strips to make up the 3in. Your joint might be invisible when cleaned up, but will nearly always show up when polished. Try to make a side, flap or top in one piece.

The simple butt joint

This is mostly used as an end grain to side grain join, which is not suitable for long lasting work. Only use where it is just impossible to work any other kind of joint in. The only butt joint you should use on quality work is a glue block.

Long edge joint

This can be used for making up backs. Figure 78a shows how to glue long strips, but only use this method if the drawing or cabinet you are studying calls for this. A back more than 2½in. (64mm) wide, made up and glued in one piece, tends to shrink later and then split. Therefore, if the back exceeds this, divide it into two panels; glue the two separate pieces in place but not down the centre vertical butt joint.

Cover this join with a thin cover strip as shown in fig. 78b.

Only glue this strip to one side: this will allow for shrinkage to take place without any splitting or gaps appearing.

The same principle applies with a large cabinet back – just add more panels and strips. Divide them evenly so that the backs look neat and allow a little extra overlap on the top to hide the ends of the cover strips.

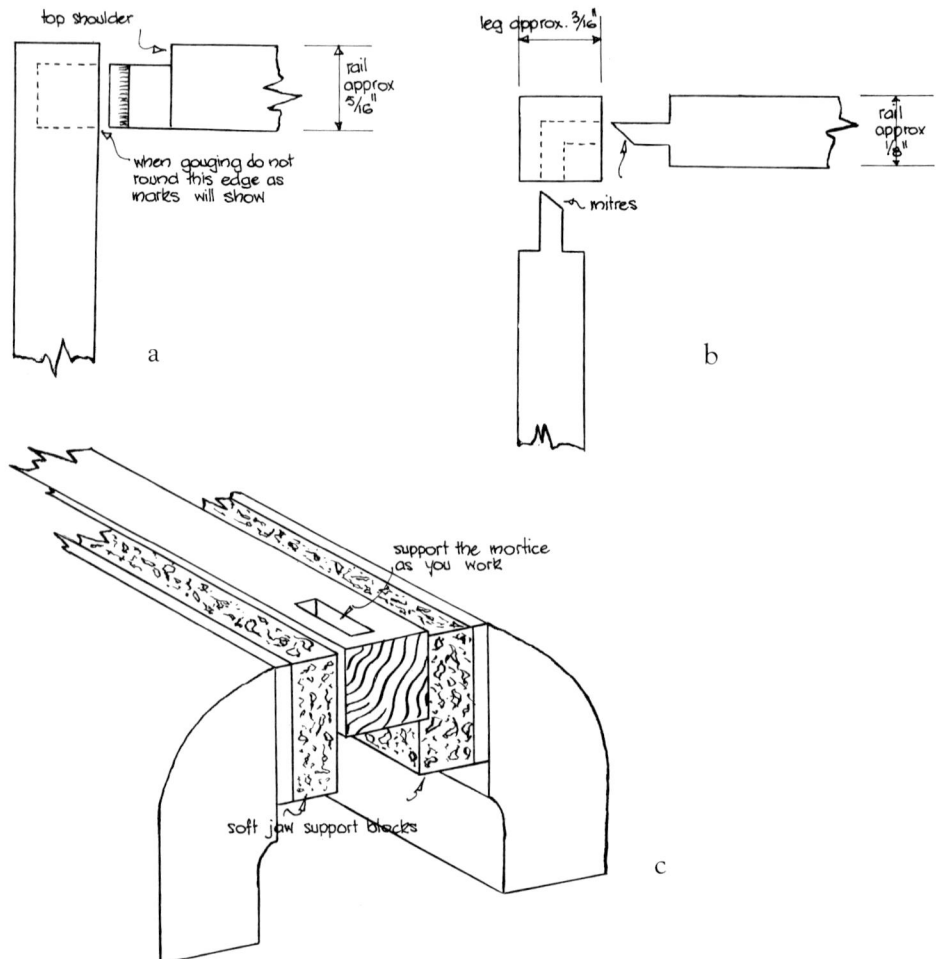

79 Mortice and tenon joint

Mortice and tenon joints

This joint is used more often than all others in woodworking, and cabinet work in miniature also. Many variations of this joint are possible; only the *main* ones are shown here. Figure 79 shows how much easier a mortice and tenon joint is to manage on a thinner leg if supported with a glue block. This is ideal for table legs if, when scaled down, the leg is not less than $\frac{3}{16}$in. (5mm) thick and the rail $\frac{1}{8}$in. (3mm) thick. If the leg and the rail are thinner, the joint can become very weak. Figure 80 shows how much easier a mortice and tenon joint is to manage on a thinner leg ($\frac{3}{32}$in. (2.5mm) leg; $\frac{1}{16}$in. (1.5mm) rail) supported with a glue block.

74

80 Mortice and tenon joint

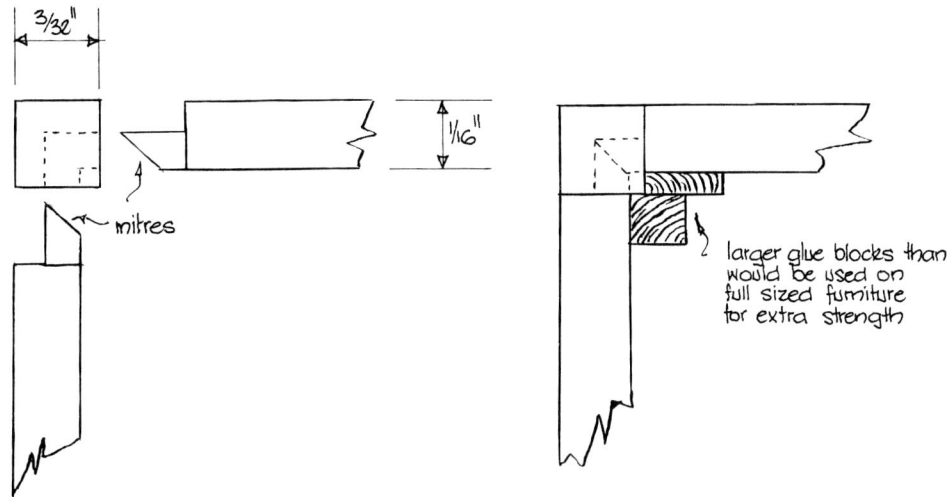

mitres

larger glue blocks than
would be used on
full sized furniture
for extra strength

The through dovetail

This is a joint used where it can be seen as a feature of the cabinet; many large
old chests show the dovetail at the corners. Drawers that are dovetailed almost
always show a through dovetail at the back; many well-made boxes will make a
feature of a dovetail as in fig. 81 and 82.

81 A through dovetail on a box where
the dovetails and pins are spaced
equally. The dovetails are cut on
the front and the pins on the sides

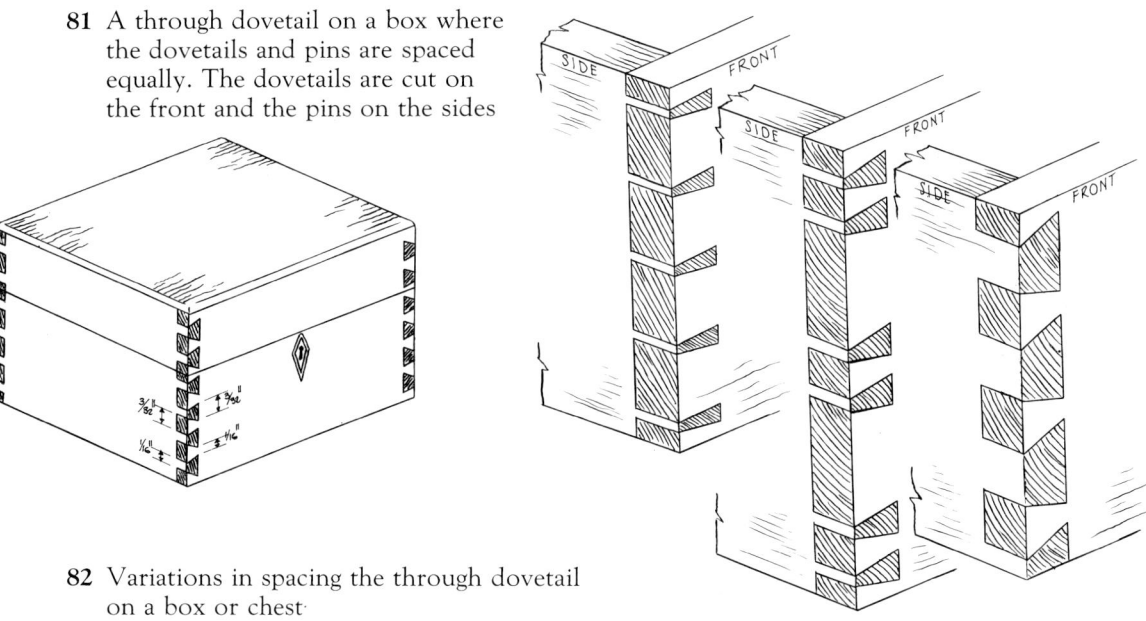

82 Variations in spacing the through dovetail
on a box or chest

The lapped dovetail

This joint is used chiefly in cabinets, carcasses and drawers. You can use housing joints on a carcass rather than dovetails for this $\frac{1}{12}$th scale, if fitted correctly, as they are quite strong. (fig. 83). But if you want to attempt the authentic reproduction of a full size antique in miniature – a chest of drawers, for example – it would be in almost all cases made with these lapped dovetails (fig. 84).

83 A simple through lap joint formed on the carcass

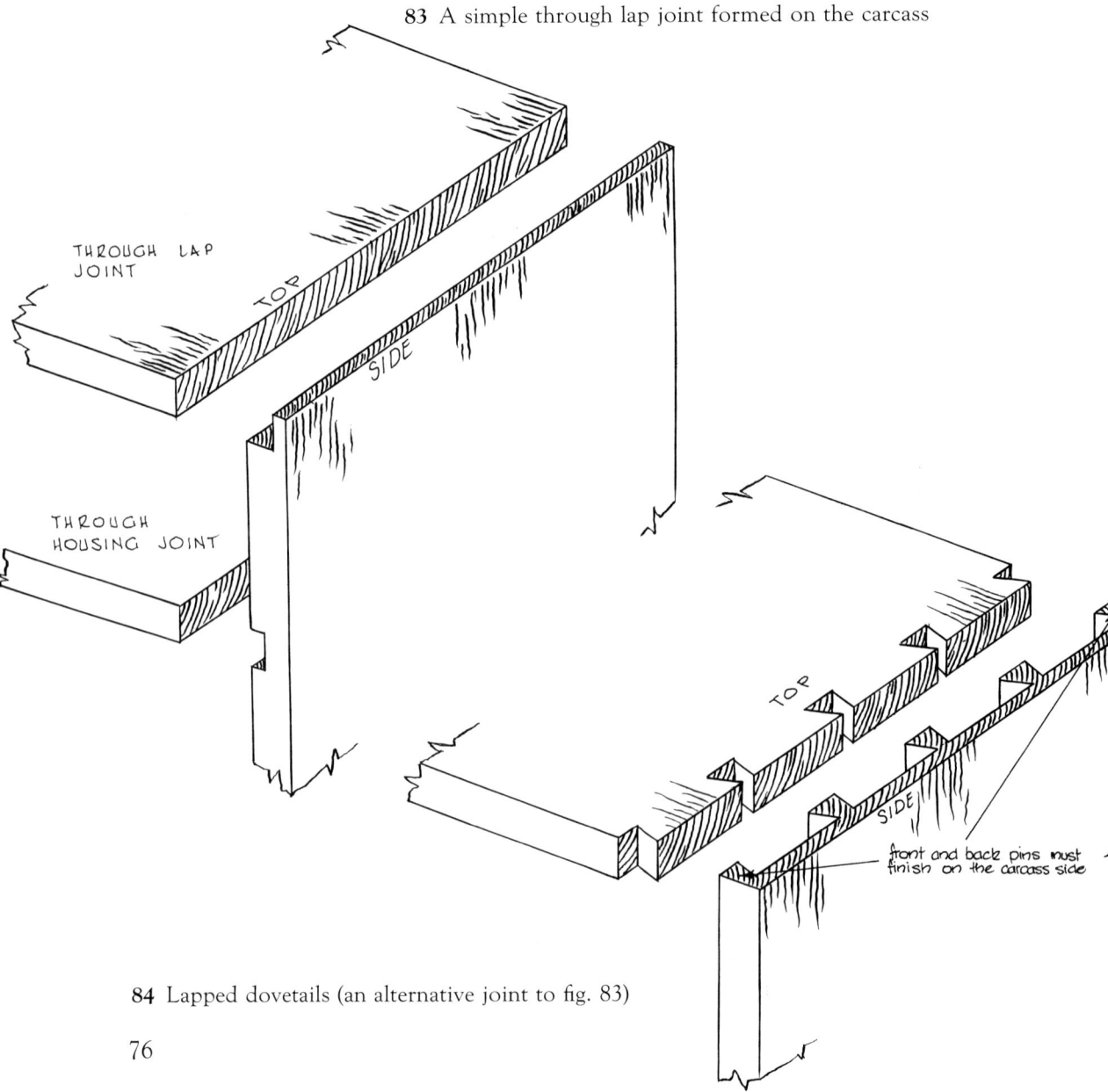

84 Lapped dovetails (an alternative joint to fig. 83)

Hidden mitred dovetails

These joints would be used on a good quality bureau, for example, to joint the sides to the top. (fig. 85). They are a little difficult to get right; if you want a

85 Hidden mitred dovetail

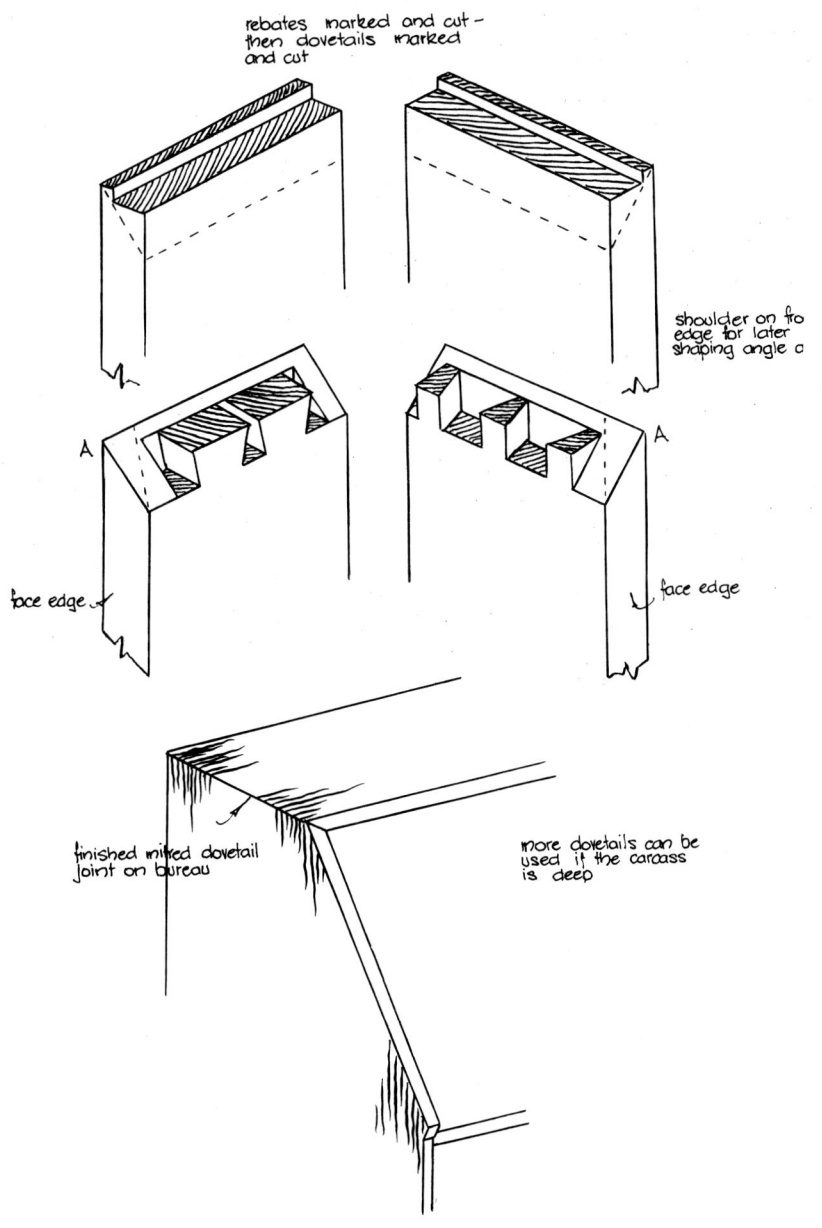

rebates marked and cut –
then dovetails marked
and cut

shoulder on fro
edge for later
shaping angle c

A

A

face edge

face edge

finished mitred dovetail
joint on bureau

more dovetails can be
used if the carcass
is deep

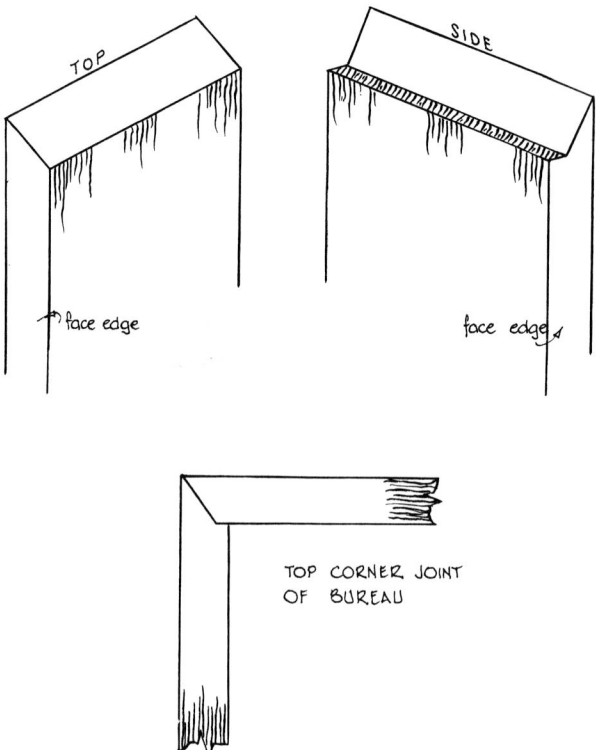

86 Alternative corner joint mitre with shoulder

neat finish without making the dovetail, the mitre with shoulder is quite strong. (fig. 86). However, for top quality work you really should use the hidden dovetails.

Housing joints

These can be used on carcasses, rails or shelving. Figure 87 shows four that can be used according to the style and quality of the miniature you are making.

Bridle joint

This joint is not seen as often, but it still has its uses. Figure 88 shows the joint on the inner leg of a six or eight leg cabinet and the front legs of a console table.

87 Housing joints – housing is never cut out
more than half-way through the frame or carcass

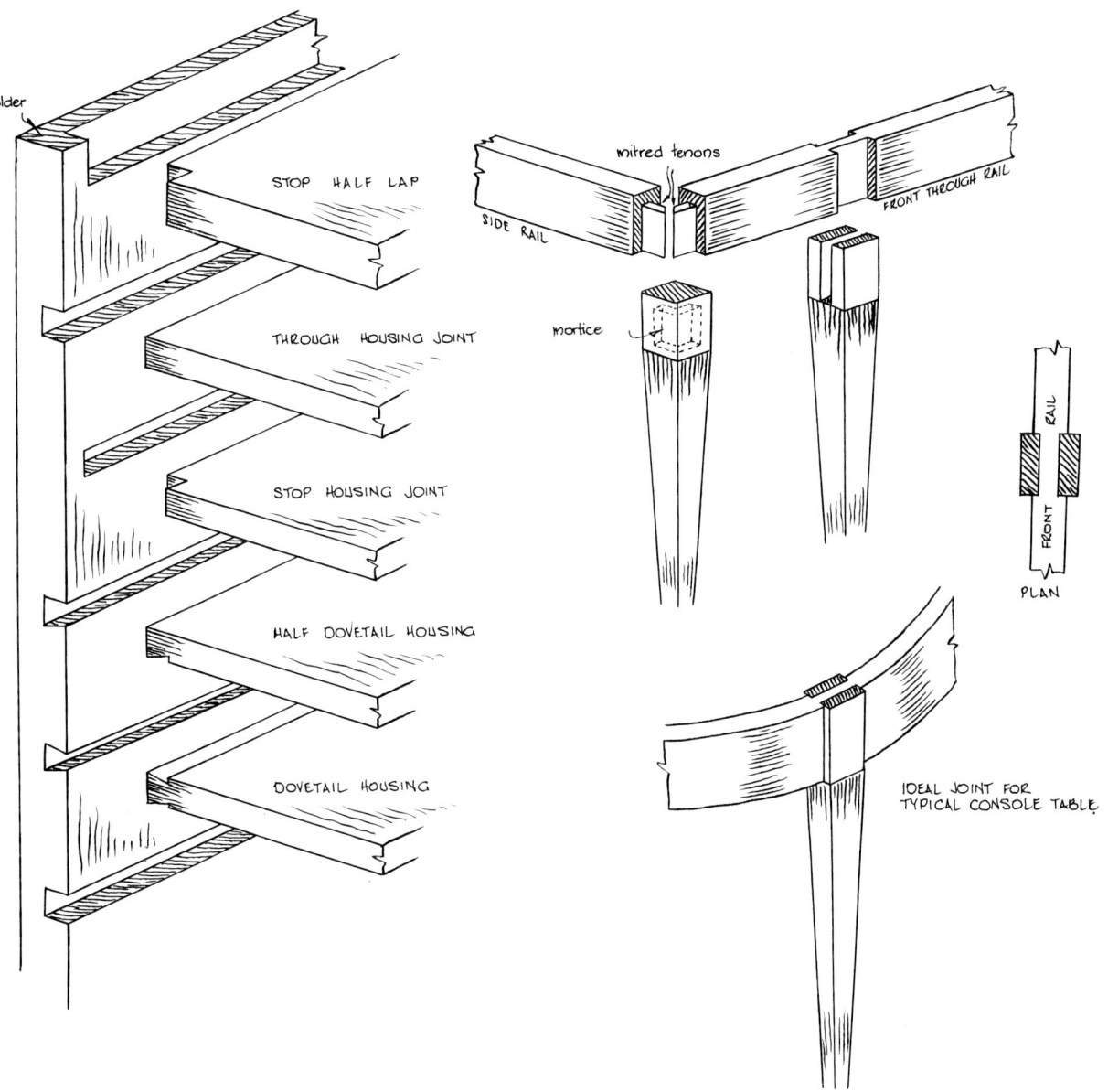

shoulder

STOP HALF LAP

THROUGH HOUSING JOINT

STOP HOUSING JOINT

HALF DOVETAIL HOUSING

DOVETAIL HOUSING

mitred tenons

SIDE RAIL

FRONT THROUGH RAIL

mortice

RAIL

FRONT

PLAN

IDEAL JOINT FOR
TYPICAL CONSOLE TABLE

88 Bridal joint on six or eight leg cabinet

79

Carcass dovetail

This can be used on the top front rail in a chest of drawers, and also, where legs in a carcass run through to the underside of a top – a sideboard, for example – where a strong corner joint is often called for (fig. 89). A *loose tongue* should be used if you are making a long curve, for example, on a round breakfast table frame. Some of the grain has to run on a slant so a tenon joint or even a half-lap in this case would be too weak (fig. 90). Even if the face of the frame is later veneered for strength and to hide the angle of the grain it should still be jointed with tongues.

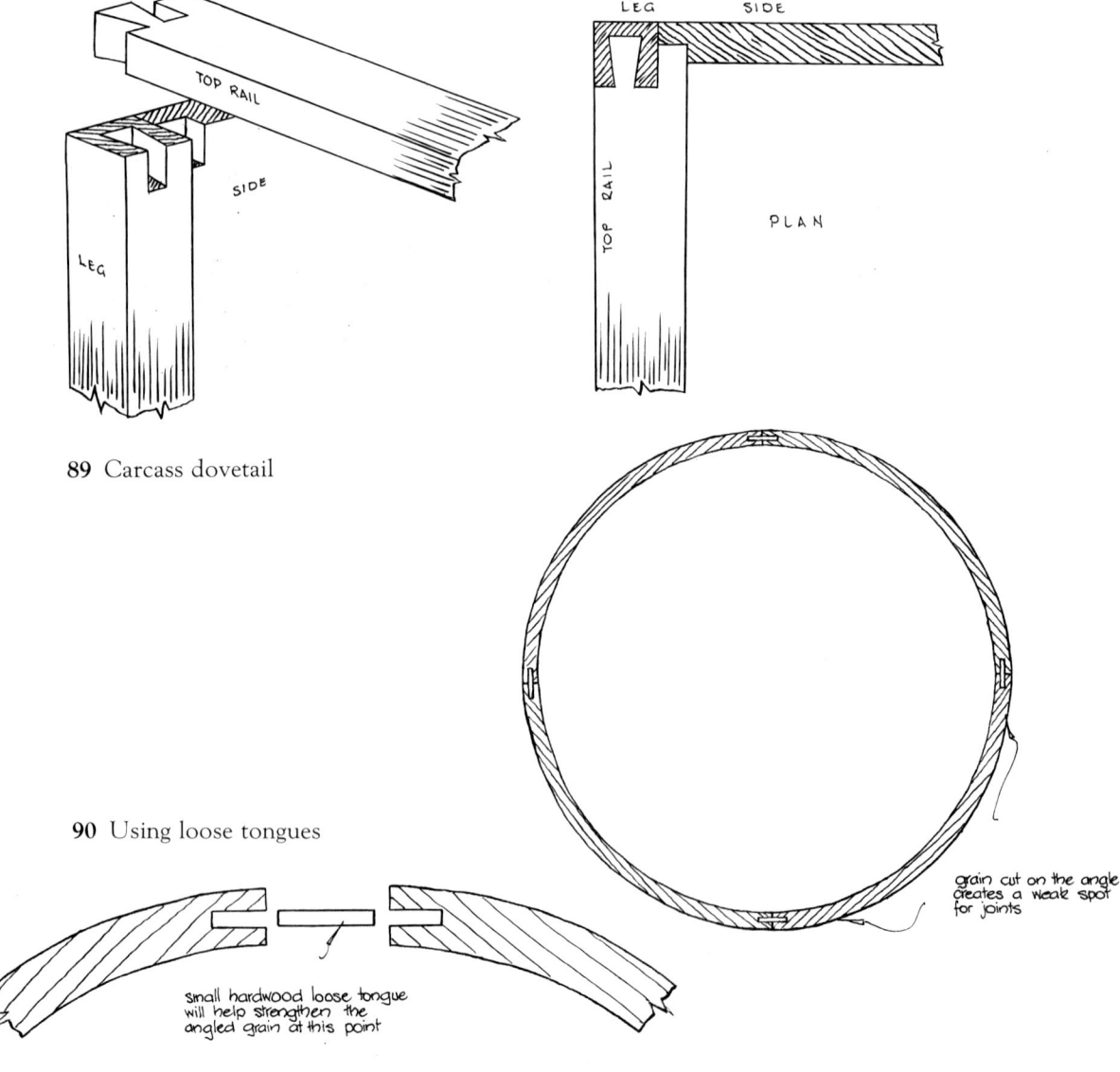

89 Carcass dovetail

90 Using loose tongues

small hardwood loose tongue will help strengthen the angled grain at this point

grain cut on the angle creates a weak spot for joints

4 A 1/12th scale Dutch bureau cabinet made in walnut and inlaid with
boxwood. With forty-three drawers in all, eight of which are secret, and
working locks. (7 in. high)

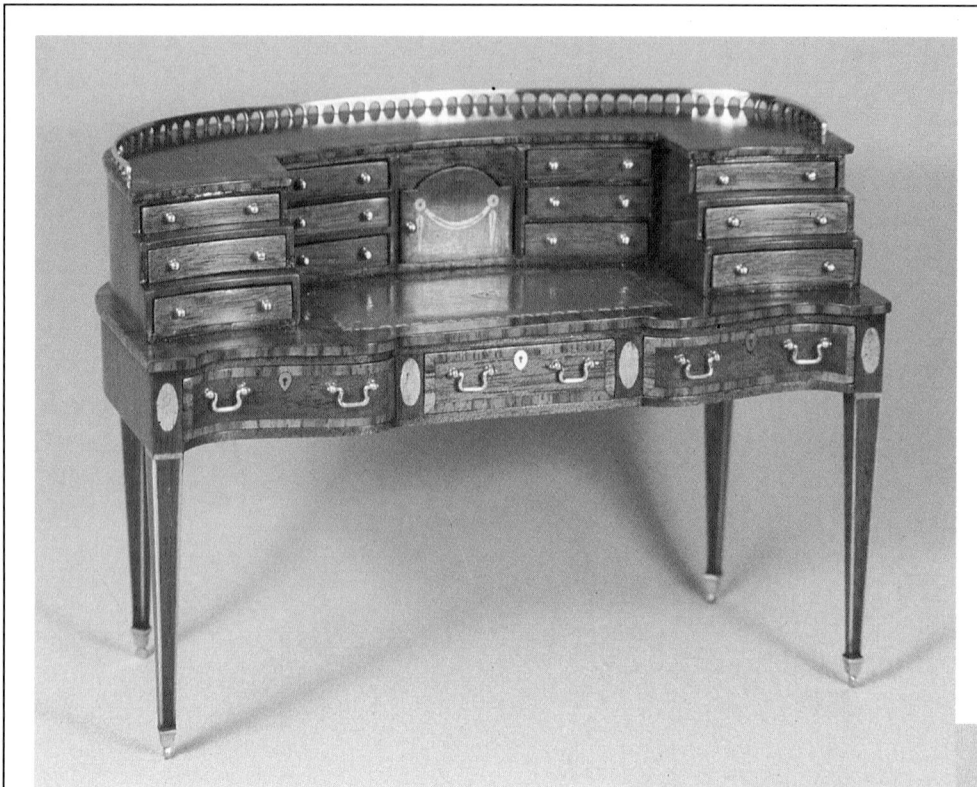

5 A 1/12th scale Carlton desk made in walnut
and banded in zebrano. Leather top tooled in
gilt, brass gallery, castors and secret drawers.
(3½ in. high)

6 A 1/12th scale teapoy made in mahogany with
ivory pateras. (2⅜ in. high)

VI *Cleaning up process*

One of the most important parts of making miniature furniture is the cleaning up stage. Too little attention at this point can ruin the finish of your piece, especially if a full grain finish is needed or you require a soft finish look.

Do not be in too much of a hurry to glue pieces together: clean up the separate parts as much as possible. Also, there are times when you will have to make the shapes and trim and so on after glueing.

I have seen so many well-made miniatures spoilt for lack of care taken on the cleaning up process. After spending so much time making a piece, there is a tendency to want to polish or varnish it immediately to see how it will look. You should be saying, I have spent all this time and work, it seems to look good so I must be careful to clean the surface properly and not spoil the polish finish. So do try to get this part of the job right. *Do not rush.* Handle holes should be worked out and drilled at this stage, but do not fit handles till polishing is completed.

Sandpaper

There are many types of sandpaper you can use; I will suggest my preferences but you may find others to your liking. Remember, never use a coarse paper of any kind.

I start the sanding process with garnet grade 5/0 and 7/0, nothing coarser than this.

For the finish I use silicon carbide lubrisil 165.

Remember always to work with the grain, never across, because much of the $\frac{1}{12}$th scale miniatures are so fragile when finished. Never forget to approach this cleaning up with a light hand and some moderation – tolerance is very limited in many places. In the case of a tapered leg, for example, the base of the leg can be less than $\frac{3}{32}$in. (2.5mm) wide.

An easy way to check your sanding if you are still not quite sure whether you have covered it all properly is to cast your magnifying glass over the work. This will soon reveal any parts missed.

When you have satisfied yourself it is now finished, wipe over with a clean cloth and blow all the dust away.

Now dip a small piece of cotton wool into methylated spirits (not white spirit). Do not have the cotton wool too wet. Wipe your miniature once over – this will raise the grain up very slightly.

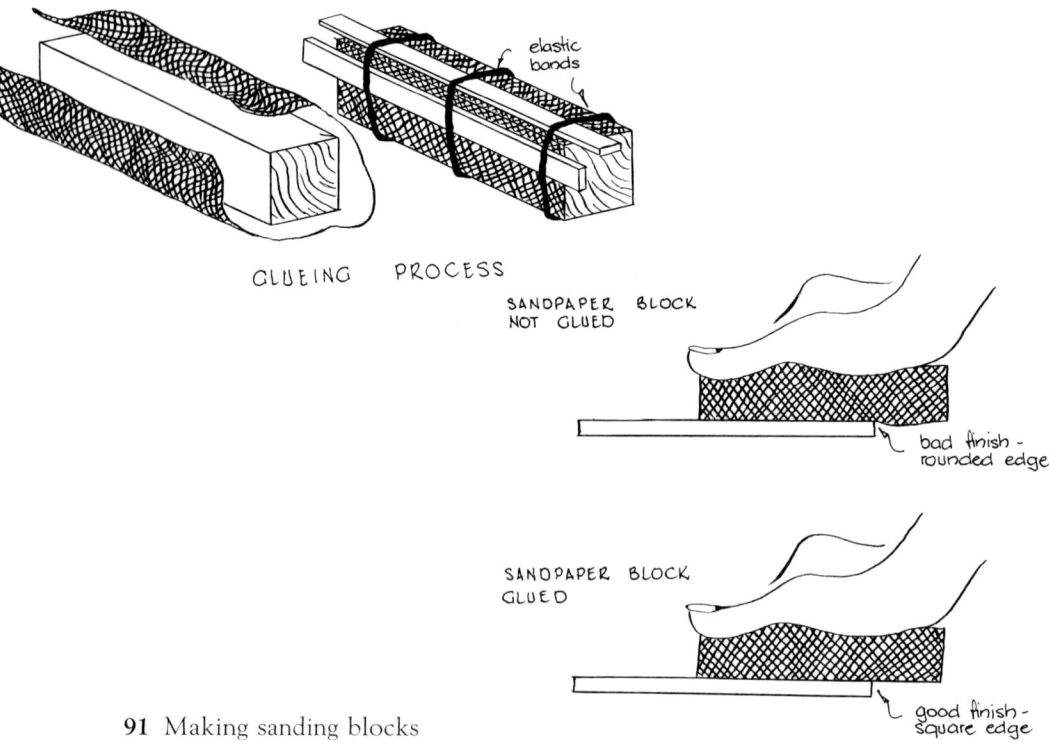

GLUEING   PROCESS

SANDPAPER   BLOCK
NOT   GLUED

bad finish -
rounded edge

SANDPAPER   BLOCK
GLUED

good finish -
square edge

91 Making sanding blocks

When dry, just touch the surface over very lightly with your finest
sandpaper – this will give it that slightly extra fine surface and will be ready for
filling the grain.

NB The smaller the piece of wood you are sanding down, the easier it will round
on the edges. There is always this tendency for slightly rounded edges to take
shape when they should finish square. One way to overcome this is to use a
small wood sanding block as shown in fig. 91.

Using sanding blocks

Glue the sandpaper round the block, using the glue sparingly. Pull the paper
tight round the block and trim; small slats will hold the ends in place with
elastic bands till the glue is dry.

The sandpaper will not last long as it becomes clogged, but while it lasts it will
give you this sharp clean edge.

A square block 1 × 1in. (25 × 25mm) and 3in. (76mm) long will give you four
sides to work with. Do not use it until the glue is completely dry and do make
sure that the four sides of the block are flat.

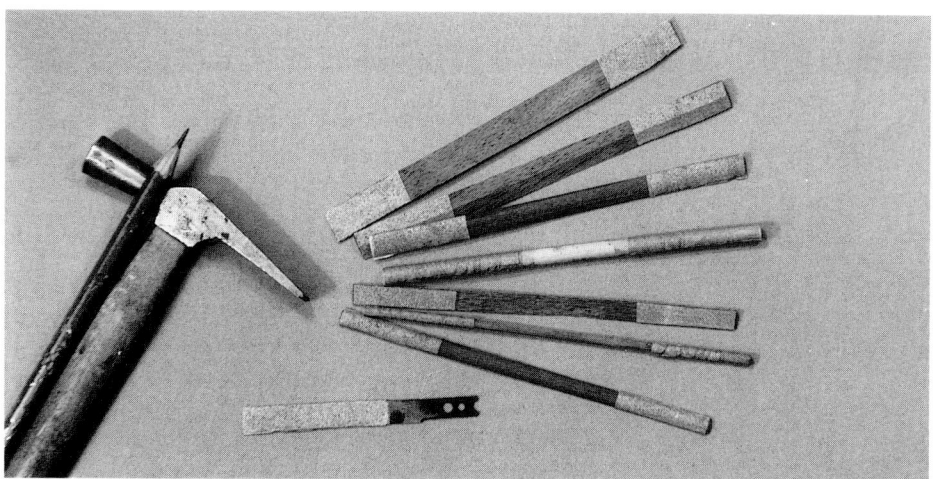

92 Sanding sticks

Sandpaper sticks in all shapes and sizes can be made up and glued in this way. They are useful to use in tight corners and for cleaning mouldings.

The sandpaper stick at the bottom of fig. 92 is a thin strip of $\frac{1}{32}$in. thick metal, ideal for awkward edges, yet still strong enough to stand up to a little pressure.

It is sometimes difficult to hold very small pieces while trying to clean them up; you will find a sandpaper block with fine sandpaper glued on a great help (fig. 93). Make sure the board is perfectly flat, and change the sandpaper when the grip has gone.

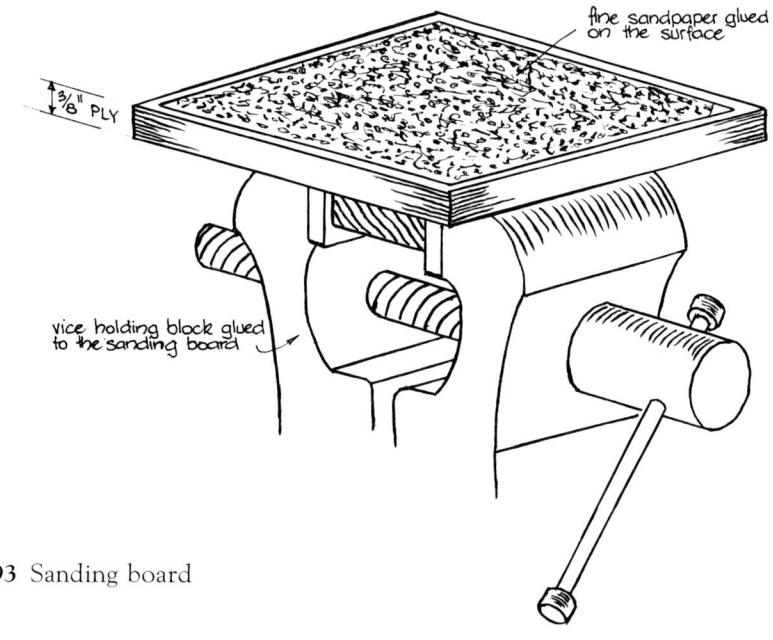

93 Sanding board

VII *Finishing*

Your finish will partly depend on the type of wood you have selected and on how skilful you have been in choosing the best cuts for your miniature.

Wood staining

If you want to obtain a slightly different colour, always stain a sample piece taken from the same stock you have made your miniature with. To chance applying stain on your finished piece will invite disaster as once too much stain has been rubbed on it is very hard to remove. Your cleaning up will have been completed and you will alter the finish thickness by sanding out stain.

Try to use the natural wood colours for staining as much as you can, although there will be times you will have to stain in a slight brown or red tint. *Colron wood dyes* have good oil stains in a vast range of colours, a few bottles giving you a colour range that will last for ages on miniatures. I do use spirit colours occasionally, but you have to send away for them and you do need a little practice to mix and get them just right.

Wood filler

Filling the grain is most important to obtain that soft, full grain finish, seen on so many fine antique pieces of furniture. For very early furniture in Europe, c.1650, resin was mixed with linseed oil and used to fill the surface, which was then polished with beeswax and turpentine. Later, lac and spirits of wine became more popular. In the early 1800s french polish (shellac and spirit mixed) was used in Europe and America to obtain that full grained, soft shiny surface look.

One good grain filler is the walnut-coloured Jecolit, (see the list of suppliers, Appendix V). There are other wood fillers on the market you can use, though I would suggest that you do not use a clear filler because as it dries the filler tends to show up in the grain, appearing as light flecks, especially if the grain is a little open. The slightly tinted fillers (walnut or mahogany) should tone down these flecks in most instances.

There is always a grain problem in miniature making: your miniature is scaled down but the grain stays the same size. Only with careful selection to improve your pieces can you alter this to any degree.

Rub the filler across the grain using a small soft cloth, then wipe all surplus filler off, still rubbing across the grain. Clear off all edges.

You now leave this for 20 minutes, then very gently sandpaper the surface, working with the grain using the finest sandpaper. Do not use a sanding block from now on. The object here is to remove all minute pieces of surface filler, leaving a fine flat surface and edges.

Now leave this for 6–12 hours before the next process.

The filler I use takes 6 hours to harden fully; other wood fillers might take longer but instructions are always on the packets or tins.

Applying French polish

After the 6 hours you can now apply your first coat; the workshop temperature should be around 21°C (70°F) and the environment as dust free as possible. I use a pale transparent polish for building up the surface. Varnish, I find, is too thick for many coats over small surfaces, encouraging an inevitable build up at the edges when it is brushed on.

Always shake up your polish well before using it; also use good brushes and clean them as soon as you have finished coating the work. I use camel or sable hair brushes, although they are expensive.

Brush your first coat on; do not lay the polish on too thick. Wait 20 minutes, then brush another coat on, taking care at all edges.

Leave the miniature now for 12 hours.

Then clean down by hand all polished surfaces with your finest sandpaper. Try not to miss any parts and do not rub through; a little practice will soon show you how much to clean without rubbing away too much.

Now coat with polish again only once this time.

Wait 12 hours then sand down a little more gently this time.

If the grain of your miniature was good to start with and well filled you should be getting a real flat surface by now.

Occasionally you might have to repeat this process four or five times – do not worry about the shine, concentrate on that filled surface.

Varnishing

When you are satisfied with the polish surface, apply your last coat with varnish (not too thick).

The workshop temperature should still be about 21°C (70°F) and your workshop should be as dust free as possible.

Do not shake up the varnish bottle or tin; instead pour the liquid into a clean, dust-free jar; stir well then pour the varnish back, just keeping enough in the jar for the work in hand. The reason for not shaking the bottle is that minute bubbles form and become trapped in the varnish just before you use it; they are hard to brush out later. This also happens in the thinner polish but does not create a problem as they rise and vanish very quickly.

You will have to wait some time for the varnish to dry; put the miniature away in a safe place and leave it for about three days.

The instructions on the varnish bottle will tell you how long to leave the piece before the coating is completely dry.

Dulling

For the soft look finish rub gently and as evenly as possible over the finished coat with 0000 steel wool; this fine grade steel wool is not always available in local hardware shops so you might have to send away for a supply. (See Appendix V.) It will have to be this fine wirewool, any other grade is just too coarse.

Dulling can also be done with a rottenstone powder and rubbing oil, but I prefer the steel wool.

Wipe off all dust when you have finished dulling the piece.

It only remains now to wax the surface with a good furniture wax polish.

If you have been successful your piece should have a finish something like that of the $\frac{1}{12}$th scale miniature in fig. 94.

94 Kneehole writing desk with a soft finish ($\frac{1}{12}$th scale)

VIII *Projects*

1: Making a carcass for a simple drawer and door

Making a carcass and a well fitting drawer are musts for the true cabinet maker. This applies to miniature cabinet work too, although the approach may differ a little. The carcass in figs 95 and 96 is not a true cabinet but the sort to begin on in order to learn how to fit your first drawer and door. Don't worry if you make mistakes – it is all good practice.

The project for making a practice carcass and adding a drawer and door is to familiarize you with the process in general and to prepare you for the inevitable problems that occur on the way. Once you have done two or three trial runs, you will be able to progress to the simple cabinet and just add a plain top. Later, you can add pieces and alter the shape and size to suit various pieces.

Figure 104 shows you how the carcass can be altered, still using the same joints, drawers and doors. Of course, you will not always be able to use the same frames and joints in all styles, but this will give you confidence before you go on to attempt more complex pieces. A general guide to the thickness on the front edge of a carcass in a full size chest of drawers is $\frac{3}{4}$in. (19mm). This would be scaled down to $\frac{1}{16}$in. (1.5mm) in a $\frac{1}{12}$th model. For your first attempt at the jointing, scale up a little, to say $\frac{3}{32}$in. (2.5mm) on the edges; only when you are more confident scale to the $\frac{1}{16}$in. (1.5mm) thickness.

First cut and trim the sides square (fig. 96).

Mark out the housing joints and cut them out (fig. 97), not forgetting the

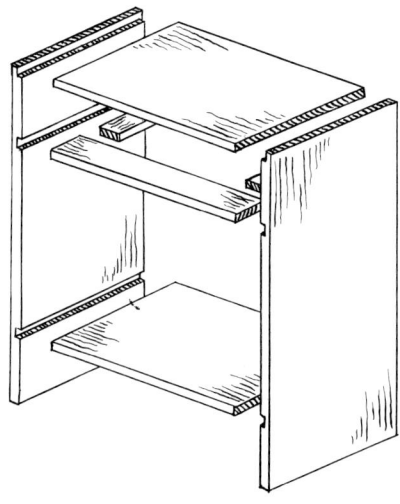

95 Practice carcass

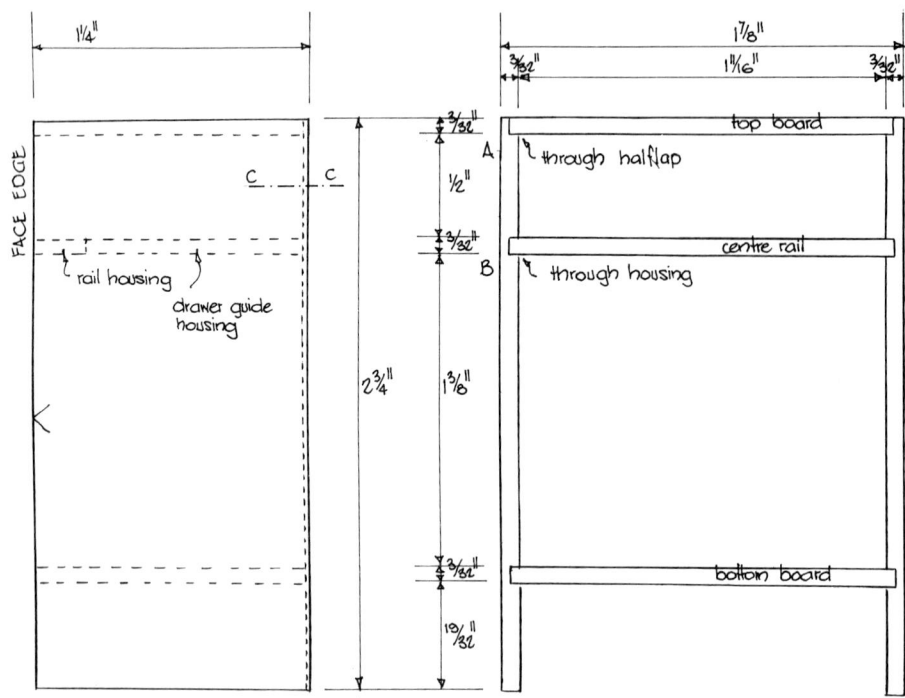

SIDE ELEVATION   FRONT ELEVATION

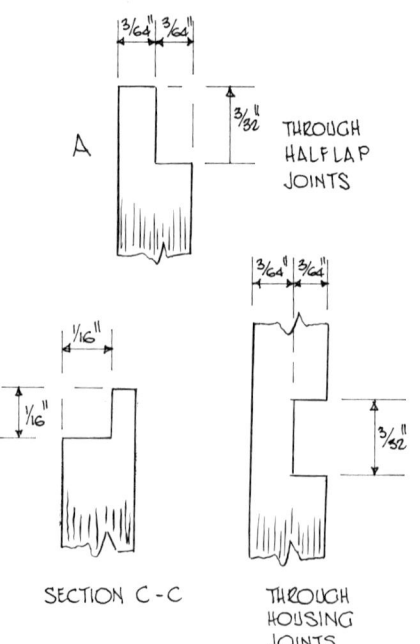

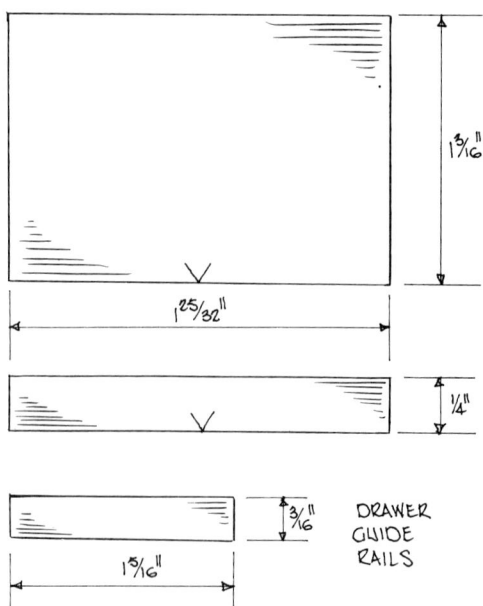

96 Detail of practice carcass

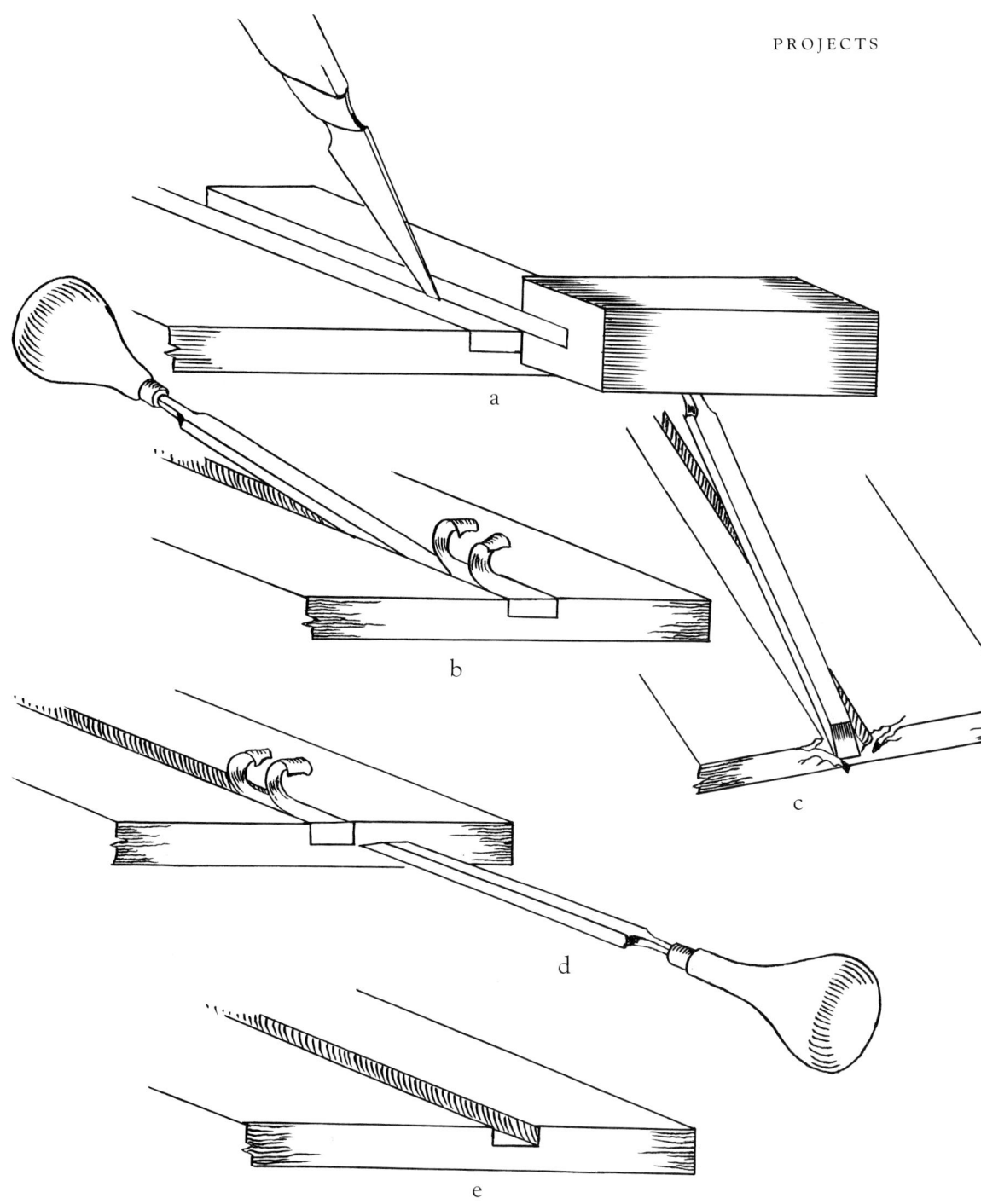

97 Cutting housing joints. (a) Cuts are not to be deeper than half-way; (b) Stop chiselling ¼in. from end; (c) Finish housing from this side; (d) Damage that occurs if you chisel right through; (e) Completed housing joints

rebate for your back panel, to be fitted later (fig. 96c–c). Be careful with the housing joints, they should not finish more than half-way through.

Chisel out the housings, shown in fig. 97b.

Stop ¼in. (6mm) from the end, then chisel in from the other side (fig. 97c).

There is a weak point here at the edges where damage can easily occur (fig. 97d).

Figure 97e shows the finished joint.

Now prepare the rest of the carcass and, when you are satisfied, glue together as in fig. 98. Do not forget the squaring block to hold the frame in place for you.

When this has set glue in the drawer runners, making sure they do not overlap the rebates made to take the back.

Do not fit a foot rail or back in until you have made the door and drawer. If the back is left out till last it will enable you to see where your drawer is catching when you are trimming, by looking through the back.

The door must be fitted and the swivel pins inserted before the feet or foot rail is glued.

The drawer

After cutting out the main pieces, mark out the rebates that must be cut on the front and sides of your drawer; be careful with your scribing here, the sides and back of the drawer are thinner than the front and without caution you will cut right through them. Use your chisel very gently and do not lose patience. Once you can make drawers that fit you are well along the road of miniature cabinet work (fig. 99).

The sides and front of the drawer should finish with no rounded edges.

A good opportunity arises here to try out the wood block with glued sandpaper when cleaning up the drawer before assembling (fig. 91).

When you have cleaned down to the right thickness, check all measurements, then glue the drawer together on the workboard as shown in fig. 100.

Lay the weight from side to side to keep the sides in alignment. When the glue is dry, trim the drawers and fit, checking they are square with the front before cutting and fitting the bottom in place.

It is important to remember the grain in a drawer bottom runs from *side to side*, never front to back; there is much less chance of shrinkage this way.

The back of your drawer bottom can be trimmed down and used as a drawer stop.

The door

This mitred door is quite strong, having braced corners. First cut your door frame out with $\frac{1}{32}$in. (1mm) overlap on all ends. Mark the face sides, then mark and cut the rebates on the inside of your door frame. Cut carefully with your chisel, working with the grain, finish with a small pillar file (fig. 101a).

Using your mitre square mark out and cut the mitres, leaving your pencil

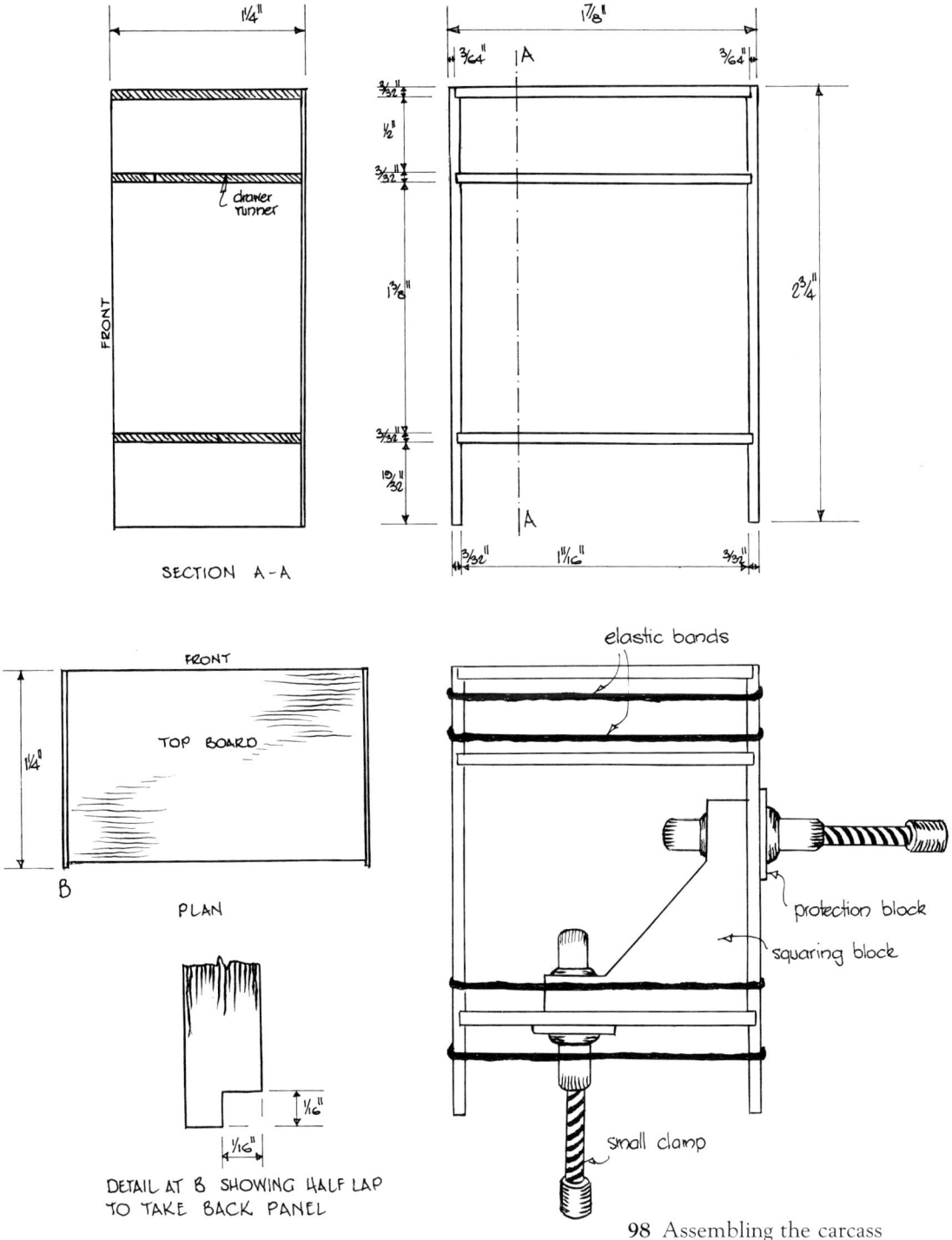

$1\frac{1}{4}''$

$1\frac{7}{8}''$

$\frac{3}{64}''$ $\frac{3}{64}''$

A

$\frac{3}{32}''$

$\frac{1}{2}''$

$\frac{3}{32}''$

drawer runner

$1\frac{3}{8}''$

$2\frac{3}{4}''$

FRONT

$\frac{3}{32}''$

$\frac{19}{32}''$

A

SECTION A-A

$\frac{3}{32}''$ $1\frac{11}{16}''$ $\frac{3}{32}''$

FRONT

TOP BOARD

$1\frac{1}{4}''$

B

PLAN

$\frac{1}{16}''$

$\frac{1}{16}''$

DETAIL AT B SHOWING HALF LAP
TO TAKE BACK PANEL

elastic bands

protection block

squaring block

small clamp

98 Assembling the carcass

91

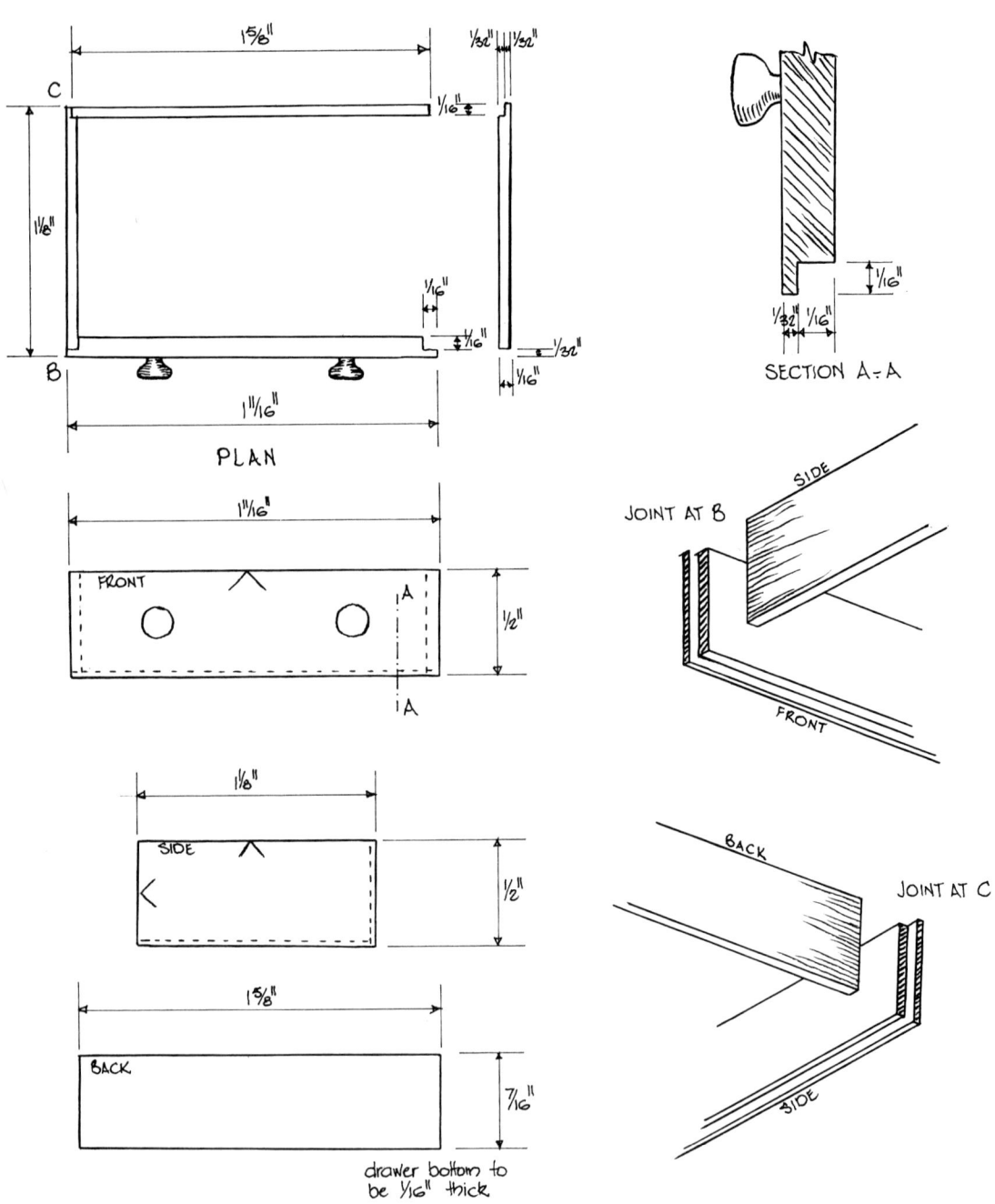

99 Easy-to-make drawer

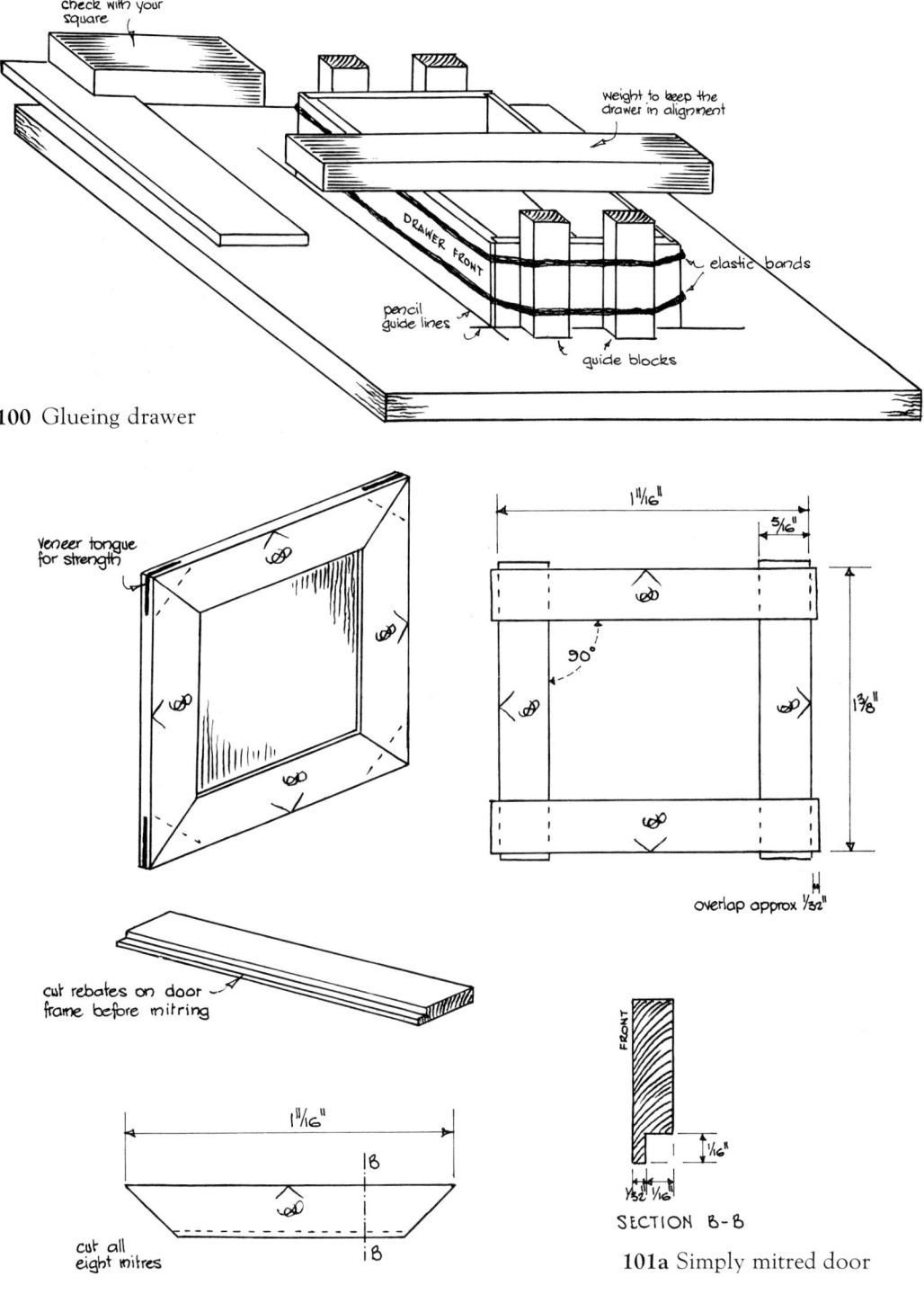

check with your square

weight to keep the drawer in alignment

DRAWER FRONT

elastic bands

pencil guide lines

guide blocks

100 Glueing drawer

Veneer tongue for strength

1¹¹⁄₁₆"

5⁄16"

90°

1³⁄₈"

overlap approx 1⁄32"

cut rebates on door frame before mitring

1¹¹⁄₁₆"

B

B

cut all eight mitres

FRONT

SECTION B-B

1⁄16"

1⁄32" 1⁄16"

101a Simply mitred door

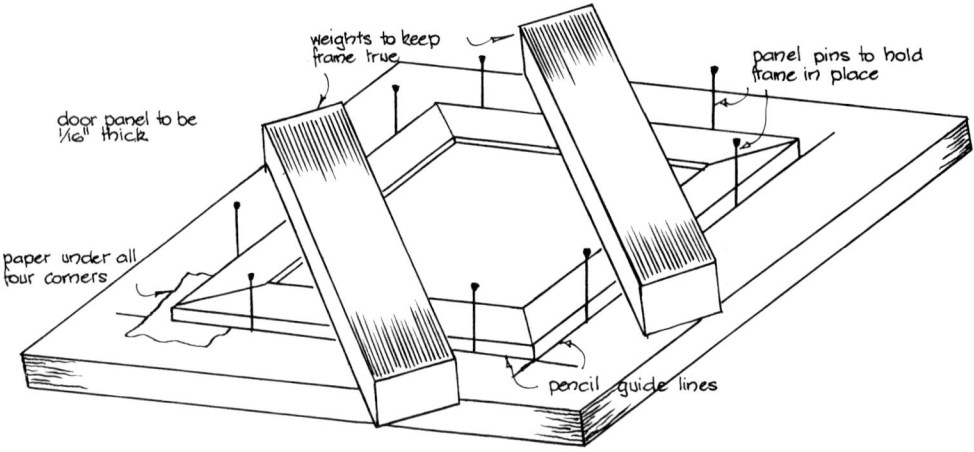

weights to keep frame true

panel pins to hold frame in place

door panel to be 1/16" thick

paper under all four corners

pencil guide lines

101b Simply mitred door

lines just showing; this will allow you a little room for trimming your mitres if your cut is a little out of line. When you are satisfied the mitres fit, place them face side up as in fig. 101b.

Slip a piece of paper under each mitre; this will prevent your frame sticking to your work board when you glue and pinch the mitres tight. Do not use newspaper as the print can come off and stain your work when in contact with the wet glue. Place a small weight on the door to keep it flat and square.

When the frame has set, cut and glue a tongue of veneer on each corner. This will add strength to the butt mitre; saw cuts should only be half-way through, however (fig. 102).

Glue and push the veneer into place but do not trim until the glue has set.

The door panel can now be cleaned up, trimmed and glued into place. When dry you can fit the door in position. It is sometimes difficult to get the correct location point to drill the hole for the swivel pin without a little practice. Make up a spare corner first to get the position just right. When you locate the swivel hole correctly transfer the measurements to your frame and drill the two holes. Do not drive the pin into the door – you may split the corner. Drill a little way down, press the pin tight just the last eighth only.

A small door stop and handle is all that is needed now. Figure 103 shows how the top swivel pin is located and drilled down through the top rail.

94

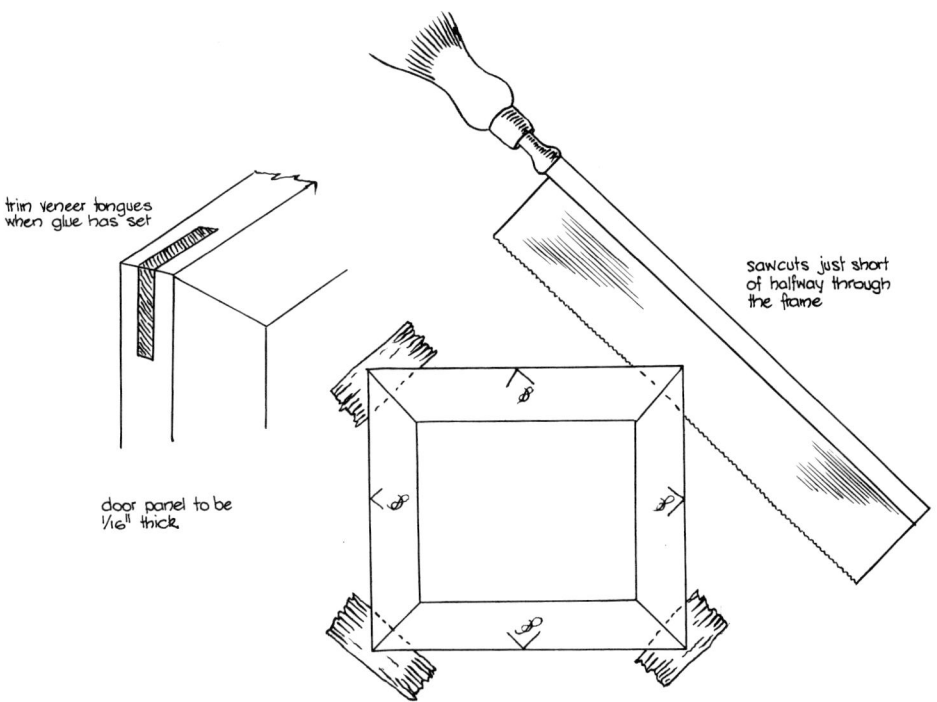

trim veneer tongues
when glue has set

sawcuts just short
of halfway through
the frame

door panel to be
1/16" thick

102 Strengthened corner joints (Project 1)

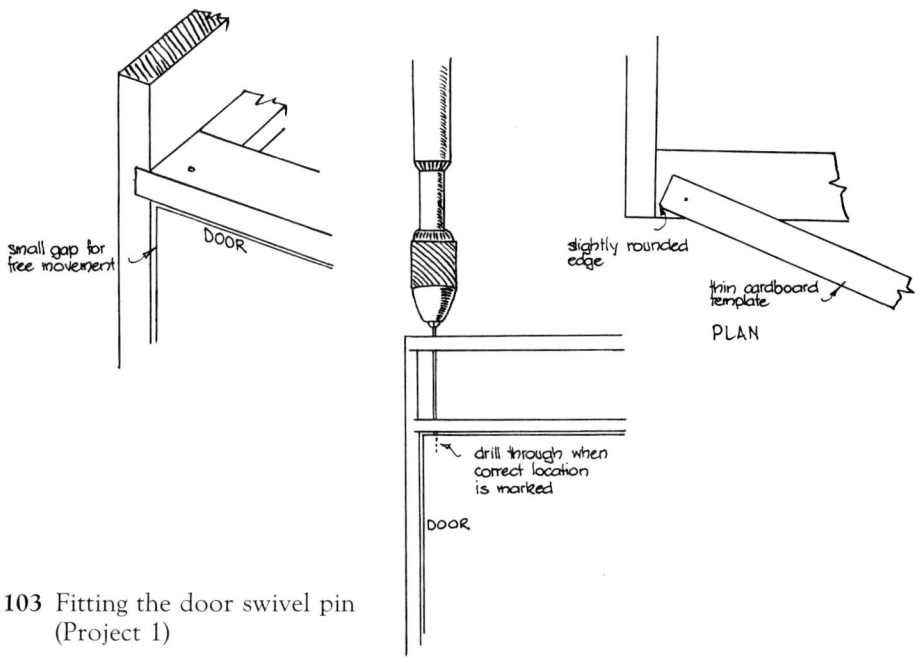

small gap for
free movement

DOOR

slightly rounded
edge

thin cardboard
template

PLAN

drill through when
correct location
is marked

DOOR

103 Fitting the door swivel pin
(Project 1)

104 Showing the simple drawer and door (Project 1)

2: The better made drawer and door

The drawer

In old furniture most drawers and runners were made in hardwoods, so that less wear would take place. I use oak for most of my drawers in miniature work, and occasionally mahogany. Walnut was very seldom used for this purpose although it was grown in the British Isles and used extensively for cabinet work. Later, walnut was imported and was probably too expensive to use, except sparingly. Hardwoods such as oak were used for the insides of drawers, backs and runners etc. Lapped dovetails are probably the most difficult joints to make in this miniature scale (except maybe for the hidden mitred dovetail). The dovetail is cut into the drawer sides and the pins into the drawer front. The old carpentry-type of dovetail is often seen on the drawer sides of old country furniture, and in many cases has been badly fitted (fig. 105a). It would be appropriate to use this type on old oak dresser drawers. Later, in the heyday of fine, handmade cabinet work many of the dovetails in drawer sides were made up to give a much neater appearance (fig. 105b). When you have the chance, look at the drawer sides of a late eighteenth-century quality piece of furniture. You will soon find this type of dovetail.

96

With the introduction of more sophisticated machinery came the machine dovetail. You can always recognize these as they are quite chunky (fig. 105c), although they do the job just as well. You will be able to use just plain half-lap joints at first on your drawers. Later, when you attempt more accuracy and detail, especially in the drawer, you will have to use these dovetails, as in fig. 108.

First the front edge of the drawer side must be squared, then fit these sides tight along the drawer runners.

Now take out and mark the depth of the dovetail using a small marking gauge. Determine the size of your dovetails, then mark spacing evenly. A small template can be used here, to ensure that the dovetail is angled at 10 degrees (fig. 106). The angle can vary considerably, but this is about average for drawer sides. Now place your work in the vice using a hardwood block at the back (fig. 107a), with the top edge resting on the bottom cutting line of the dovetail. This will stop your fretsaw undercutting this line.

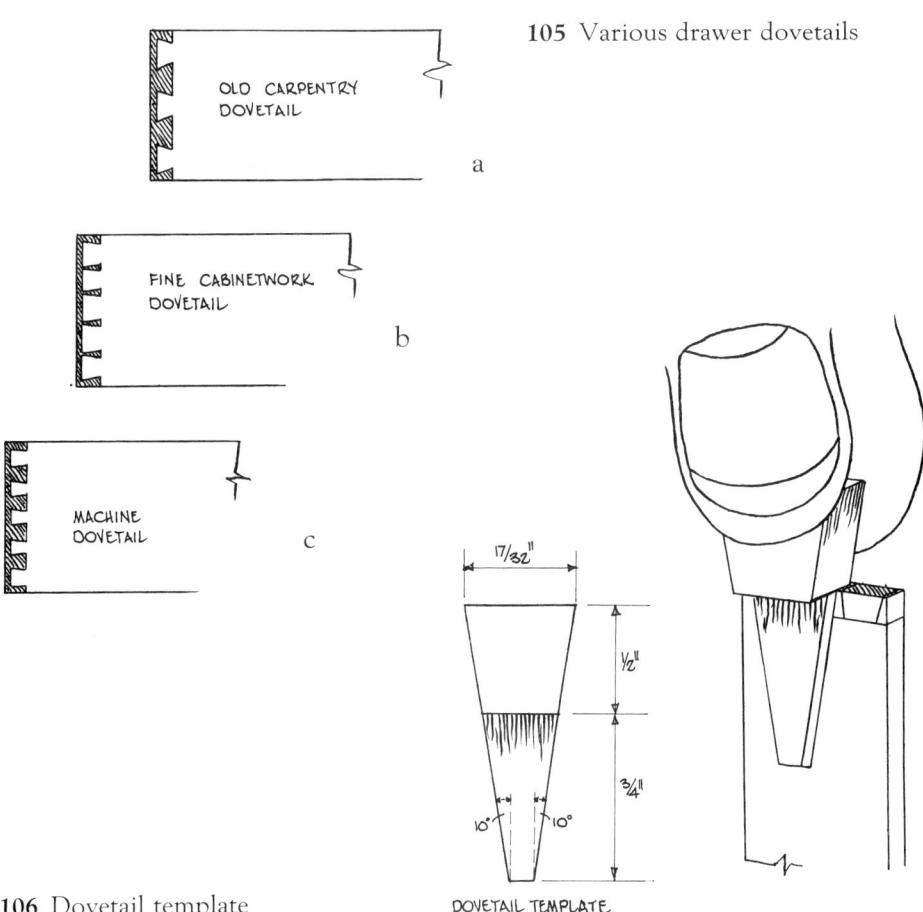

OLD CARPENTRY DOVETAIL

a

FINE CABINETWORK DOVETAIL

b

MACHINE DOVETAIL

c

105 Various drawer dovetails

17/32"

½"

¾"

10° 10°

DOVETAIL TEMPLATE

106 Dovetail template

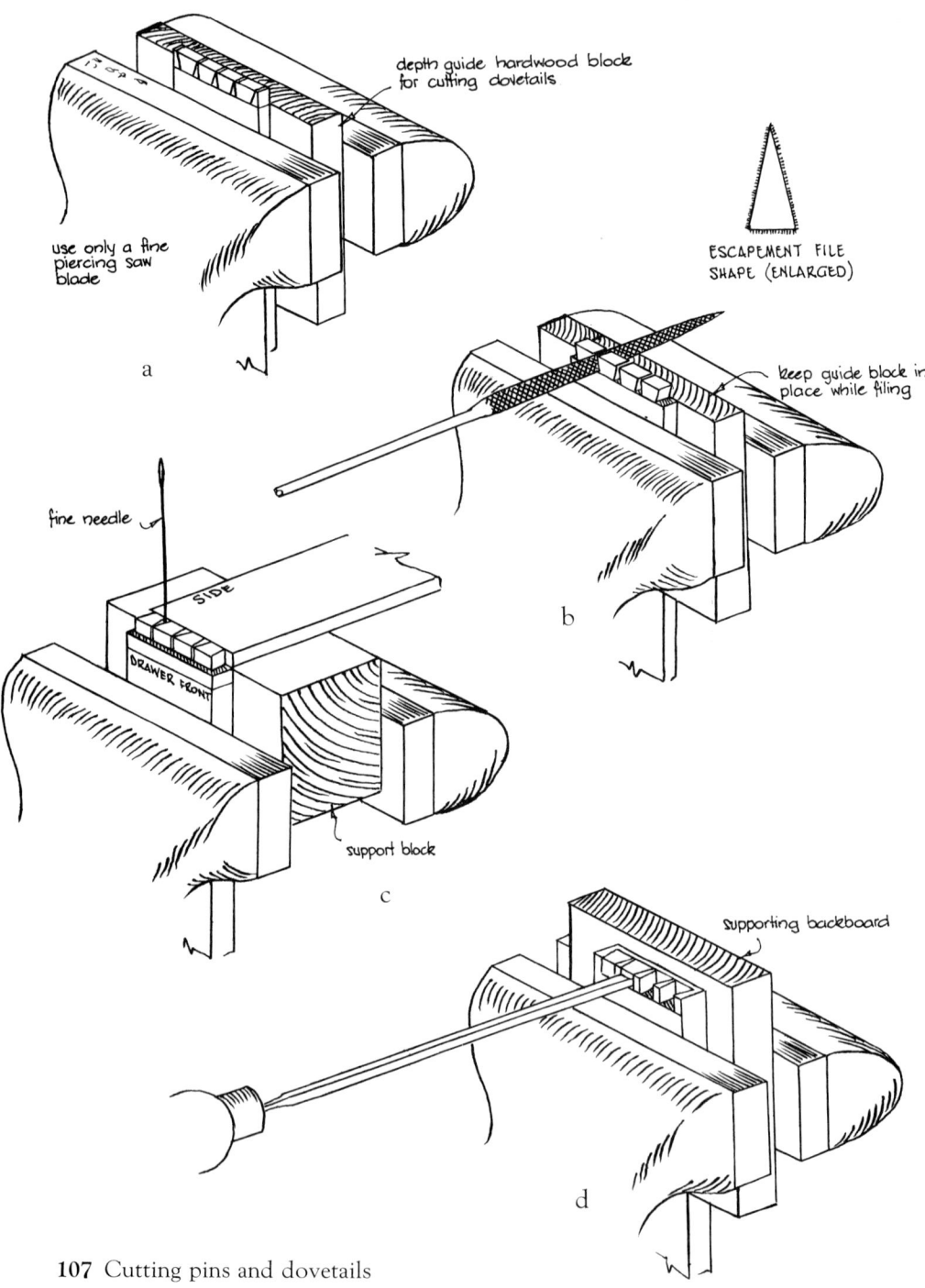

depth guide hardwood block
for cutting dovetails

use only a fine
piercing saw
blade

a

ESCAPEMENT FILE
SHAPE (ENLARGED)

keep guide block in
place while filing

b

fine needle

SIDE

DRAWER FRONT

support block

c

supporting backboard

d

107 Cutting pins and dovetails

When you have cut all dovetails, trim with a very fine escapement or miniature file (fig. 107b).

Secure your drawer front to be marked in the vice, and lay the side in place for marking the pins – the side must be held as still as possible here and a fine needle can be used (fig. 107c). Now remove the drawer side and improve these marks, transferring these guide lines down the inside of the drawer front.

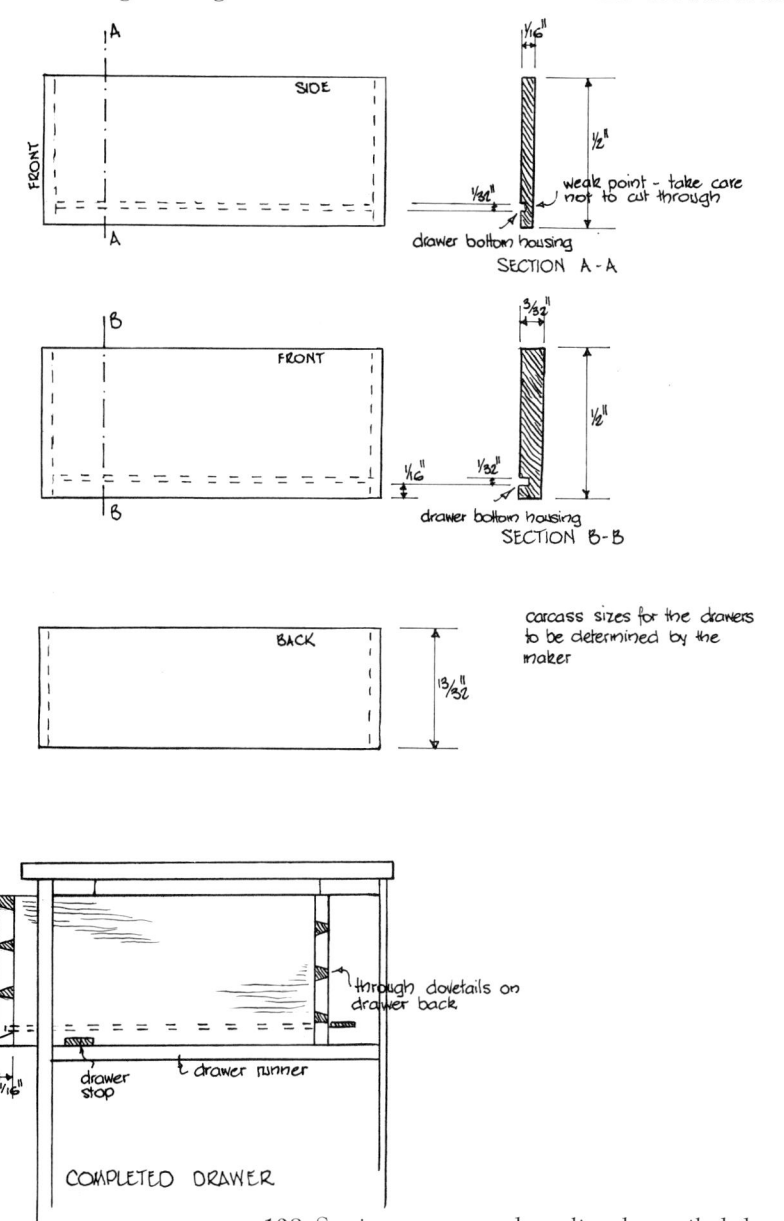

108 Setting out a good quality dovetailed drawer

109 Marking out door joints

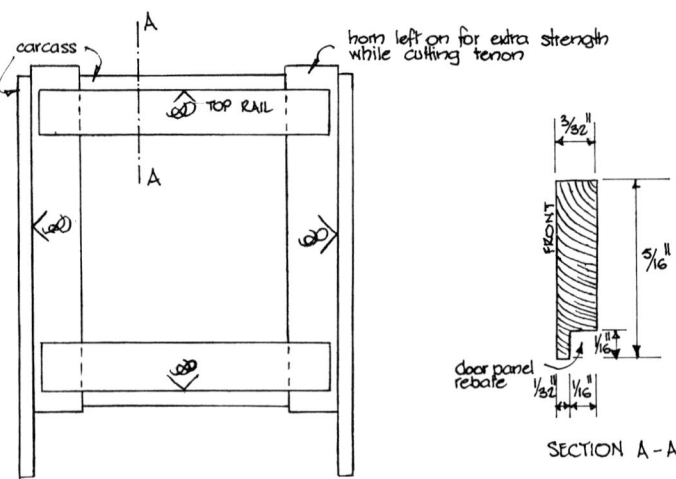

Support drawer front in the vice with a backboard (fig. 107d) while you cut these pins out with a $\frac{1}{16}$in. (1.5mm) or less chisel (and it must be sharp).

Great care must be taken not to cut through to the front of the drawer; also, the pins are so fine they will break if the chisel is pressed home too hard (fig 107d). Fitting the two parts together is also delicate work: apply no pressure here either. It is better to trim the joints slightly again than to push them home. (See fig. 108 for the finished joints.)

The door

This type of door will be much stronger than the butt-mitred door. When you have decided on the door sizes, cut the top, bottom and side rails; square them to the required size for the frame, then cut the side rails $\frac{1}{8}$in. (3mm) longer than actual size required. (The top and bottom rails are $\frac{1}{8}$in. shorter than the frame size, as the tenons must finish short of the full width of the rails.)

110 Squaring and making mortice and tenons

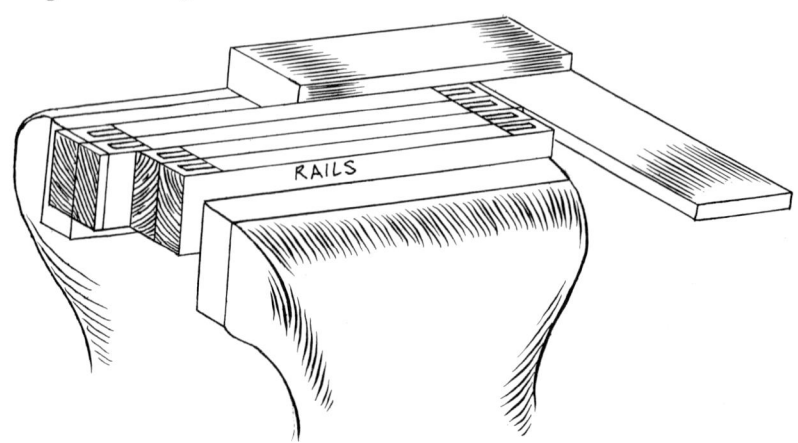

Mark all face sides.

Place the rails in the vice, keeping them square and mark all leading edges for the mortice and tenons (fig. 110).

Then take each separate rail, squaring all lines round, and with a marking gauge scribe the mortice and tenons for cutting. Remember that the tenon should not take up more than $\frac{1}{3}$ in. (8mm) of the overall thickness of the frame. It is important to mark the depth of the tenon on the drill; as a guide to stop you cutting right through it put a small strip of tape on the drill.

Check frequently as you cut that the joints are kept square.

There remains now just the rebate on the back to take your panel – push the frame gently together, then mark out for this rebate.

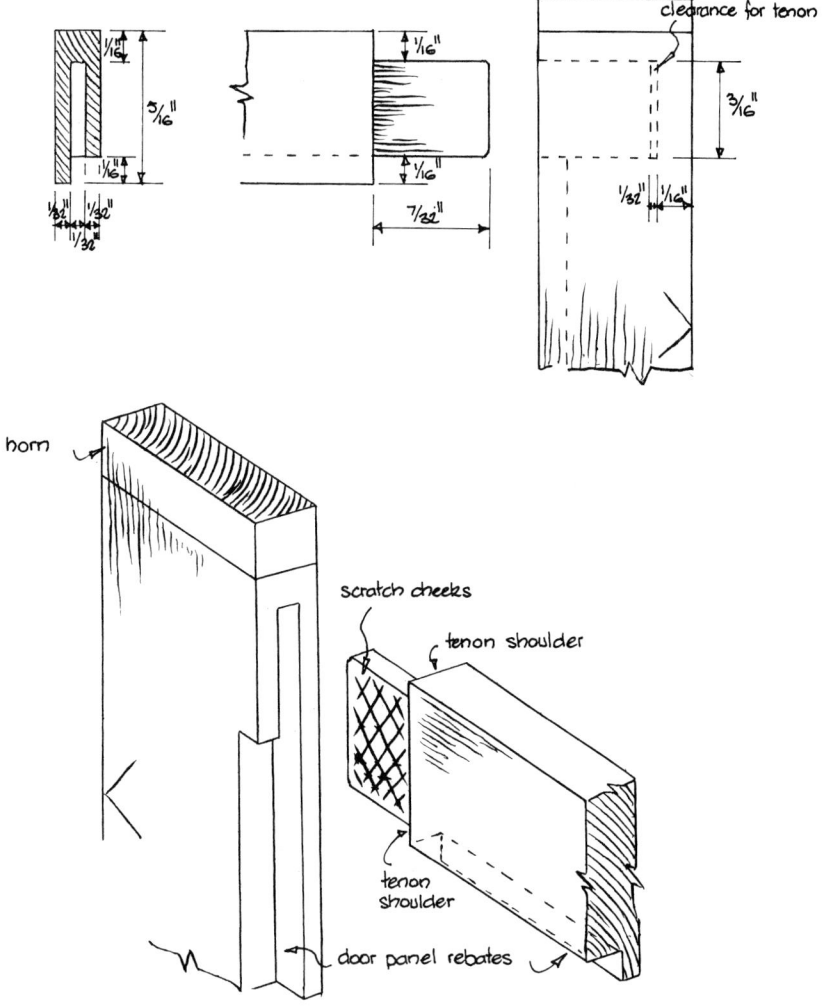

111 Typical mortice and tenon for cabinet door

101

112 Single banding

Take the frame apart and scribe a guide line on the back edges just to the depth of your panel, then chisel it out carefully.

Later, if you purchase a drill on a stand you will be able to cut this type of rebate out with small burrs.

Before glueing, always cross scratch the cheeks of each joint; this will give the glue a much better grip (fig. 111). The area covered by the glue is so small in this miniature work that you need all the help you can get for more strength (see page 105 for glueing method).

The panel is glued in later.

NB You can put hinges on the door instead of using swivel pins.

Cross banding

Because you will be cutting across the grain in bandings, there is a tendency for the veneer to split along the natural grain lines. This particularly applies to many hardwood veneers, rosewood, tulip and satinwood, to name just a few. Mahogany and walnut, although both considered hardwoods, are much easier to work with for this purpose; use these at least for your first attempts. Use adhesive tape to stop the thin strips falling apart – masking tape will do this same job but clear tape is better as you can see if the veneer is bedding down correctly before clamping. Where small splits do occur, before you lay the strip in place, make sure a small slip of glue is let into each one. This will stop any curl or lift at these points later (fig. 113a).

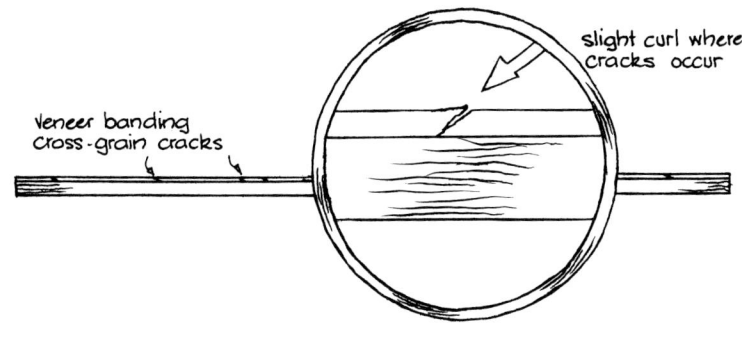

slight curl where
cracks occur

Veneer banding
cross-grain cracks

a

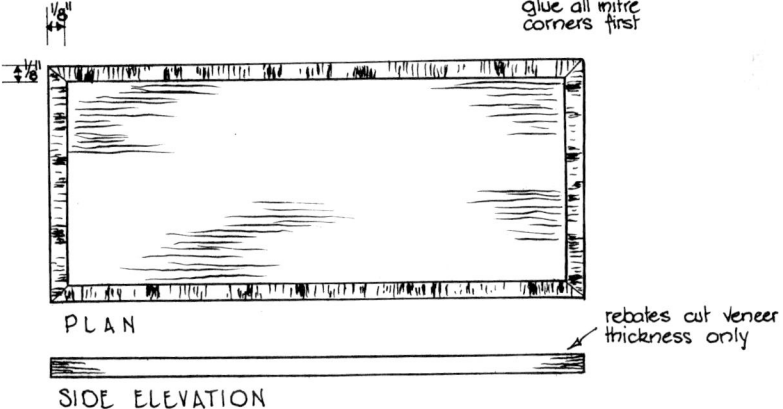

1/8"

1/8"

glue all mitre
corners first

PLAN

rebates cut veneer
thickness only

SIDE ELEVATION

b

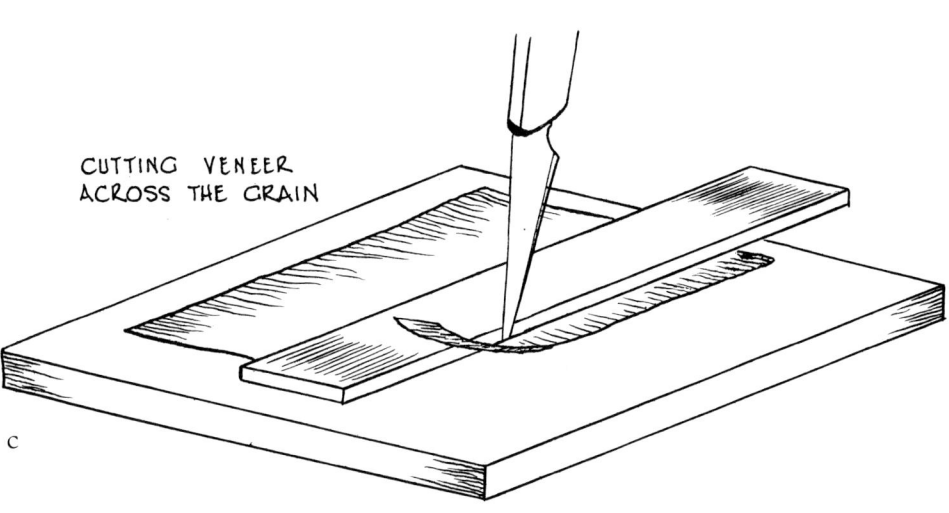

CUTTING VENEER
ACROSS THE GRAIN

c

113 Cutting cross bandings

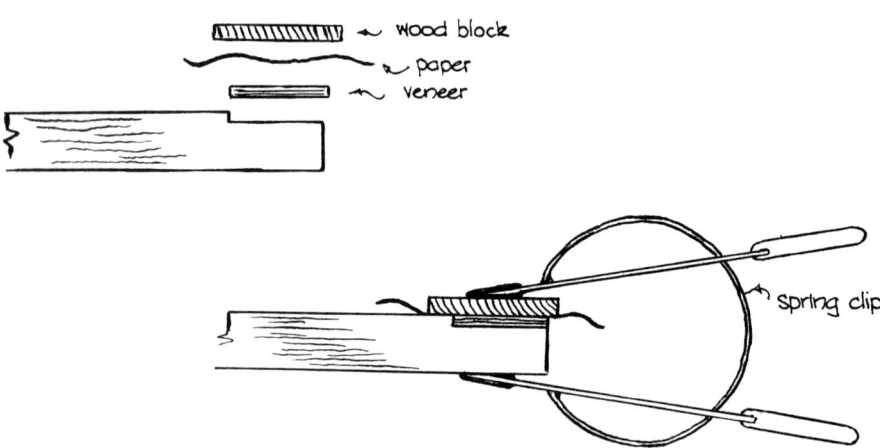

114 Glueing bandings

The above principles all apply to banding round the edge of a drawer, table top or door. Try banding this coffee table for practice (fig. 113b).

Use your marking gauge to scribe a line round $\frac{1}{8}$in. (3mm) from the edge of the coffee table. Working with the grain, cut carefully with your chisel until you have a rebate all round – check you are not cutting too deep (veneer thickness only).

Finish the rebate with a flat needle file – not sandpaper.

Now stick down strips of clear adhesive tape on one side of the small piece of veneer you have selected, joining each strip to form a complete cover.

115 Clips for holding bandings

104

116 Double banding on a $\frac{1}{12}$th scale walnut chest in rosewood and satin wood

Then turn the veneered tape face down on the cutting board; mark out a $\frac{1}{8}$in. strip (across the grain) using your marking gauge.

With a fine knife cut along this line (fig. 113c).

Repeat this until you have enough veneer – do not attempt to take off the adhesive tape yet.

Cut out all your mitre corners first and glue them in place. Fix them in place using bulldog clips (fig. 114).

With these clips in place it takes about 20 minutes to dry using Resin W.

You can then remove the clips and glue more veneer; do not however, try, to fix too many pieces in one go with this method.

When all the veneer is in place leave for about 24 hours before peeling the tape off and cleaning up the top.

Bear in mind as you clean up, that the veneer is very thin – if you round the edge while sanding you will quickly rub through it.

I use adhesive Resin W (Evo-stik) for most jointing and veneering, but choose the adhesive that suits you best.

3: Collector's cabinet

General tips

I have chosen this piece for the $\frac{1}{12}$th scale miniature maker who has started, but is still in the early stages of progress, and would now like to make a fairly impressive piece with door and drawers etc. You will only have to make straight lines – no turning, carving or curves are involved. The doors and tray (drawers) can be made up as shown earlier in the book.

If you wish to fit knobs or handles on the trays, allow extra clearance on the overall depth of the tray for these, otherwise the door will foul the handles when they are closed; also cut the tray runners back to finish flush with the tray fronts before you glue them in place.

Allow enough stock for at least six legs when you prepare your wood – a mistake can easily be made in tapering legs down. The cabinet has $\frac{1}{8}$in. (3mm) thick sides to allow for tray clearance past the swivel doors.

Fit the swivel pins and adjust the doors before glueing the top and base boards to the carcass. Swivel pins are shown at H.

The cabinet has $\frac{1}{8}$in. thick sides to allow for tray clearance when they slide out.

If you wish to fit hinges on the doors, the sides can be made $\frac{3}{32}$in. (2.5mm) as less clearance will be needed, but remember to make the inside width $\frac{1}{16}$in. (1.5mm) wider. Mark out and drill holes for the handles before finishing, but fit the handles only when the polishing is finished and the surface completely dry.

Method

Stage 1
Cut out all parts to rough sizes, selecting the grain carefully. Do not mix dark or light shades when choosing your stock and allow extra for mistakes or breakages. Leave these parts on a shelf to settle down (see page 26). Later trim all parts down much closer to finished sizes and thicknesses, leaving just a little extra thickness for final sandpapering down.

Stage 2
Assemble the carcass when you have trimmed the two sides to the right measurements. Place them together and mark out the guide lines for the tray runners. Check these lines carefully – they must run parallel. Now cut out the half-lap on the inside of the sides that will later take the back (shown at A–A). Prepare the top and bottom of the carcass and try them in place, checking all measurements. Now glue the carcass together.

117 Small collector's cabinet. Recommended wood – close-grained mahogany, darkish colour

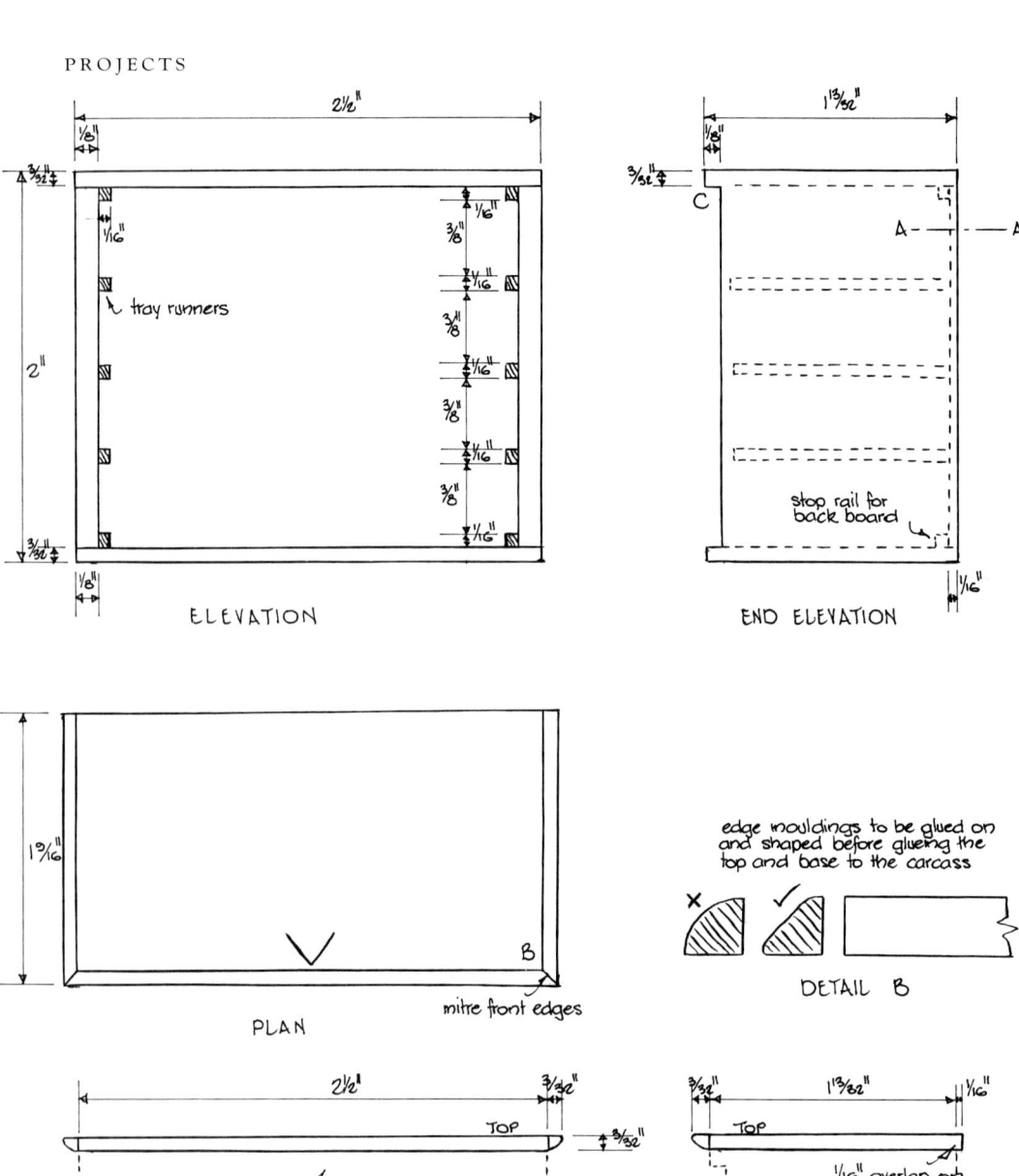

ELEVATION

END ELEVATION

tray runners

stop rail for
back board

2½"

1¹³⁄₃₂"

³⁄₃₂"

¹⁄₈"

¹⁄₁₆"

³⁄₈"

³⁄₈"

³⁄₈"

2"

1⁹⁄₁₆"

PLAN

mitre front edges

edge mouldings to be glued on
and shaped before glueing the
top and base to the carcass

DETAIL B

TOP

glue to carcass only after
doors have been fitted

2½"

3⁄₃₂"

BASE

2½"

TOP

1¹³⁄₃₂"

¹⁄₁₆" overlap on
this back edge

BASE

1¹⁵⁄₃₂"

118 Small collector's cabinet – carcass

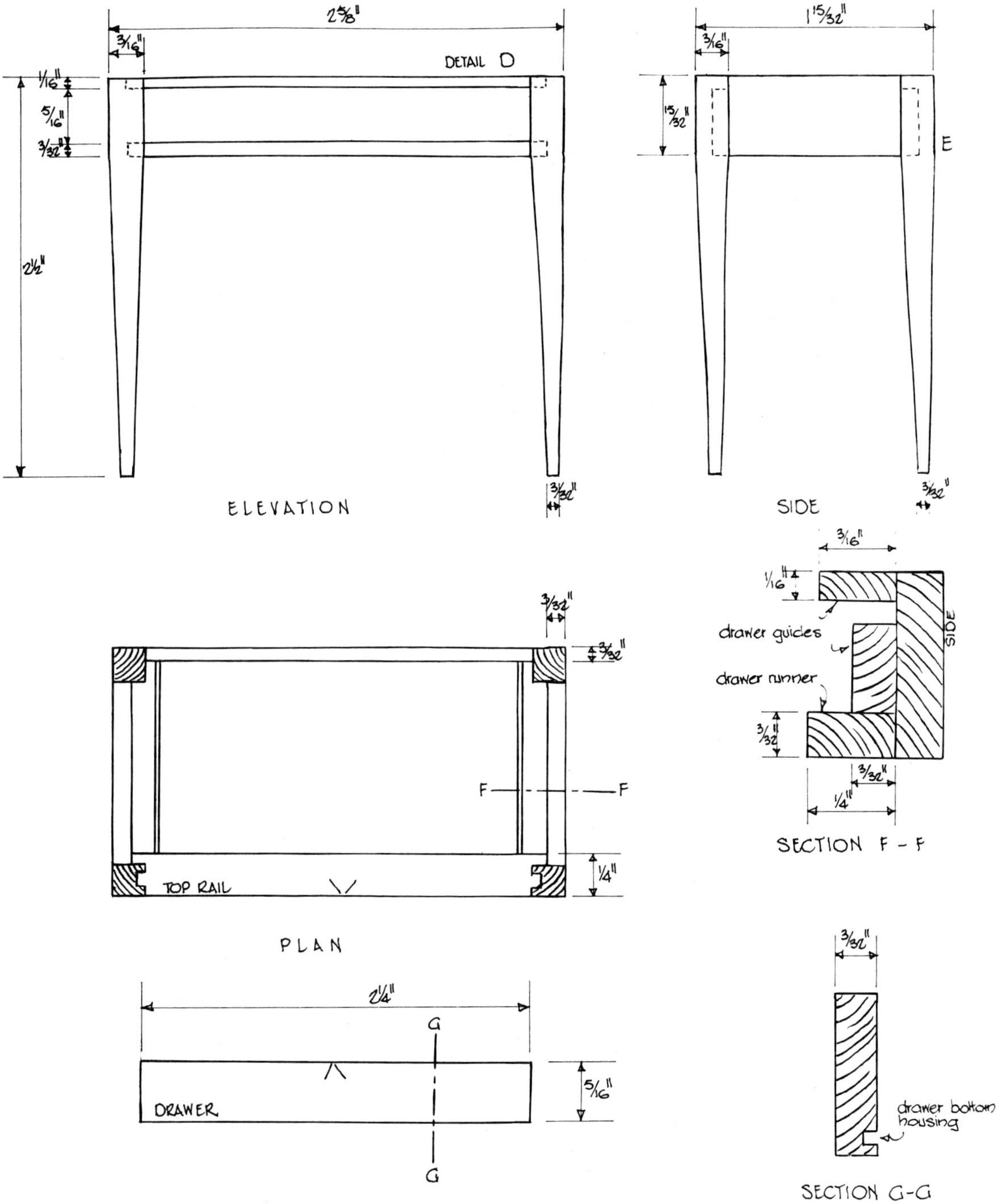

2⁵⁄₈"

3⁄₁₆"

DETAIL D

1⁄₁₆"

5⁄₁₆"

3⁄₃₂"

2½"

3⁄₃₂"

ELEVATION

1¹⁵⁄₃₂"

3⁄₁₆"

¹⁵⁄₃₂"

E

3⁄₃₂"

SIDE

3⁄₃₂"

3⁄₃₂"

TOP RAIL

F — — — F

¼"

PLAN

3⁄₁₆"

1⁄₁₆"

drawer guides

drawer runner

3⁄₃₂"

3⁄₃₂"

¼"

SIDE

SECTION F – F

2¼"

G

5⁄₁₆"

DRAWER

G

3⁄₃₂"

drawer bottom housing

SECTION G-G

119 Small collector's cabinet – supporting legs and frame

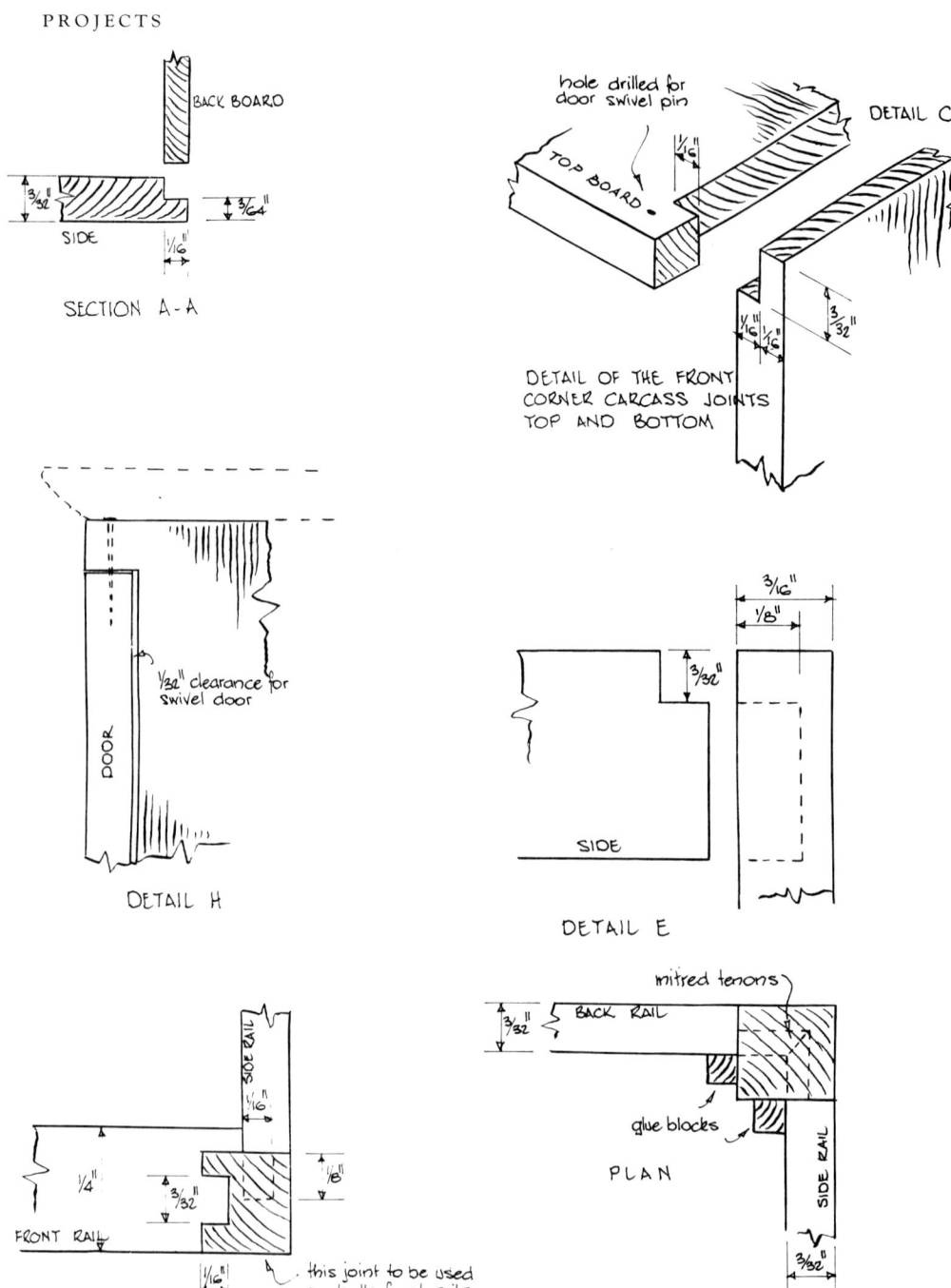

SECTION A-A

BACK BOARD

SIDE

3/32"

3/64"

1/16"

hole drilled for
door swivel pin

TOP BOARD

DETAIL C

1/16"

3/32"

1/16" 1/16"

DETAIL OF THE FRONT
CORNER CARCASS JOINTS
TOP AND BOTTOM

DOOR

1/32" clearance for
swivel door

DETAIL H

SIDE

3/16"

1/8"

3/32"

DETAIL E

SIDE RAIL

1/16"

1/4"

3/32"

1/8"

1/16"

FRONT RAIL

this joint to be used
on both front rails

DETAIL D

mitred tenons

BACK RAIL

3/32"

glue blocks

PLAN

SIDE RAIL

3/32"

120 Small collector's cabinet – joints and construction

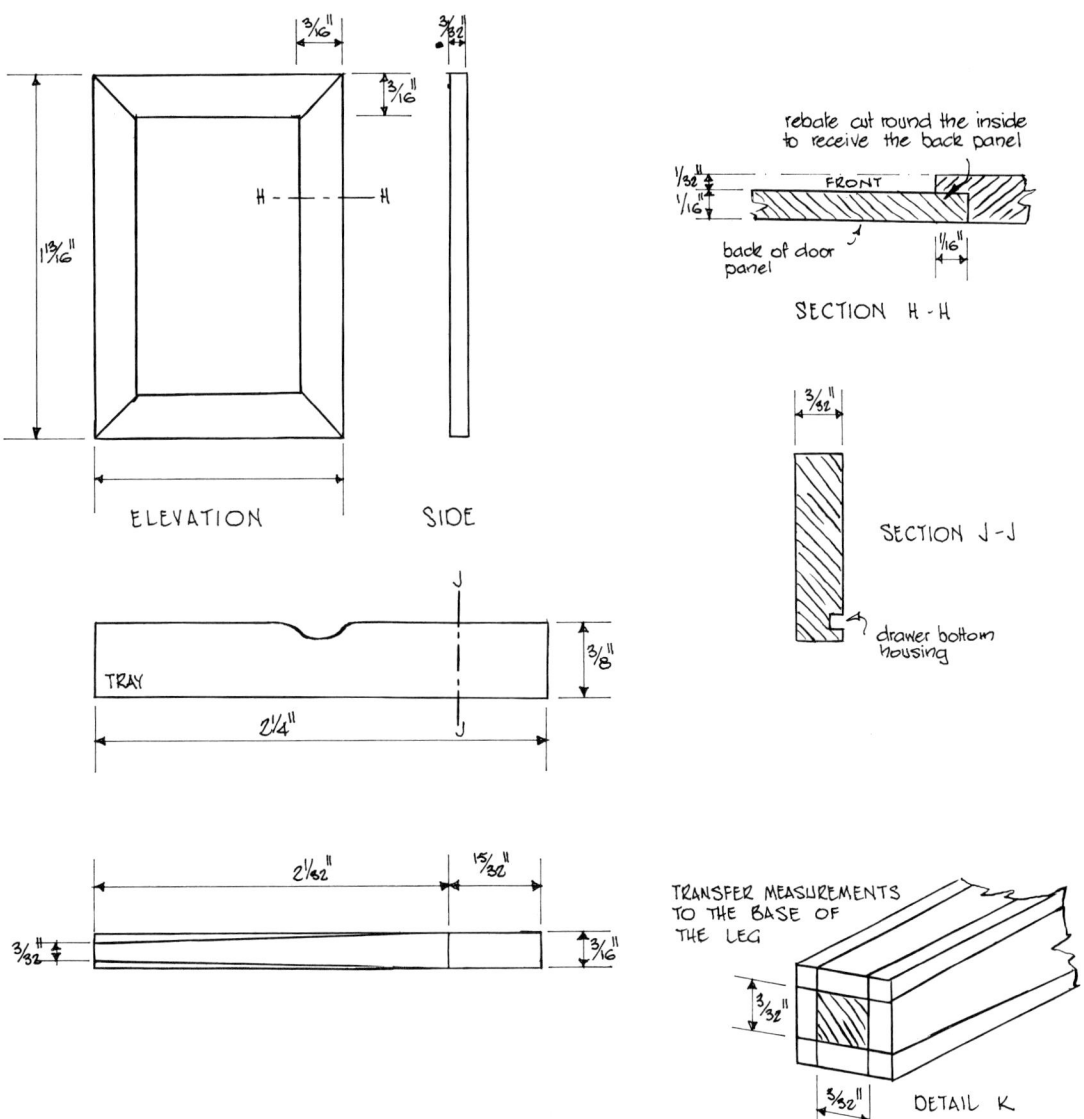

121 Small collector's cabinet – cabinet doors and tapered leg

Stage 3

The top and base can now be fitted in place and trimmed. Cut the mouldings to shape and glue them on (as shown at B, page 108). When these are dry, only glue on the base. The top must be placed aside and glued on later when the doors have been fitted.

111

Stage 4

Trim down all tray runners to the right thickness. As you glue them to the guide lines in the carcass use a $\frac{3}{8}$in. (9mm) strip template to check your spacing When they have set, the back can be fitted. Make sure you sandpaper the inside of the back before glueing it in place.

Stage 5

The four legs can now be trimmed and cleaned up. Use the small plane for tapering the legs. Go carefully here – the lines on the tapers must be kept straight. Set the adjustable plane iron to fine and when you are nearly down to the tapered marks finish cleaning to these final marks with sandpaper, taking care not to round off the edges. Complete the side, back and front rails of the leg frame to the appropriate sizes and cut all joints. Then glue the side rails to the legs, checking they are square; later when these sides have set glue the front and back rails in place. When set glue the drawer guides and runners as shown at F–F.

Stage 6

Glue the carcass to the leg frame.

Stage 7

Make up the trays and drawers using the method of assembly described on page 92). In the drawing you will notice only the front measurements are shown for the trays and drawer. I have left the rest out purposely to enable you to try your hand at marking out drawer sizes. If you have made a drawer and door by now this should be fairly easy, with the collector's cabinet carcass and leg frame made up tray and drawer guide runners all in place for you to take measurements from.

The trays and drawer, when made up, should finish at least $\frac{3}{32}$in. (2.5mm) short of the back (inside the carcass). When the bottom of the drawer is fitted leave $\frac{5}{32}$in. (4mm) overlap at the back; the bottom board can now be trimmed down and used as a drawer or tray stop, as shown on page 99.

Stage 8

The doors can now be made up using the method of assembly shown on pages 93 and 94. Do not forget to clean up the door panel before glueing in place. When the doors are completed, fit them in place with the swivel pins shown at H (page 110). (See fitting door swivel pins, page 96.)

Stage 9

The cabinet top made and then put aside can now be glued in place. The miniature should be ready for a last cleaning down with fine sandpaper before starting the polishing process.

122 Victorian davenport desk

4: Victorian davenport desk

Introduction

Making a davenport desk is just a little more challenging than the collector's cabinet, with shaped columns, gallery and turned bun feet.

Early davenport desks were made rather square in shape without columns, looking somewhat like a box stood on end with a slide or swivel leather desktop to allow legroom for writing. A set of drawers usually fitted down the right side, with small cupboard door or set of dummy drawers on the left side. Later, more elaborate pieces were developed with supporting front columns and carved wood or brass galleries.

Many of the finer quality pieces have lift-up sections on the top, revealing small drawers and pigeon holes. Almost all davenport desks are polished on all sides enabling them to present a finished surface from any position in a room. You can buy small brass knobs and escutcheon plates but do mark and cut any holes required before starting the polishing of any miniature piece you make.

Stage 1
As in the preparation of the collector's cabinet, first cut all stock (I recommend close-grained walnut) to rough sizes, remembering to allow extra for mistakes and breakages. Leave the cut stock to settle down as shown in fig. 12.

113

Stage 2
Trim all parts much closer now to the finished sizes required. Prepare the front, back, top and bottom sizes and thicknesses of the bottom carcass. Place the front and back of the carcass together, carefully marking the spacings between the drawers.

Cut out the housings for the rails and then the through half-lap joint for the top and bottom. When you have checked all joints, glue the top bottom front and back (keeping the carcass square). When this has set, glue in the three drawer rails on the right side. Later glue in the six drawer runners – these must be the same thickness as the drawer rails and all $\frac{1}{8}$in. (3mm) wide and $1\frac{3}{16}$in. (30mm) long. The left side is to be made the same measurement as the drawer width at the right side, trimmed in top and bottom and glued in place. The grain on this blank side is to be horizontal.

Stage 3
Now prepare the front back and two sides of the top carcass; the small drawer aperture on the left side must be marked and cut out at this stage. Then place

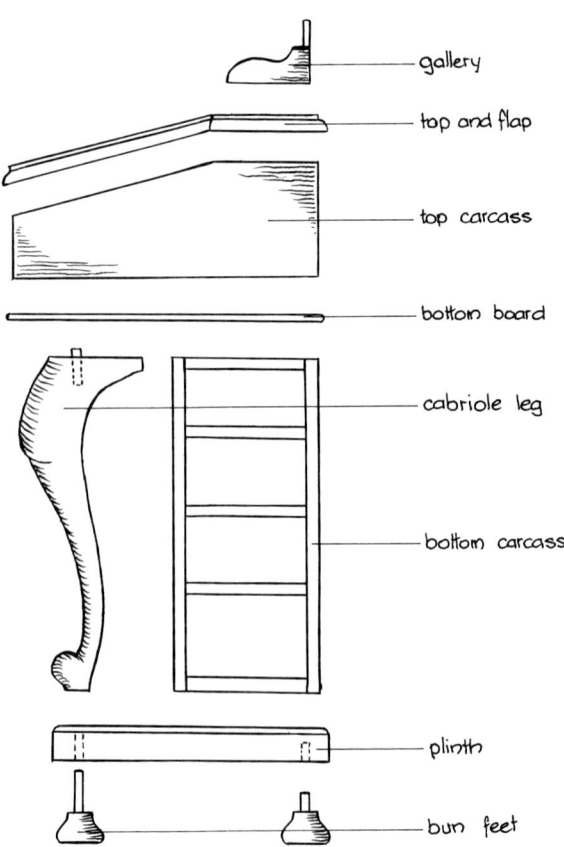

gallery

top and flap

top carcass

bottom board

cabriole leg

bottom carcass

plinth

bun feet

123 Victorian davenport desk – breakdown of main parts

114

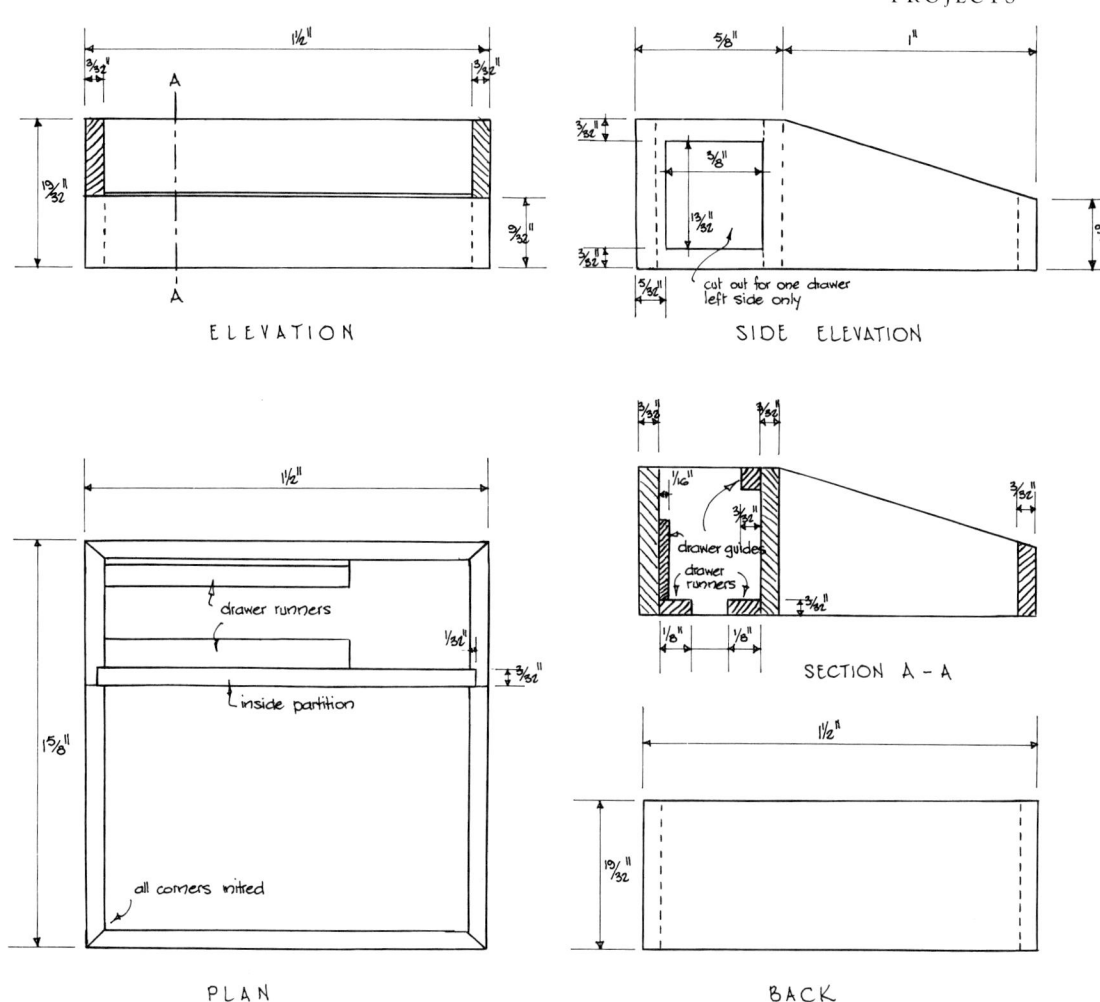

124 Victorian davenport desk – top carcass

the sides together and mark out for the mitres and partition housing joints. Then cut these joints. If you have difficulty keeping the mitre square when cutting, practise with a spare piece of stock of the same size and thickness until you are more confident to cut your set work. When you have cut them, check that all the joints are in place. Then glue the carcass. Later glue in the partition and trim your mitre edges.

Stage 4
Cut, fit and glue the bottom board. The grain on this board should run from side to side. Now make up the half-round moulding to form a lip round the bottom edge of this carcass. Mitre all corners of the moulding and glue in place. Trim the small drawer aperture and fit the drawer guides and runners (A–A).

115

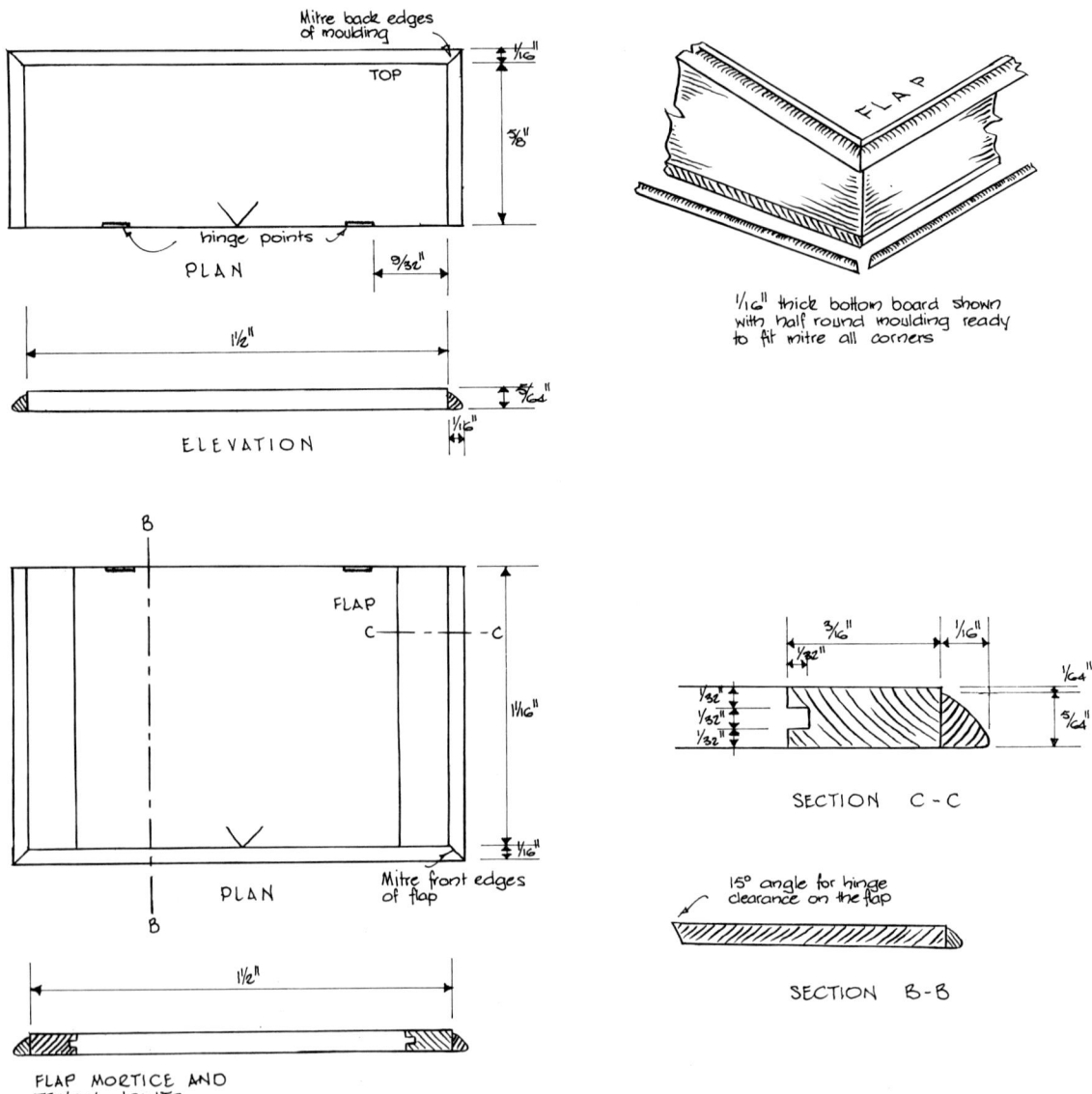

125 Victorian davenport desk – top, flap and mouldings

Stage 5
Glue top and bottom carcass together. Make quite sure they are placed on square. If they are out of line the leg alignment will be affected.

Stage 6
Make up the base frame (or plinth). Cut all four pieces to the correct sizes and place the two sides together. Mark out the shoulder mitres and front rail

116

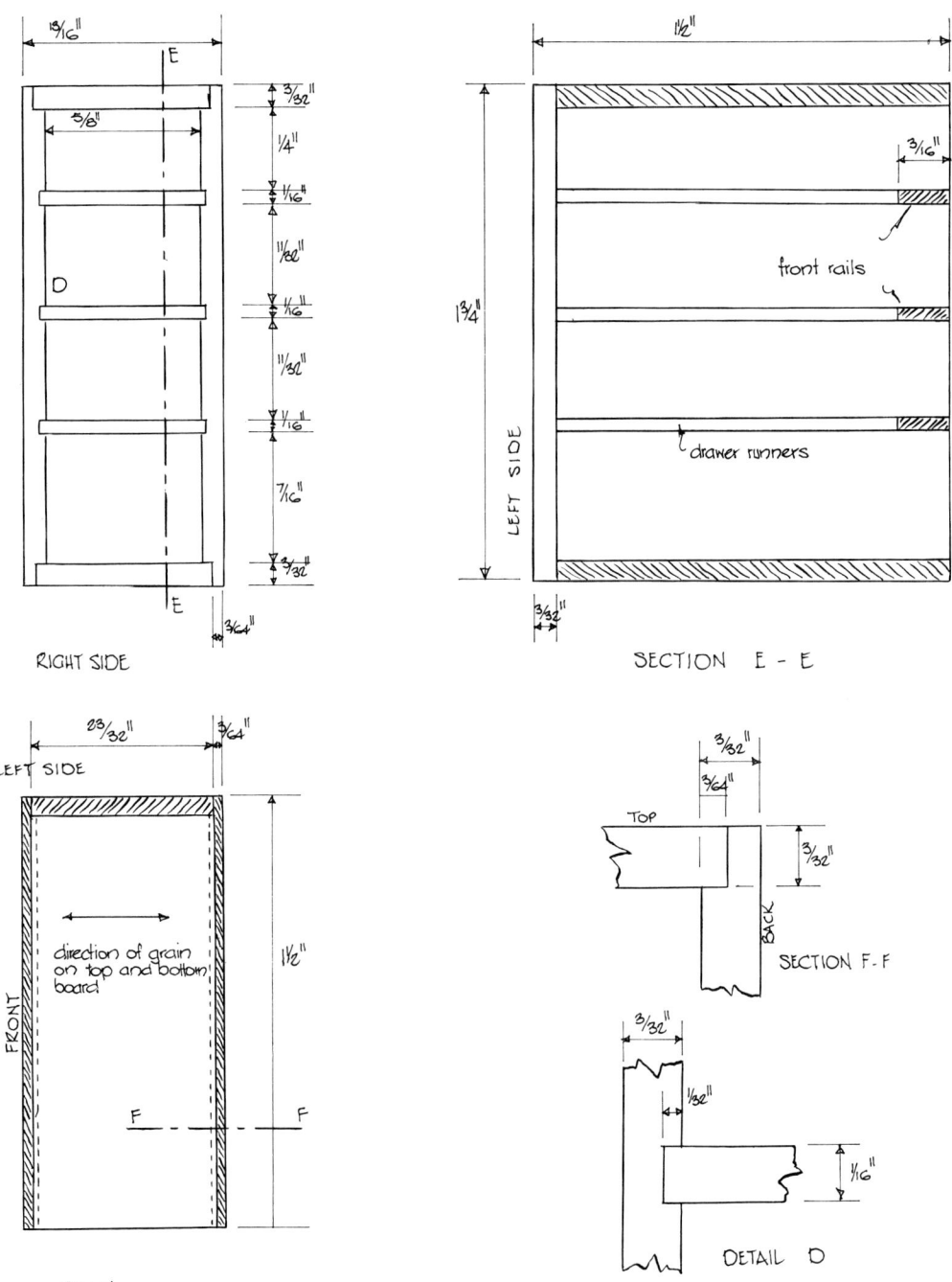

RIGHT SIDE

SECTION E - E

LEFT SIDE

PLAN

SECTION F - F

DETAIL D

126 Victorian davenport desk – bottom carcass

Cut at least an extra cabriole leg to allow for mistakes or breakages

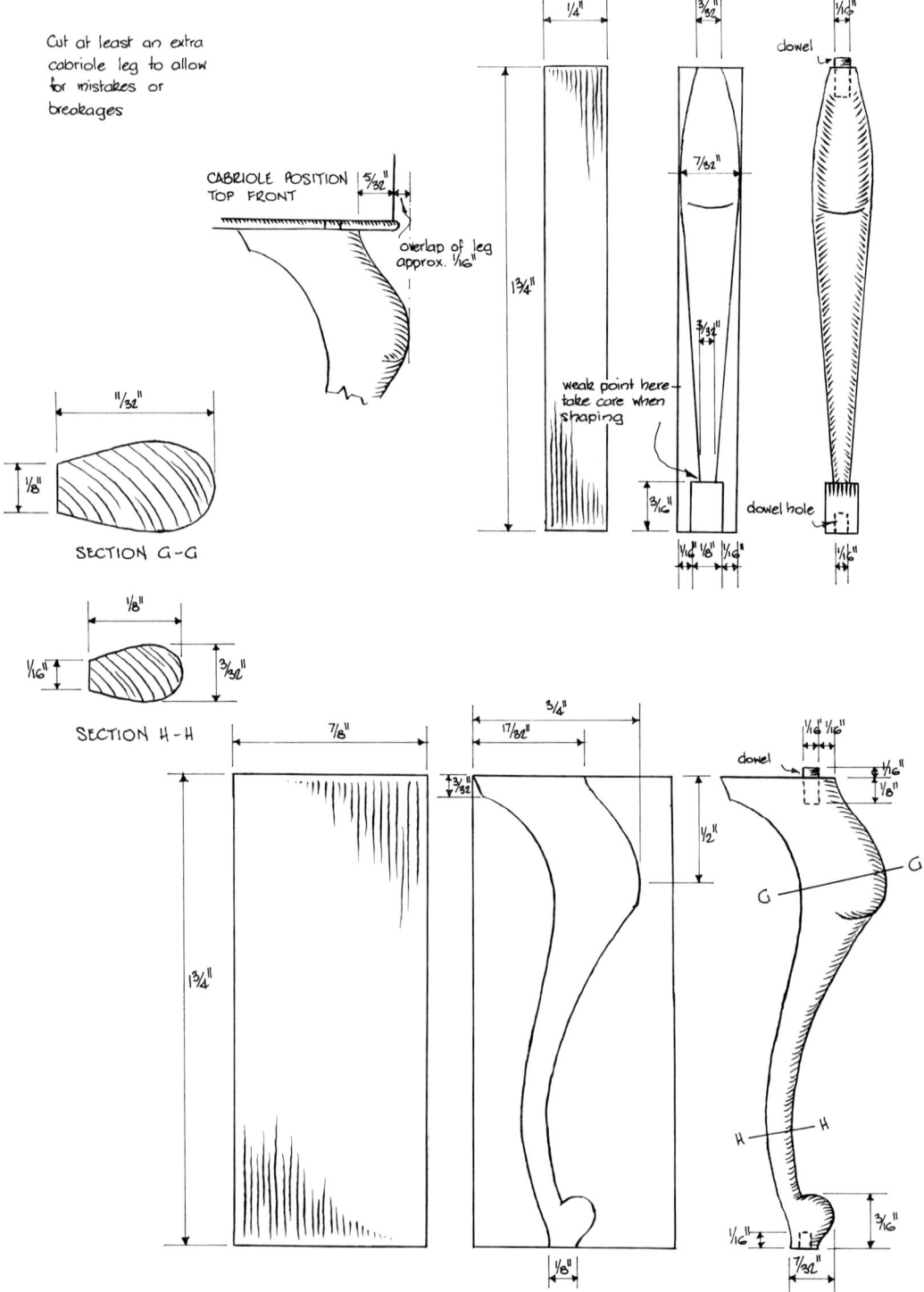

CABRIOLE POSITION TOP FRONT

overlap of leg approx. 1/16"

SECTION G-G

SECTION H-H

weak point here — take care when shaping

dowel

dowel hole

dowel

G

G

H   H

127 Victorian davenport desk – front support cabriole legs

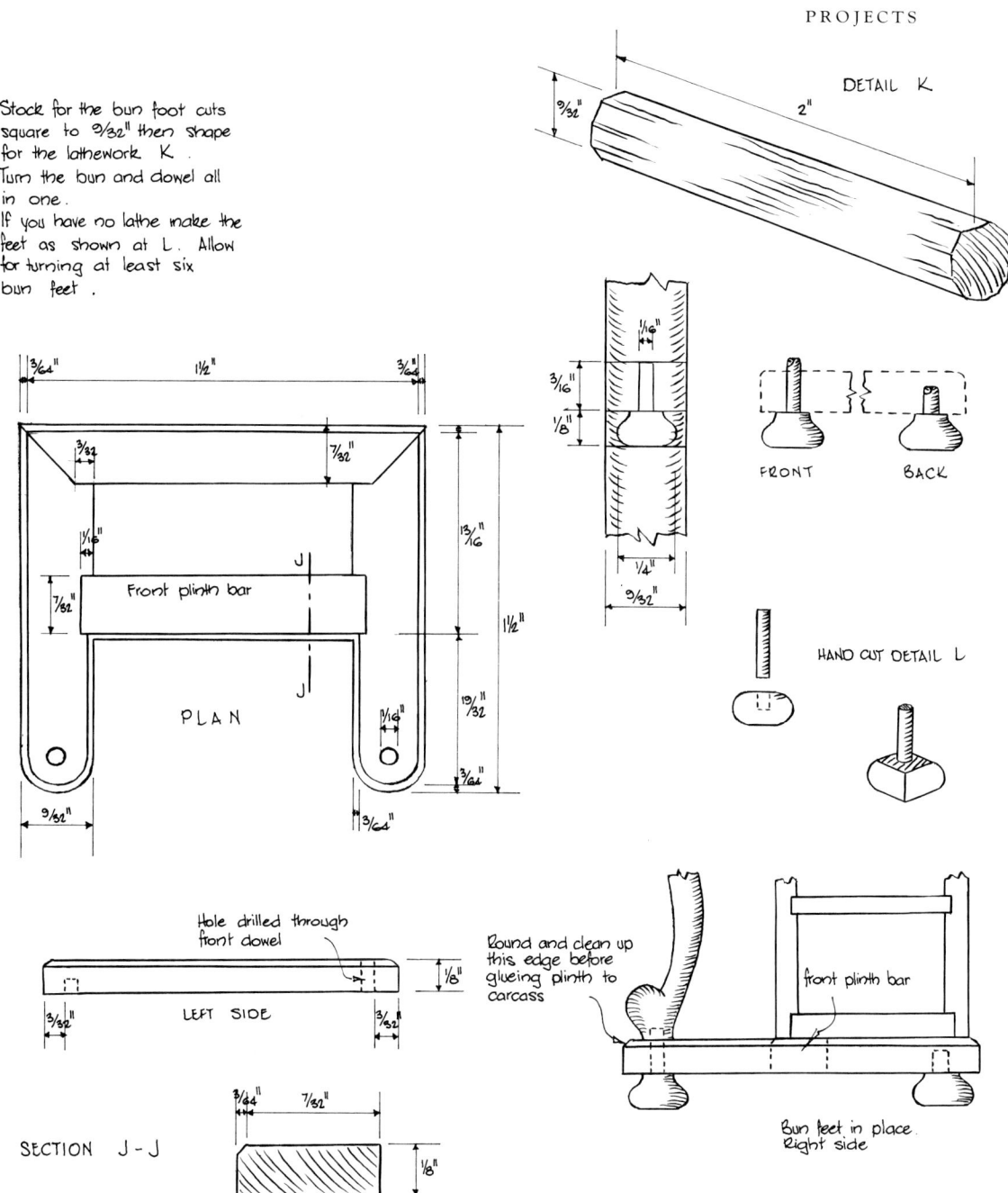

DETAIL K

Stock for the bun foot cuts
square to 9/32" then shape
for the lathework K .
Turn the bun and dowel all
in one.
If you have no lathe make the
feet as shown at L. Allow
for turning at least six
bun feet .

FRONT   BACK

HAND CUT DETAIL L

PLAN

Front plinth bar

J — J

Hole drilled through
front dowel

LEFT SIDE

SECTION   J - J

Round and clean up
this edge before
glueing plinth to
carcass

front plinth bar

Bun feet in place.
Right side

128 Victorian davenport desk – plinth and bun feet

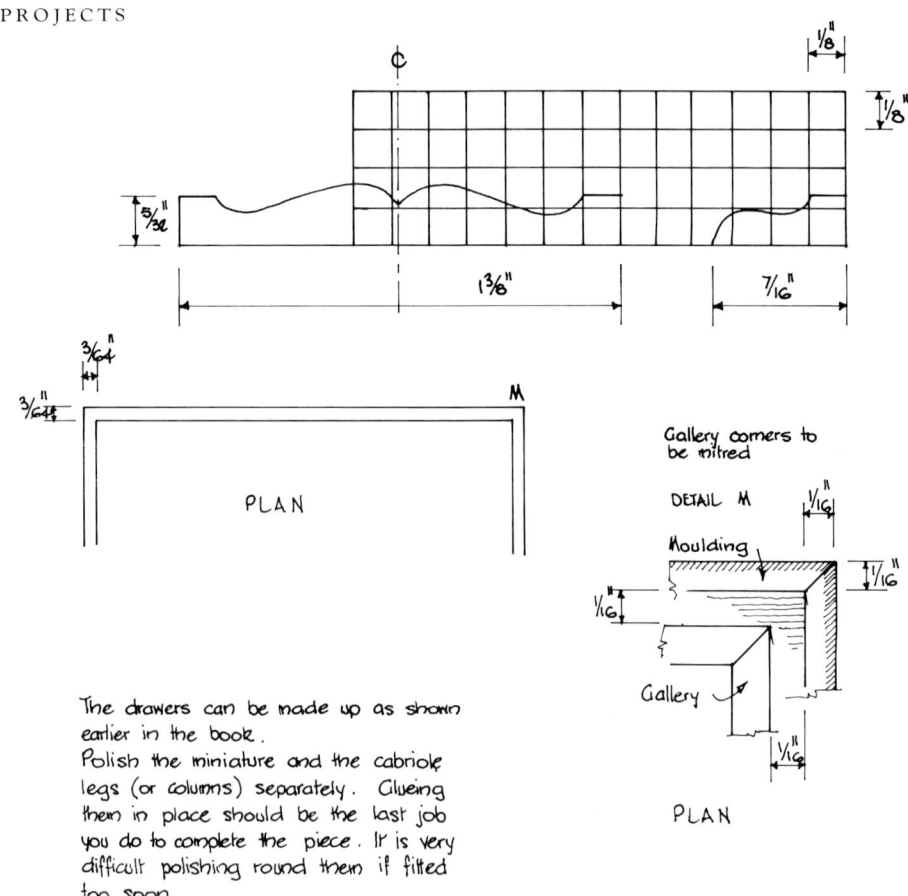

The drawers can be made up as shown earlier in the book.
Polish the miniature and the cabriole legs (or columns) separately. Glueing them in place should be the last job you do to complete the piece. It is very difficult polishing round them if fitted too soon

129 Victorian davenport desk – gallery

housing joints and cut them out. Round the two front protruding parts of the base frame that support the legs and place them together to check they are both evenly rounded.

Cut the back mitres and when you have checked all joints glue the frame together, keeping it square. When this has set round the top edge of the frame as shown. Be careful not to round off too much. The dowel holes can now be drilled in the frame.

Stage 7
Glue this base frame to the bottom carcass.

Stage 8
Making up the top and flap (fig. 125). This flap is made up with tongue and groove side straps. Full size flaps were usually made like this for strength and to stop warping. These long joints can be a little difficult so try cutting this tongue and groove joint on a practice piece before using your selected stock. If you

120

DOUBLE DOMED

BROKEN ARCH

TRIPLE DOMED ARCH

BROKEN CIRCULAR

GOOSE NECK OR SWAN NECK

LATTICE OR FRET CUT

QUEEN ANNE STYLE

TYPICAL DUTCH STYLE

130 Different style of pediments used on bureau bookcases or secretaires

cannot master it at this stage use a plain butt joint, but a long joint is much stronger.

Glue the flap together, then cut the top in place and trim them both ready for fitting. At this stage cut the 15 degree angle on the inside of the flap for later hinge clearance. Now shape the edge mouldings for the flap and top; cut all mitres and glue mouldings in place. When these have set, glue the top on.

Stage 9
Mark the gallery shape half-way only on a piece of graph paper (fig. 129). Cut out along this shape to the centre line (as shown in drawing) then fold the graph paper over on this centre line and transfer this to the other side. Cut the whole

121

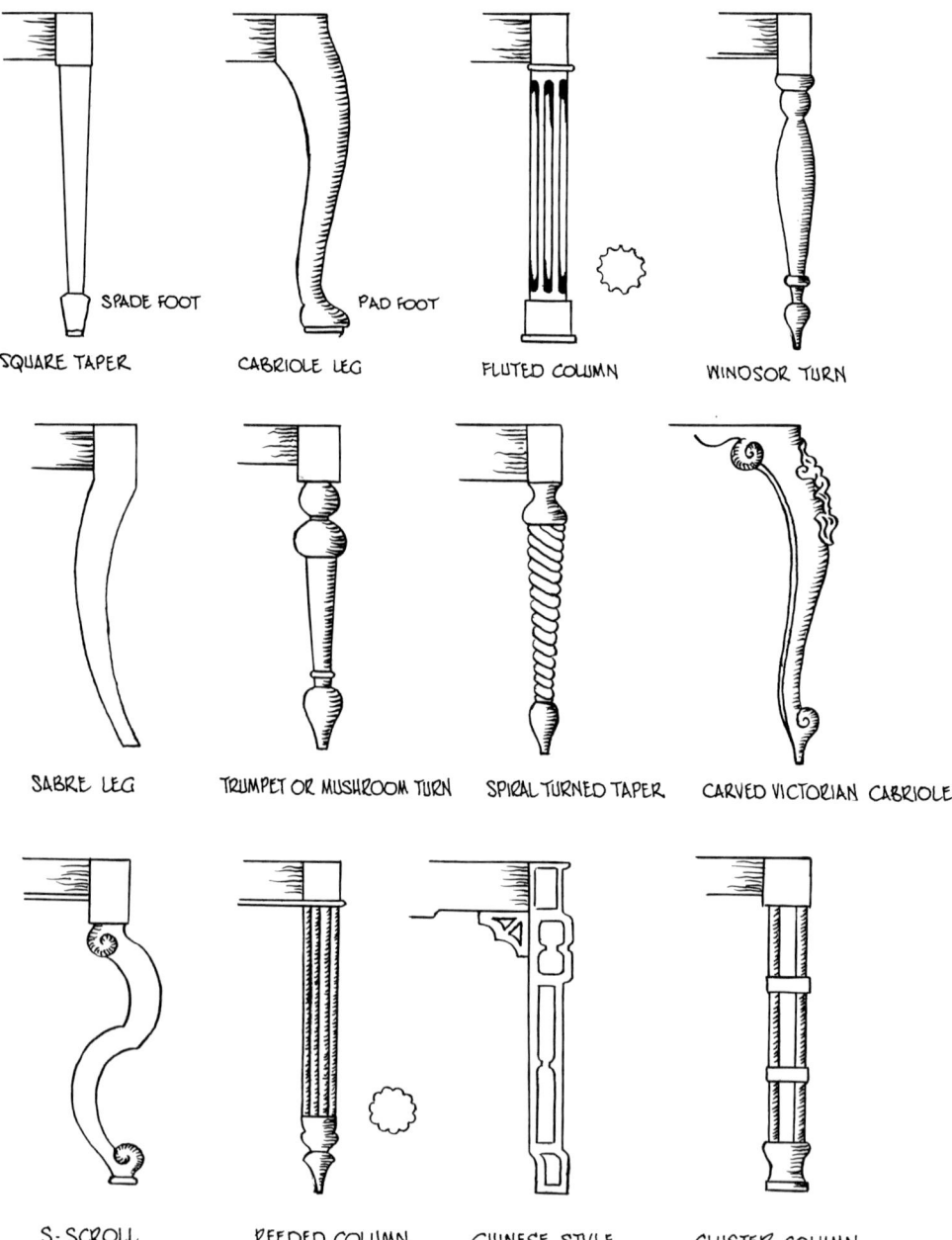

SPADE FOOT

SQUARE TAPER

PAD FOOT

CABRIOLE LEG

FLUTED COLUMN

WINDSOR TURN

SABRE LEG

TRUMPET OR MUSHROOM TURN

SPIRAL TURNED TAPER

CARVED VICTORIAN CABRIOLE

S-SCROLL

REEDED COLUMN

CHINESE STYLE

CLUSTER COLUMN

131 Various styles of period chair

template out and transfer the shape to your selected stock to make up the gallery back. Make up the two side pieces and mitre the back edges as shown. Half round the top edges then glue the mitres together. When these have set, clean the back and sides, checking the bottom edge is flush. Now glue the gallery in place.

Stage 10
Cut and shape the two cabriole legs roughly, then finish trimming and sanding down just one. When you are satisfied with the shape, start the second one, using the first one now as a template. Only work with fine files and the finer grades of sandpaper to shape down from the rough cuts. Note that these thin legs will not take a great deal of pressure. Finish sanding the legs completely then drill and fit the two top dowels in place. Drill the two holes that will locate the bun feet, dowel $\frac{1}{16}$in. deep only. The leg base is very fine here so take care when drilling these holes. Then put them aside ready for glueing later.

Stage 11
When starting on the five drawers use the method of assembly shown on page 91. Measurements for the sizes of the drawers can be taken from your two made-up carcasses, as in the collector's cabinet. Allow the drawer to finish just short of the back. When pushed in place the overlap on the back of the drawer bottom can now be trimmed and used as the drawer stop (see fig. 108).

Stage 12
Cut and fit the bun feet as shown (fig. 128). As you dowel the bun feet in place, the legs must also be fitted. Try them in place first and check for alignment – no altering can be made here after glueing. When this has been done it only remains to hinge the top. When fitting these hinges, be careful not to make the cut-outs too deep or the hinge pins will pull out when you close the lid. If you are not quite sure, try a practice fitting on two pieces of your spare stock. When you are satisfied you have the right depth cut hinges in place and pin them in.

The davenport should be now ready for the last clean down with fine sandpaper before starting the polishing process.

Appendix I: Supplementary Tools

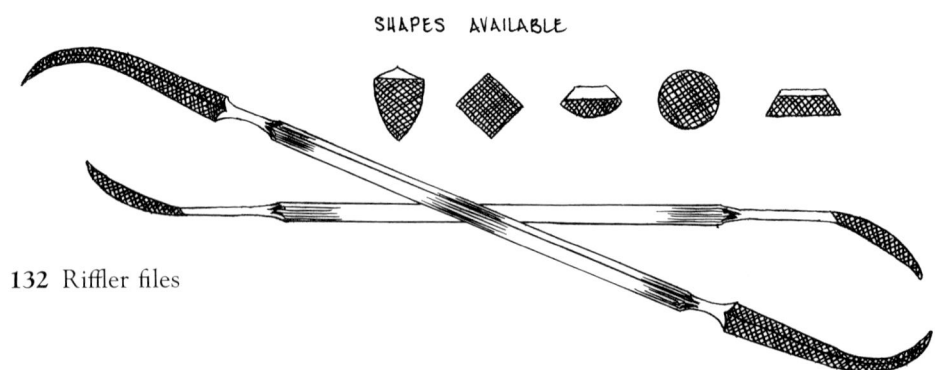

SHAPES AVAILABLE

132 Riffler files

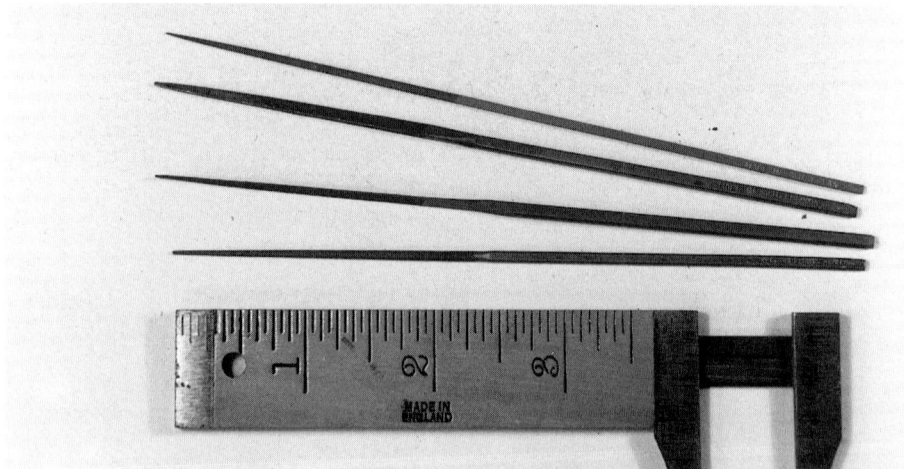

133 Fine escape
files

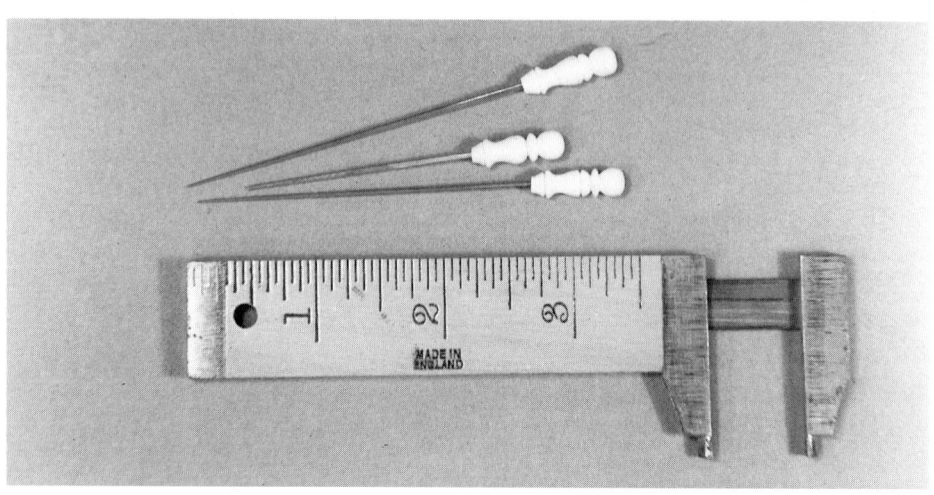

134 Miniature f

Rifflers (fig. 132)

These files are useful for cleaning inside shapes and awkward corners when it is just not possible to get a straight file in. They come in various lengths and shapes. You will only be interested in the smallest sizes.

Escapement files (fig. 133)

Slightly smaller and finer than the general size of needle files, some of the many shapes are not always available. I use one of these smaller files to trim the pins on drawers with fine dovetails.

Miniature files (fig. 134)

Ideal for cleaning out fine fretwork or very small holes that must be shaped or cleaned inside, I use these files to clean up much of my ivory fretwork. Being so tiny they can easily be mislaid so it is a good idea to fit a small bright handle on each one. Treat them gently as they are very thin and will easily break.

135 Hatakane clamps

Hatakane clamps (fig. 135)

Ideal for miniature cabinet work because of their light weight. Large G clamps and quick action joinery clamps are not suitable for this miniature work.

Panavice (fig. 136)

A small bench vice with the ability to move and lock at the angle you require. I have found this vice so useful in carving small pieces.

136 Panavice

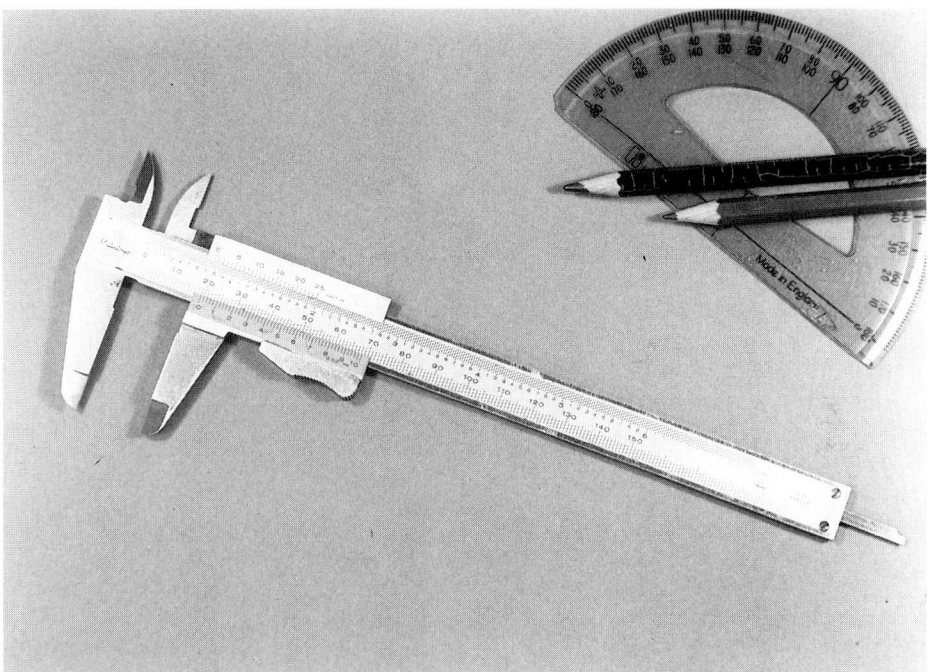

137 Easy, adjustable vernier callipers

Vernier callipers (fig. 137)

This particular type is very easy to use with this fine work. It has a thumb lock and release operation, instead of the usual screw operation, but these are expensive.

Jewellers' or watchmakers' drill stock (fig. 138)

This is so useful where the hand drill is just too cumbersome and the standard hand pin chuck is too slow.

Very fine pencil ($\frac{1}{100}$in.) (fig. 139)

This is not needed for the general $\frac{1}{12}$th scale work but useful for marking out very intricate work, such as a small set of drawers to be made and fitted inside a cabinet, working in $\frac{1}{2}$in. scale or less. Staedtler make a very fine $\frac{1}{100}$in. (0.3mm) pencil.

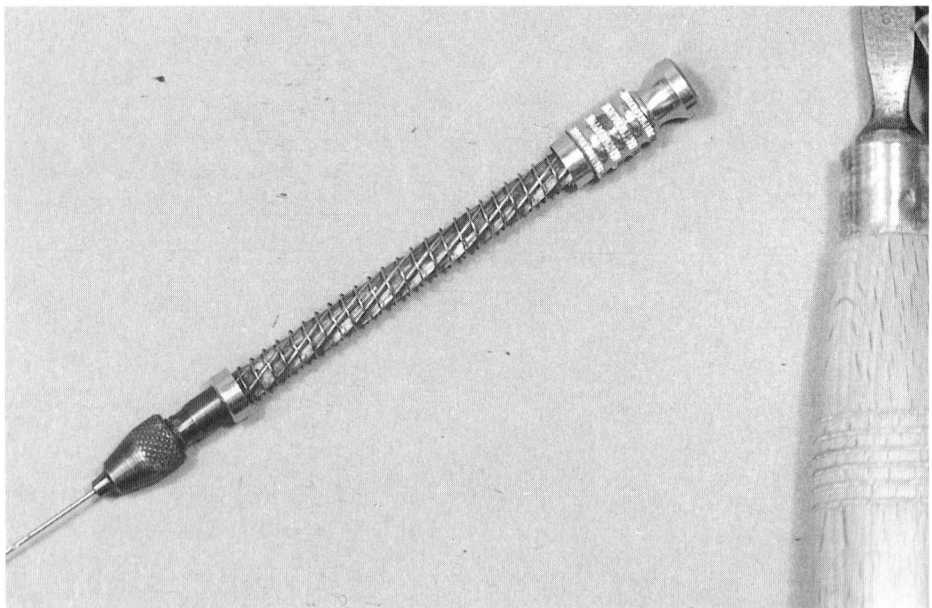

138 Spring-loaded drill stock

139 Pencils for fine marking

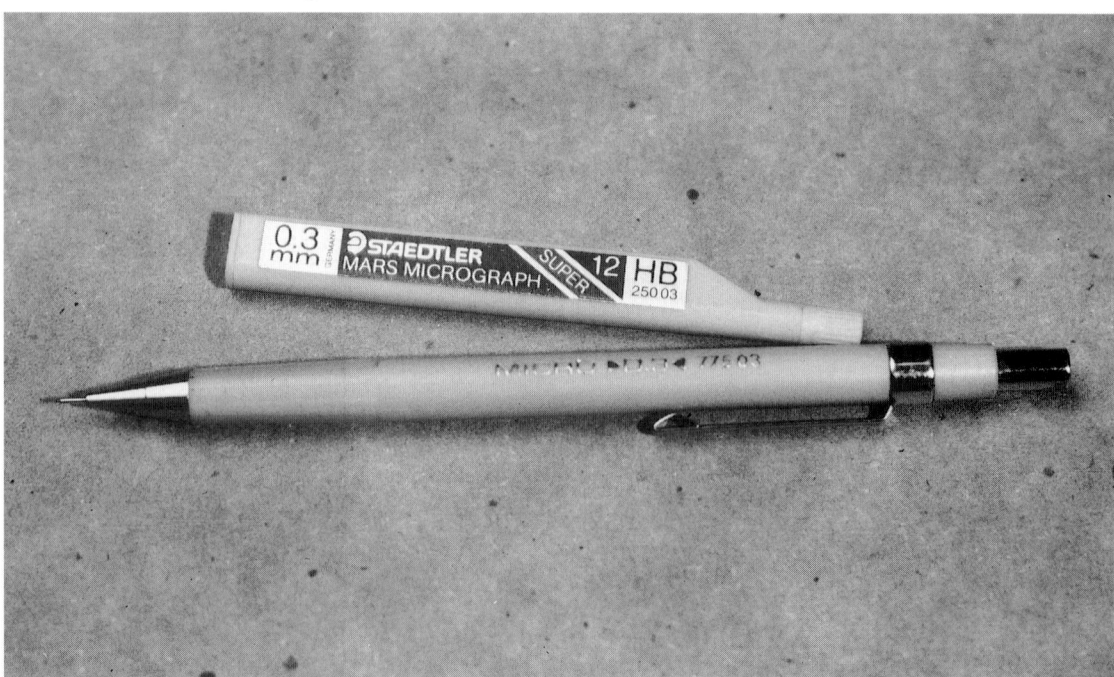

Appendix II: museums to visit in Britain

This list has been compiled by *International Dolls' House News*.

* denotes National Trust

*Nostell Priory, Wakefield. Tel: 0924 863892. Nostell baby house with original fittings, Open Apr, May, June, Sept, Oct Sat 12–5p.m. Sun 11–5p.m. July & Aug Mon–Sat 12–5p.m. Sun 11–5p.m. Closed Fri.

Windsor Castle, Windsor, Berks. Tel: 07535 68286. Queen Mary's dolls' house with all original furniture and fittings. Normally open daily but subject to occasional closure.

Uppark, South Harting, Petersfield, Hants. Tel: 073 085 317. Uppark dolls' house, Early eighteenth century with original furnishings. Open Apr–Sept Wed, Thur, Sun 2–6 p.m.

Wilton House, Nr Salisbury, Wilts. The Pembroke Palace dolls' house (now also on show a Victorian dolls' house). Open Apr–Oct, Tues–Sat 11–6p.m. Sun 1–6p.m.

Avon

American Museum in Britain, Claverton Manor, Nr Bath. Tel: 0225 60503. Miniature Rooms. Open Apr–Oct, Tues–Sun, 2–5p.m.

Blaise Castle House, Henbury. Tel: 0272 506789. Victorian dolls' house, fully furnished. Open all year, Sat–Wed,10–1p.m. & 2–5p.m.

Burrows Toy Museum, York St, Bath. Tel: 0225 21819. Social history of toys with many dolls' houses. Open daily.

Cambridge

Cambridge and County Folk Museum, 2/3 Castle St, Cambridge. Tel: 0223 355159. Several houses incl 1 beautiful German dolls' house. Open Tues–Sat 10.30–5p.m., Sun 2.30–4.30p.m.

Channel Islands

Lihou Island, off Guernsey. Large collection of dolls' houses. Open Summer subject to tidal conditions.

Cleveland

Preston Hall Museum, Yarm Rd, Stockton-on-Tees. Large toy gallery with several dolls' houses. Open Mon–Sat, 9.30–5.30p.m., Sun 2–5.30p.m.

Cumbria

Abbot Hall Museum of Lakeland Life & Industry, Kendal. Tel: 0539 22464. Period rooms, costume, etc., 2 dolls' houses. Open Mon–Fri, 10.30–5p.m., Sat & Sun 2–5p.m.

Doll & Toy Museum, Bank's Court, Market Place, Cockermouth. Tel: 0900 8529/823254. Ethnic dolls, miniature room settings and Kentish weald model house. Open Mar–Oct, 10–5p.m.

Derbyshire

*Museum of Childhood, Sudbury Hall, Sudbury, DE6 5HT. Tel: 028 378 305. New display including the Betty Cadbury 'playthings past' collection. Open Apr–Oct, Wed–Sun 1–5.30p.m. As at 25.4.87 we are told that the collection is still not yet on view due to 'electrical faults'.

Devon

*Castle Drogo, Nr Chagford. Tel: 064 73 3306. One Victorian dolls' house, furnished. Open Apr–Oct daily 11–6p.m.

Merchant's House, 33 St Andrew's St Plymouth. Large Victorian dolls' house. See

IDHN Autumn 1984. Open Mon–Sat 10–5p.m. (Closed 1–2), Sun Apr–Sept 3–5p.m.

Powderham Castle, Nr Exeter. Tel: Starcross 0626. The Castle's own model house with furniture, Courtenay family nursery items and The Baby House with the Eveline Sole memorial room (see IDHN Winter 1986). Open Tues, Wed & Thurs from end May until mid Sept, 2–5.30p.m.

*Overbecks, Sharpitor, Nr Salcombe. Tel: 054 884 2893. Room with dolls and dolls' house furniture. Open Apr–Oct, 11–1,2–6p.m. daily.

The Elizabethan House, 70 Fore St, Totnes. Tel: 0803 863821. Two dolls' houses (1 Georgian I Victorian) with furniture. Open Apr–Oct 10.30–1, 2–5.30p.m. weekdays.

Dorset

Redhouse Museum & Art Gallery, Quay Rd, Christchurch. Tel: 0202 482860. 2 Victorian dolls' houses, selection of furniture. Open Tues–Sat 10–1, 2–5p.m., Sun 2–5p.m.

Dorset County Museum, Dorchester. Tel: 0305 62735. Early nineteenth-century dolls' house with furniture and dolls. Open Mon-Sat, 10–5p.m.

Sherborne Museum, Sherborne. Tel: 0935 812252. Large Victorian dolls' house, well furnished. Open Mon–Sat 10.30–12.30 & 2.30–4.30p.m.

Co. Durham

The Bowes Museum, Barnard Castle. Tel: 0833 37139. Collection of toys and dolls' houses. Open Mon–Sat 10–5.30p.m. (Nov–Feb, 1–4p.m.) Sun 2–5p.m.

Essex

Saffron Walden Museum, Museum St. Tel: 0799 22494. Collection of toys, dolls and dolls' houses. Open Mon–Sat 11–5p.m. Sun 2.30–5p.m. Oct–Mar 11–4p.m.

Gloucestershire

*Snowshill Manor, Broadway. Tel: Broadway 852410. Room full of toys, dolls and dolls' houses. Open May to end Sept, Wed–Sun 11–1, 2–6p.m., Apr & Oct, Sat & Sun 11–1, 2–5p.m.

Greater Manchester

Monks Hall Museum, 42 Wellington Rd, Eccles, Salford. Tel: 061 789 4372. Permanent display of toys inc miniature kitchen equipment and very large Victorian dolls' house. Open Mon–Fri, 10–12.30, 1.30–5p.m. Sun 2–5p.m.

Ordsall Hall Museum, Taylorson St, Salford. Tel: 061 872 0251. Toys and late Victorian dolls' house. Open Mon–Fri 10–12.30, 1.30–5p.m., Sun 2–5p.m.

Hampshire

The Curtis Museum, High St, Alton. Tel: 0420 82802. Victorian dolls' house, 1920s house and small display of Victorian furniture. Open all year, Mon–Sat 10–5p.m.

Tudor House Museum, St Michael's Square, Southampton. Tel: 0703 24216. From August 1987 collection of dolls' houses and dolls never exhibited in public before, (see IDHN Summer 1987). Open Tues–Sat 10–12, 1–4p.m. Sun 2–5p.m.

Isle of Wight

Arreton Manor, Arreton. Tel: 0983 528134. Collection of dolls' houses inc the Pomeroy Regency house. Open Apr–Oct, Mon–Sat 10–6p.m., Sun 2–6p.m.

The Lilliput Museum of Antique Dolls & Toys, High St, Brading. Tel: 0983 407231. Collection of toys, dolls and some dolls' houses. Open daily Summer 9.30a.m.–10p.m. Winter 10–5p.m. Closed Jan–Mar inc.

Kent

Lympne Castle, Nr Hythe. Tel: 0303 67571. Pollock's Toy Museum Reserve Collection. Open June–Sept 10.30–6p.m. daily.

Municipal Museum & Art Gallery, Civic Centre, Mount Pleasant, Tunbridge Wells. Tel: 0892 26121 Ext 171. Large collection of toys and the Riggs' dolls' house and others. Open Mon–Fri 10–5.30p.m. Sat 9.30–5p.m. Closed Bank Holidays.

The Precinct Toy Collection, 38 Harnet St, Sandwich. Collection of toys and large number of dolls' houses, all furnished. Open daily Apr–Sept, Mon–Sat 10–5p.m., Sun 2–5p.m., Oct Sat & Sun 2–5p.m.

Lancashire

Leighton Hall, Yealand, Carnforth. Tel: 0524 734474.The Gay Nineties Mansion made in 1870s and furnished over 30 years. Open May–Sept, Tues, Wed, Thur, Fri & Sun, 2–5p.m.

The Judges Lodgings Museum of Childhood, Church St, Lancaster. One dolls' house and large collection of dolls. Open Apr–Oct, Mon–Fri 2–5p.m. (July/Aug Sat 2–5p.m. also)

Ribchester Dolls' House & Model Museum, Church St, Ribchester Nr Preston. Tel: 025484 520. Large collection of dolls' houses and other toys. (See IDHN Summer 1987) Open Tues–Sat all year,10–5p.m.

London

Bethnal Green Museum of Childhood, Cambridge Heath Rd, E2 9PA. Tel: 01 980 2415. Noted for its large collection of toys, games and dolls and many dolls' houses, inc. The Tate Baby House. Open Mon–Thur & Sat 10–6p.m. Sun 2.30–6p.m.

Gunnersbury Park Museum, Gunnersbury Park, W3 8LQ. Tel: 01 992 1612. Collection of toys, dolls and 2 Victorian dolls' houses and furniture. Open Mar–Oct, Mon–Fri 1–5p.m. Sat & Sun 2–6p.m., Nov–Feb, Mon–Fri 1–4p.m. Sat & Sun 2–4p.m.

London Toy and Model Museum, 23 Craven Hill, W2. Tel: 01 262 9450/7905. Collection of mechanical toys, trains, Victorian dolls' houses, furniture and dolls. Open Tues–Sat 10–5.30p.m. Sun 11–5.30p.m.

Museum of London, London Wall, EC2Y 5HN. Tel: 01 600 3699. Collection of dolls and Blackett Baby House. Open Tues–Sat 10–6p.m. Sun 2–6p.m.

Pollocks Toy Museum, 1 Scala St. London W1. Tel: 01 636 3452. Collection of dolls' toy theatres and 4 English dolls' houses, Victorian–1960. Open all year Mon–Sat 10–5p.m.

Norfolk

Museum of Social History, 27 King Street, King's Lynn. Tel: 0553 775004. 2 dolls' houses. Open all year Tues–Sat 10–5p.m.

Stranger's Hall, Charing Cross, Norwich. Tel: 0603 611277 Ext 275. Three large dolls' houses, Victorian. Open daily Mon–Sat 10–5p.m.

Northumberland

*__*Wallington House__, Cambo. Tel: 067 074 283. Very large collection of dolls' houses inc The Hammond House which has 36 rooms and dates from 1886. Open Apr–Sept daily except Tues 2–5p.m. (Oct, Wed, Sat & Sun 2–5p.m.).

Oxford

The Rotunda Museum of Antique Dolls' Houses, Grove House, Iffly Turn, Oxford. Large collection of dolls' houses from 1700–1900, all furnished, also display of antique miniature furnishings and accessories. No children under 16. Open Sun from 1st May to mid Sept from 2.15–5p.m.

Suffolk

Christchurch Mansion, Christchurch Park, Ipswich. Tel: 0473 53246. Collection of nursery items and toys and 2 Victorian dolls' houses. Open daily Mon–Sat 10–5p.m. Sun 2.30–4.30p.m.

Jacobs Farm Children's Museum, St Jacobs Hall, Laxfield. Tel:098 683 657. Large collection of antique toys, dolls, Teddy bears. Open Apr–Oct Tues, Thurs, Sun 10–5p.m.

Southwold Museum, Bartholomews Green, Southwold. Mid-Victorian dolls' house lent to the museum, fully furnished with accessories & dolls. Open daily during the Summer 2.30–4.30p.m.

Surrey

Farnham Museum, Willmer House, 38 West St, Farnham. Tel: 0252 715094. Local history inc one eighteenth-century dolls' house and one Victorian. Open all year Tues–Sat 11–5p.m.

Sussex

Arundel Toy & Military Museum, 23 High St, Arundel. Tel: 0903 883101/882908. Collection of toys, dolls and dolls' houses. Open most days Apr–Sept.

Hove Museum & Art Gallery, 19 New Church Road, Hove. Tel: 0273 779410. Collection of dolls, toys and one Edwardian dolls' house. Open Tues–Fri 10–5p.m. Sat 10–4.30p.m.

Michelham Priory, Upper Dicker, Hailsham. Tel: 0323 844224. Two dolls' houses (see IDHN spring 1986 p. 24). Open daily Apr–Oct 11–5.30p.m.

The Grange Art Gallery & Museum, The Green, Rottingdean. Tel. 0273 31004. Large display of toys including 2 dolls' houses. Open Mon, Thurs, & Sat 10–5p.m. Tues & Fri 10–1 & 2–5p.m.

Worthing Museum & Art Gallery, Chapel Rd, Worthing. Tel: 0903 39999 Ext 121. Dolls, toys & 4 dolls' houses from 1905 approx to 1930s. Open Apr–Sept Mon–Sat 10–6p.m. (Oct–March Mon–Sat 10–5p.m.).

Warwickshire

Doll Museum, Oken's House, Castle St, Warwick, Antique dolls, toys, many old dolls' houses. Open daily 10.30–5p.m.

Wiltshire

Longleat House, Warminster. Tel: 098 53 551. Two dolls' houses one 1870 made for the daughters of the 4th Marquess of Bath and one earlier. Open daily Apr–Sept 10–6p.m. Oct–Mar 10–4p.m.

Yorkshire

Ecastle Museum, Tower St, York. Tel: 0904 53611. Museum of social history with many toys and baby house early eighteenth century possible Vanbrugh design, also late Victorian house. Open daily 9.30–5p.m. approx.

Museum of Childhood, Haworth. Tel: 0535 43825. Dolls, tinplate toys, Victorian dolls' house, furniture and accessories. Open daily Apr–Oct 10.30–5.30p.m. Nov–Mar 11–4.30p.m.

*Nunnington Hall, Helmsley. Tel: Nunnington 283. The Carlisle collection of miniature rooms and an early Victorian dolls' house in the nursery. Open Apr–Oct, Tues, Wed, Thurs, Sat & Sun 2–6p.m.

Wales

Doll Museum and Model Railway, Masonic St, Llandudno. Large collection of toys, prams and Victorian dolls' house. Open Apr–Sept, Mon–Sat 10–1 & 2–5.30p.m. Sun 2–5.30p.m.

*Erdigg, nr Wrexham, Clwyd. Tel: 0978 355314. Large Victorian dolls' house, furnished. Open Apr–Sept, daily except Fri

12–5.30p.m. Oct, Wed, Sat & Sun
12–3.30p.m.

*Penrhyn Castle, Bangor, Gwynned. Tel: 0248
353 084. Doll exhibition with large Victorian
dolls' house, furnished. 4 dolls' houses
altogether, not all on display at the same time.
Open Apr–Oct, daily (except Tues) 12–5p.m.

Scotland

Museum of Childhood, 38 High St,
Edinburgh. Large collection of dolls, toys and
games, display of dolls' house furniture, the

'Stanbrig Earls' house and others. Open all
year Mon–Sat 10–5p.m.

**Thirlstane Castle & Border Country Life
Museum**, Lauder, Berwickshire. Tel: 05782
254. Pollocks Toy Museum Reserve
Collection is in the Nursery Wing. Open
May, June & Sept, Wed & Sun 2–5p.m., July
& Aug, daily except Fri 2–5p.m.

A World in Miniature, North Pier, Oban,
Argyll. Ever increasing collection of the finest
modern miniatures. Open Apr–Oct, Mon–Sat
10–5p.m., Sun 2–6p.m.

Appendix III: museums to visit in America

This state by state listing includes museums and permanent displays of miniatures, dollhouses, dolls and toys nationwide. To assure a pleasant visit, call ahead for specific hours. For information on where to buy miniatures, refer to advertisements in *Nutshell News* and other miniatures publications, or check your local telephone directory.

Arizona

Carolyn's Dreamland Doll Museum, Box 285, Sedona, AZ 86336.

Phoenix Art Museum, 1625 N. Central Ave, Phoenix, AZ 85004.

California

Angel's Attic, 516 Colorado Ave, Santa Monica, CA 90401.

Henderson Doll Museum, 40571 Lakeview Dr., Big Bear Lake, CA 92315.

Hobby City, 1238 S. Beach Blvd, Anaheim, CA 92804.

Maynard Manor at the Miniature Mart, 1807 Octavia St, San Francisco, CA 94109.

Mott's Miniatures, Knott's Berry Farm, Buena Park, CA 90620.

N.A.M.E. Museum, Arlington Ridge Rd, Arlington, VA 22210.

World of Miniature, 1375 South Bascom Ave, San Jose, CA 95128.

Colorado

Denver Art Museum, 100 West 14th Ave Pkwy, Denver CO 80204.

Miniature Doll & Toy Museum of Denver, 217–221 12th Ave, Denver, CO.

Connecticut

Barnham Museum, 820 Main St, Bridgeport, CT 06604.

Crafty Owl Shop & Doll Museum, 470 Washington Ave, North Haven, CT 06473.

Historical Museum of the Gunn Memorial Library, Wykeham Rd, Washington, CT 06793.

Memory Lane Doll & Toy Museum, Olde Mystick Village, Mystic, CT 06355.

Wilton Heritage Museum, 249 Danbury Rd, Wilton, CT 06897.

District of Columbia

Smithsonian Institution Museum of History & Technology, 12th & 14th Sts, NW, Washington, DC 20560.

Washington Dolls' House & Toy Museum, 5236 44th St, NW, Washington, DC 20015.

Florida

Henry Morrison Flagler Museum, Whitehall Way, PO Box 969, Palm Beach, FL 33480.

Museum of Old Dolls & Toys, 1 mile north of downtown Winter Haven, FL on US Hwy 17.

Museum of Yesterday's Toys, 52 St George St, St Augustine, FL.

Oldest House Museum, 322 Duval St, Key West, FL 33040.

The Lord's Little House of Miniatures, Rt 2, Box 834, Santa Rosa Beach, FL 32459.

Georgia

Enchanted Palace, Hwy 129, Blairsville, GA 30512.

Illinois

Art Institute of Chicago, Michigan Ave at Adams St, Chicago, IL 60603.

Klehm's Pink Peony Doll & Mini Museum, 2 East Algonquin Rd, Arlington Heights, IL 60005.

Museum of Science and Industry, 57th St & Lake Shore Drive, Chicago, IL 60637.

Time Was Village Museum, 1325 Burlington Rd, Mendota, IL 61342.

Indiana

Children's Museum of Indianapolis, 3000 N. Meridian, Indianapolis, IN 46208.

Iowa

Museum of Amana History, PO Box 81, Amana, IA 52203.

Big Doll House Museum, RR 2, State Center, IA 50247.

Maryland

Potpourri Miniatures, 7811 Montrose Rd, Rockville, MD 20850.

Massachusetts

The Children's Museum, 300 Congress St, Boston, MA 02210.

Children's Museum, 276 Gulf Rd, So. Dartmouth, MA 02748.

Toy Cupboard Museum, 57 E. George Hill Rd, So. Lancaster, MA 01561.

Essex Institute, 132 Essex St, Salem, MA 01970.

Fairbanks Doll Museum, Hall Rd, Sturbridge, MA 01566.

Plymouth Antiquarian Society, 27 North St, Plymouth, MA 02360.

Sturbridge Village, Sturbridge, MA 01566.

Wenham Historical Association & Museum, Inc., 132 Main St, Wenham, MA 01984.

Yesteryear's Museum, Main & River Sts, PO Box 609, Sandwich, MA 02563.

Michigan

Children's Museum, 67 East Kirby, Detroit, MI 48202.

Henry Ford Museum, 20900 Oakwood Blvd, Dearborn, MI 48121.

Minnesota

Minnesota Historical Society, 690 Cedar St, St Paul, MN 55101.

Missouri

Historic Hermann Museum, Inc., Box 88, Hermann, MO 65041.

Toy and Miniature Museum of Kansas City, 5235 Oak St, Kansas City, MO 64112.

Missouri Historical Society, Lindell & DeBalivier, St Louis, MO 63112.

Nebraska

Louis B. May Museum, 1643 N. Nye Ave, Fremont, NE 68025.

Old Brown House Doll Museum, 1421 Ave F, Gothenburg, NE 69138.

New Hampshire

The Bunthaus, Main St, Swanzey Center, NH.

Harrison Gray Otis House, Langdon Mansion, Portsmouth, NH 03801.

New Jersey

Monmouth County Historical Association, 70 Court St, Freehold, NJ 07728.

New Mexico

Museum of New Mexico, International Folk Art Museum, 706 Camino Lejo, Santa Fe, NM 87504–2087.

The Playhouse, Museum of Old Dolls & Toys, 1201 N. Second St, Las Cruces, NM 88005.

Gila Faerieland Museum, Gila Hot Springs Vacation Center, State Hwy No 15, NM

New York

Aunt Len's Doll & Toy House, 6 Hamilton Terrace, New York, NY 10031.

Brooklyn Children's Museum, 145 Brooklyn Ave, Brooklyn, NY 11213.

Hyde Park Doll Museum, Rt 9 G, Hyde Park, NY 12538.

Museum of the City of New York, 5th Ave, & 103rd St, New York, NY 10029.

The Museum at Stony Brook, 1208 Rt 25a, Stony Brook, NY 11790.

New York Historical Society, 170 Central Park W., New York, NY 10024.

Shaker Museum, Shaker Museum Rd, (1 mile south of Old Chatham), Old Chatham, NY 12136.

Margaret Woodbury Strong Museum, 700 Allen Creek Rd, Rochester, NY 14618

Yorktown Heights Museum, 1974 Commerce, Yorktown Heights, NY 10598.

Cooper-Hewitt Museum, 2 East 91st St, New York, NY.

North Carolina

Angela Peterson Doll & Miniature Museum, Wesleyan Arms Adm. Bdlg, 1911 N. Centennial St, High Point, NC 27260.

Ohio

Allen County Historical Society, 620 W. Market St, Lima, OH 45801.

Rutherford B. Hayes State Memorial, 1337 Hayes Ave, Fremont, OH 43420.

Western Reserve Historical Society, 10825 East Blvd, Cleveland, OH 44106.

Oklahoma

Eliza Cruce Doll Museum, Grand St at East Northwest, Ardmore, OK 63401.

Pennsylvania

Strawberry Mansion's Attic Museum, Fairmont Park, Philadelphia, PA.

Chester County Historical Society, 225 No. High St, West Chester, PA 19380.

Dollhouse & Rag Doll Museum, Cresco, PA 18326.

Happiest Angel Doll Shoppe & Museum, Newfoundland, PA 18445.

Memory Town, HCR 1, Box 10, Mt Pocono, PA 18344.

Mary Merrit Doll Museum, RD 2, Douglasville, PA 19518.

Perelman Antique Toy Museum, 270 S. Second St, Philadelphia, PA 19106.

Rhode Island

Newport Historical Society, 82 Touro St, Newport, RI 02840.

South Dakota

Stuart Castle, Rt 16, Box 54, Rockerville, SD 57701.

Tennessee

Dulin Gallery of Art, 3100 Kingston Pike, Knoxville, TN 37919.

Vermont

Shelburne Museum, U.S. Rt 7, Shelburne, VT 05482.

Abby Aldrich Rockefeller Folk Art Center, 307 S. England St, Williamsburg, VA.

Arlington Historical Society Museum, Arlington Ridge Rd, Arlington, VA 22210.

Lee-Fendall House, 429 N. Washington St, Alexandria, VA.

Woodlawn Plantation, 9000 Richmond Hwy, Mt Vernon, VA.

Washington

Museum of History & Industry, 2700 24th Ave, East, Seattle, WA 98112.

Wisconsin

Milwaukee County Historical Society, 910 N. Third St, Milwaukee, WI 53203.

Milwaukee Public Museum, 800 W. Wells St, Milwaukee, WI 53202.

Mrs Gray's Doll Museum, Harbor Village, Algoma, WI 54201.

Appendix IV: shops selling miniature furniture

This list has been compiled by *International Dolls' House News*.
* denotes private showroom.

Kristin Baybars, 7 Mansfield Rd, London NW3. Tel: 01 267 0934. Tues–Sat 11–5.30p.m. *Dolls' house items in quantity.*

*Carol Black Miniatures, 'Sunhill'. Great Strickland, Penrith, Cumbria, CA10 3DF. Tel. 093 12 330. By appointment. *A large range of miniatures, some exclusive.*

Blackwells, 733 London Rd, Westcliffe-on-Sea, Essex, SS0 9ST. Tel: 0702 72248. Mon, Tues, Thur, Fri, & Sat 9–1, 2–5.30p.m. (Closed Wed.) *Furniture kits, tools, mouldings and lighting.*

Cambridge Dolls Hospital, 1 Jesus Terrace, Cambridge. Tel: 0223 350452. Mon–Sat 9.30–4.30p.m. (half day Thurs.) *Doll repairs and many miniature accessories.*

The China Doll, 31 Walcot St, Bath, Avon. Tel: Bath 65849. Mon–Sat 10–5p.m. *Range of miniatures and larger dolls.*

Claire's Crafts, 21 Pallister Rd, Clacton-on-Sea, Essex. Tel: 0255 423767. 9–5.30p.m. 7 days in summer, closed Wed half day & Sun in winter. *Many miniature accessories.*

Pamela Crawford, Showroom at rear of No. 93 Phoenix Cottage, up Nursery Lane, Hursley, Winchester, Hants. Tel: Hursley 75551. Tues–Sat 10–3p.m. *Selection of furniture and accessories.*

Crownland Miniatures, White House, Crownland Rd, Walsham le Willows, Bury St Edmunds, Suffolk, IP31 3BU. Tel: 035 98 692. Tues, Thur, Fri, Sat & Sun 10–5p.m. *Wide range of houses, furniture and accessories.*

Dolls and Miniatures, 54 Southside St, Barbican, Plymouth, Devon. Tel: 0752 663676. Mon–Sat 10.30–5.30p.m. *Very large range of furniture and accessories and larger dolls.*

The Dolls' House, 29 The Market, Covent Garden, London WC2E 8RE. Tel: 01 379 7243. Mon–Sat 10–8p.m. *Vast selection of houses, furniture and all accessories.*

The Dolls' House at Bromley, 49 Homesdale Rd, Bromley, Kent. Tel: 01 290 0616. Mon–Sat 10–5.30p.m. (Closed Wed.) *Large selection of houses, furniture, accessories and larger dolls.*

The Doll House Fowey, 5 The Esplanade, Fowey, Cornwall, PL23 1HY. Tel: Fowey 2606. Mon–Sat 10–5.30p.m. *Good selection of houses, furniture and accessories, larger dolls & Teddy Bears.*

*Dolls' House Corner, 'Salmaur', Gipsy Hill, Weymouth. Tel: 0305 786141. Showroom by appointment. *Specialist in miniature millinery, large range of other items and D.I.Y.*

The Dolls' House Estate Agents, 18 Crown Rd, St Margaret's, Twickenham, Middx TW1 3EE. Tel: 01 891 3035. Thur, Fri & Sat 10–5.30p.m. *New shop with selection of houses, shops, furniture and accessories.*

*Dolphin Miniatures, Myrtle Cottage, Greendown, Membury, Axminster, Devon. Tel: 040 488 459. Private showroom, appointment only. *Own specialist items of houses, furniture and accessories.*

Dorking Dolls' House Gallery, 23 West St, Dorking, Surrey, RH4 1BY. Tel: 0306 885785. Tues, Thur, Fri & Sat 10–5p.m.
Large range of houses, shops, furniture and all accessories.

Elm Hill Craft Shop, 12 Elm Hill, Norwich, Norfolk. Tel: 0603 621076. Mon–Sat 9.30–5p.m.
Houses, kits and furniture.

Fiddly Bits, 24 King St, Knutsford, Cheshire WA16 6DW. Tel: 0565 51119. Tues, Thur, Fri & Sat 10–5p.m.
Good selection of houses, furniture and all accessories.

Jennifer's of Walsall, (part of Graingers), 51 George St, Walsall, WS1 1RS. Tel: 0922 23382. Mon–Sat 9.30–5 p.m. (Half day closing Thur.)
Houses, shops, kits, plans and many D.I.Y. items.

Lilliput Miniatures, 8 School Close, St Columb Minor, Newquay, Cornwall TR7 3EN. Tel: 0637 874036. Open throughout the summer, winter, by appointment only.
Specialist in miniature photographs, leather trunks, handbags and other small items.

Lovin' Givin', 86 Lower Fold, Marple Bridge, Stockport, Cheshire, SK6 5DU. Tel: 061 427 7460. Mon–Sat 9.30–5.30p.m. (Closed Weds.)
Houses, furniture, large range of accessories, plans – also toys and other gift items.

*Mini Mansions, 10 The Hawthorns, Great Ayton, Middlesborough, Cleveland, TS9 4BA. Tel: 0642 723060. By appointment.
Large range of miniatures and many items made by owners.

Minster Miniatures, 68 Goodramgate, York, YO1 2LF. Tel: 0904 51622. Mon–Sat 10–5.30p.m.
Range of furniture, wallpapers, lighting and accessories.

The Miniature Scene in York, 37 Fossgate, York, YO1 2TF. Tel: 0904 38265. Mon–Sat 9.30–4.30p.m.
Good range of furniture and all accessories and D.I.Y.

Miniature World, 37 Princess Victoria St, Clifton, Bristol BS8 4BX. Tel: 0272 732499. Tues–Sat 9.30–5.30p.m.
Wide range of houses, furniture and accessories, some exclusive.

The Model Shop, 6 Westminster House, Kew Rd, Richmond, Surrey. Tel: 01 940 7489. Mon–Sat 9.30–6p.m. (Late night Fri 8p.m.)
Large amount of D.I.Y. items and kits.

The Mulberry Bush, 25 Trafalgar St, Brighton, Sussex BN1 4EQ. Tel: 0273 600471 or 493781. Tues, Thurs, Fri & Sat 10–5p.m.
Houses, furniture and large selection of accessories, D.I.Y. Specialist in dolls' house books.

Parkinsons of Broadway, 32A High St, Broadway, Worcs. Tel: 0386 853527. 7 days a week 9–5.30p.m.
Houses, shops, kits, furniture and large range of accessories.

Patricia's Dollshouses, 120 Lower Galleries, Eastgate International Shopping Centre, Basildon, Essex. Tel: 0268 293169. Mon–Sat 10–6p.m.
Houses, furniture, accessories, D.I.Y.

The Pied Piper, 54 Cross Street, Islington, London, N1 2BA. Tel: 01 226 4766. Mon–Sat 10–5p.m.
Houses, furniture and all accessories.

Leo Pilley, Chy-an-Chy Studio, The Harbour, St. Ives, Cornwall. Tel: 0736 797659. Mon–Sat 10–5p.m. (Half day Thurs.)
Own range of miniature glass, from a decanter to a chandelier.

*Polly Flinders, P.O. Box 82, Dorking, Surrey RH5 5YS. Tel: 0306 712257. Private showroom, open Wed 10–2p.m.
Houses, furniture, accessories, some exclusive.

Royal Mile Miniatures, 154 Canongate, Royal Mile, Edinburgh EH8 8DD. Tel: 031 557 2293. Mon–Sat 10.45–5p.m.
Large selection of houses, furniture, accessories.

The Secret Garden, 109 Camden Rd, Tunbridge Wells, Kent. Tel: 0892 41332. Mon, Tues, Thur, Fri & Sat 10.30–1, 2–5p.m.
Houses, furniture, accessories and miniature garden items.

Singing Tree, 69 New King's Rd, London SW6. Tel: 01 736 4527. Mon–Sat 10–5.30p.m.
Old and new houses, furniture and accessories, some exclusive, and D.I.Y.

Stamford Poste, 1 Stamford Walk, St Mary's St, Stamford, Lincs. Tel: 0780 65944. Mon–Sat 10–5p.m. Sundays July–Oct. 2–5p.m.
Ever increasing range of miniatures.

Tiger, Tiger, 219 Kings Rd, Chelsea, London SW3 5EJ. Tel: 01 352 8080. Mon–Sat 10–6p.m.
Houses, furniture and accessories.

Tiny T'ings, 884 Christchurch Rd, Boscombe, Bournemouth. Tel: 0202 429891. Mon–Sat 10–5p.m.
Houses, furniture and accessories.

Tollgate Miniatures, Bosham Walk, Old Bosham, West Sussex. Tel: 0243 572205. Open 7 days a week 10–5p.m.
Own range of houses, furniture and accessories, plus other miniature items.

Tom Thumb Miniatures, Antique Centre, 22 Haydon Place, Guildford, Surrey. Tel: 0483 67817. Tues, Thurs, Fri & Sat 10–5p.m.
Houses, furniture and accessories, antique toys.

Torbay House Miniatures, 11 The Quay, Exeter, Devon. Tel: (Evenings) 0803 33393. Summer Tues–Sun 10.30–5p.m. Winter Fri, Sat & Sun only.
Houses, furniture, accessories and own range of miniatures.

Trad Toys and Miniatures, Hales Yard, Market Place, Diss, Norfolk. Tel: 0842 61684. Mon, Tues 9.30–1p.m. Wed, Thur, Fri & Sat 9.30–5p.m. (Closed 1–2.)
Houses, shops, furniture and accessories.

*Peter Valentine, 350 London Rd, South Stifford, Grays, Essex RM16 1AB. Tel: 0375 76677. Showroom by appointment
Range of furniture and accessories, houses (some Triangs).

Wansbeck Hobbies, Holt, Norfolk NR25 6BA. Tel: Holt 713933. Mon–Sat 9–5.30p.m. (Half day Thurs.)
Houses and shops, kits, furniture and accessories, D.I.Y. and plans.

*Wentway Miniatures, Wentways, West End, Marden, Kent TN12 9JA. Tel: 0622 831765. Private showroom by appointment.
Own range of furniture kits, food and stained glass. Other accessories.

Wheelwright Miniatures, Westgate Galleria, The Island, Westgate Street, Gloucester GL1 2RU. Tel: 0452 411319. Tues–Sat, 10–5p.m.
Houses, furniture, kits and accessories.

Willowherb, 52 Station Rd, Stoke D'Abernon, Cobham, Surrey KT11 3BN. Tel: 0932 66966. Mon–Fri, 10–5.30p.m. Sat 10–4p.m. (Half day Wed & some Sats.)
Houses, furniture, accessories, D.I.Y. and many small gift items.

Woodlanders, 4 Queen St, Southwell, Notts. Tel: 0636 815172. Mon–Sat 9.15–5p.m.
Good range of furniture, accessories always on the increase.

Appendix V: tool suppliers

R. Areonson Ltd, 45 Redchurch St, London E2. Tel: 01 739 3107.
Veneers.

Bucken and Ryans, Tottenham Court Rd, London W1.
Tools.

J. Crispin and Sons, Timber Merchants, 92–96 Curtain Rd, Shoreditch, London EC2A 3AA.
Machines (Unimat 3).

Emco Maier Ltd, 10 Woodsots Meadow,
Croxley Centre, Watford, Herts WD1 8YZ.
Tel: 0923 50051.
Machines (Unimat 3).

Eme Ltd, Bec House, Victoria Rd, London
NW10 GNY. Tel: 01 965 4050.
Unimat 3.

Euro Precision Tools Ltd, 259–263 London
Rd, North End, Portsmouth, Hants.
Tel: 667331.
Machines (Unimat 3).

J. Hodgson, 25 Sands Lane, Bridlington,
North Humberside YO15 2JG. Tel: 0262
674066.
Brass handles.

W.S. Jenkins & Co. Ltd, Industrial Wood
Finishes, Jeco Works, Tariff Rd, Tottenham,
London N17 0EN.
Polishing materials.

Microflame Ltd, Vinces Rd, Diss, Norfolk
IP22 3HQ. Tel: 0377 989 4813.
Dremel tools.

Milliput Co., Unit 5, The Marian, Dolgellau,
Mid Wales II4O 1UU. Tel: 0341 422562.
Modelling materials.

Nathan Shestopal Ltd, Unit 2, Sapcote
Trading Centre, 374 High Rd, Willesden,
London NW10 2DH. Tel: 01 451 6188.
Fine tools.

New England Hobby Supply, 70 Hilliard St,
Manchester CT 06040, U.S.A.
$\frac{1}{12}$ *scale rules and small tools.*

Frank Pike, 15 Hatton Wall, Hatton Garden,
London EC1N HJE. Tel: 01 405 2688.
Fine tools.

J. Simbol and Sons, The Broadway,
Queens Rd, Watford, Herts. WD1 2LD.
Tel: 0923 26052.
Tools and machines.

Henry Taylor Tools Ltd, Lowther Rd,
Sheffield S6 2DR.
Fine Tools.

Timberline, Unit 7 Munday Works, 58–66
Morley Rd, Tonbridge, Kent TN9 1RP.
Tel: 0732 355625.
Hardwoods.

Garrett Wade Co., 161 Avenue of the
Americas, New York, N.Y. 10013, U.S.A.
Tools.

H.S. Walsh & Sons, 243 Beckenham Road,
Beckenham, Kent BB3 4TS.
Fine tools.

Appendix VI: magazines

Nutshell News, 1027 North Seven Street,
Milwaukee WI, United States of America.
Tel: 53233 9972.
(Published monthly)

Miniature Showcase, address as **Nutshell
News**.
(Published quarterly)

International Dolls House News, PO Box 79,
Southampton, Hants, SO9 7E2.
(Published quarterly)

The Home Miniaturist, 2 Croft Courtyard,
The Croft, Haddenham, Bucks, HP17 8AS.
(Bi-monthly)

Bibliography

Lillian Baker   *Creative and Collectable Miniatures*

Susan Braun   *Miniature Vignettes*

Margaret Duda   *Miniature Shops*

John Gray   *Think Small*

Vivien Greene   *English Dolls' Houses*

John Weymouth Horrell   *Measured Drawings of Old English Oak Furniture*

Dorie Krusz   *Building Miniature Houses and Furniture*

Gerald Jensen   *Buildings in Miniature*

McCall's Big Book of Dollshouses and Miniatures

Marian O'Brien   *Make Your Own Dollhouse and Dollhouse Miniatures*
                 Make and Furnish Your Own Miniature Rooms
                 Collector's Guide to Dollhouses and Dollhouse Miniatures

Ann Pipe   *Reproducing Furniture in Miniature*
            Mastercrafting Miniature Furniture and Rooms

Harry Rinker   *Warman's Antiques and their Prices*

Cynthia and Jerome Rubin   *Shaker Miniature Furniture*

Helen Ruthberg   *The Book of Miniatures*

Herbert and Peter Schiffer   *Miniature Antique Furniture*

Suzanne Slesin and Stafford Cliff   *English Style*

Leonie Von Wilkens   *Mansions in Miniature – Four Centuries of Dolls' Houses*

Marie Woodruff   *Early American Miniatures*

142

Index

Adjustable sliding bevel 42, 43
Apprentice pieces 9, 10, 16, 22, 26

Bandings
   double 105
   single 102
Bandsaw 54
Block plane 30, 31
Bulldog clips 104, 105
Burrs for shaping 62, 65

Cabriole legs 122
Callipers (Vernier) 127
Carcass (simple) 87–89
Chair legs (period) 122
Chisels 33–35
Clamps 45, 46, 125
Cleaning process 81
Collector's cabinet 106–112

Davenport desk 113–123
Door
   simple 90–94
   with swivel pins 95, 96
Dovetails 75, 76, 80, 95, 99
   fitting of 98, 99
   template 96
   through 75
Dulling 86

Felt boards 69
Files 31, 32, 124
   maintenance of 33
Fretwork 35, 40, 41

Glue 105
Gravers 34, 35
Grinder and polisher 64

Knives 36, 37

Lathe 55
   internal turning 57, 58
   jeweller's 59
Lighting 13, 14

Machinery, care of 14, 15
Mahogany 21, 26
Marking gauge 44, 45
Masterpieces 19
Milling and drilling machine 65
Miniatures, $\frac{1}{12}$th scale 11, 24, 25, 95, 105
Mitre box 71–73
Mitred door 90–94
Mortice and tenon door 100, 101
Mortice and tenon joint 74, 75

Pediments 121
Pencil (very fine) 128
Pendant drills 15, 16
Pin chucks 52
Planing board 66
Protecting delicate work 47, 48

Rosewood 22, 24
Rulers ($\frac{1}{12}$th scale) 41, 42

Salesman's samples 17
Sanding
   blocks 82, 83
   sticks 83
Sandpaper, grades of 81
Sawing block 67
Saws 36–40
Sharpening stone 49, 51
Square (tiny) 51
Squaring block 70

Timber
   preparation 21, 28
   selection 21, 28

Tools (basic kit) 30
Tweezers, grip 53

Varnishing 85
Vibrosaw 63
Vices 47, 48, 52, 126

Walnut 21, 22, 26, 27
Wood
  filling 84
  joints 73–80
  staining 84
Workshop 20